LAWYER 3.0

A Guide to Next-Wave Lawyering

Ray Brescia

BRISTOL
UNIVERSITY
PRESS

First published in Great Britain in 2025 by

Bristol University Press
University of Bristol
1–9 Old Park Hill
Bristol
BS2 8BB
UK
t: +44 (0)117 374 6645
e: bup-info@bristol.ac.uk

Details of international sales and distribution partners are available at bristoluniversitypress.co.uk

© Bristol University Press 2025

British Library Cataloguing in Publication Data
A catalogue record for this book is available from the British Library

ISBN 978-1-5292-4325-3 hardcover
ISBN 978-1-5292-4326-0 ePub
ISBN 978-1-5292-4327-7 ePdf

Cover design: Nicky Borowiec Design
Front cover image: AdobeStock/Inna

For my students

Contents

About the Author

Ray Brescia is Associate Dean for Research and Intellectual Life and the Hon. Harold R. Tyler Chair in Law and Technology at Albany Law School, where he has been on the faculty since 2007. His other books include *The Private Is Political: Identity and Democracy in the Age of Surveillance Capitalism* (2025); *Lawyer Nation: The Past, Present, and Future of the American Legal Profession* (2024); and *The Future of Change: How Technology Shapes Social Revolutions* (2020). He is also co-editor of *Crisis Lawyering: Effective Legal Advocacy in Emergency Situations* (2021); and *How Cities Will Save the World: Urban Innovation in the Face of Population Flows, Climate Change and Economic Inequality* (2016). Prior to joining the legal academy, he served as a staff attorney at the Legal Aid Society of New York and the New Haven Legal Assistance Association; as Associate Director of the Urban Justice Center; and law clerk to the Hon. Constance Baker Motley, U.S. District Judge, Southern District of New York. He received his law degree from Yale Law School and his undergraduate degree in Political Philosophy from Fordham University.

Acknowledgments

I am grateful to many people for their assistance with this work. First and foremost, I want to thank those who provided insights as interviewees for this project: Nicole Black, Rodrigo Camarena, Meghan E. Cook, Richard DiBona, Colin Levy, Adrián Palma, Kara Peterson, Jonathan Pyle, David Rosen, and Adam Stofsky. My research assistants, John Brady, Andrew Fay, and Breann Scoca, provided excellent support for my work. My legal assistants, Barbara Jordan-Smith and Sherri Meyer, as always, were indefatigable. My colleagues at Albany Law School are a constant source of encouragement and inspiration, especially Pam Armstrong, Ava Ayers, Jermaine Cruz, Ted De Barbieri, Keith Hirokawa, Rosemary Queenan, Patricia Reyhan, and Sarah Rogerson. Support from the administration at Albany Law, especially current President and Dean Cinnamon Carlarne, is unwavering. Friends also offered constant encouragement throughout this process, especially Tom Bongiorno, Graham Boyd, Adam Bramwell, Dana Carstarphen, Charles Chesnut, Chris Coons, Beth Garrity-Rokous, Gates Garrity-Rokous, Mitch Glenn, Mark Napier, Richard Newman, Kurt Petersen, Richard Pinner, Nicole Theodosiou, and Mike Wishnie. In addition, throughout this writing process, I had an "accountability team" of several dear friends who texted one another each morning to report on the progress we were making (or not making as the case may have been) toward our personal and professional goals; in many ways, this work is a product of the mutual support we gave each other. This group included Gates, Eamon, Gavin, and Liam Garrity-Rokous and Harrison Lapides. One thing I should note: while working with Bristol University Press to add the finishing touches to the book, I was fortunate to come across Dr Peter Attia's wonderful book, *Outlive: The Science and Art of Longevity*.[1] In it, he uses the framework "Medicine 2.0" and "Medicine 3.0" to describe the current and potentially future state of health care and wellness. Since I use a similar framework here, I want to note that this is purely coincidental, but

---

[1]   Peter Attia, Outlive: The Science and Art of Longevity (2022).

I am deeply gratified that someone in another discipline is looking at that field in a way similar to how I am viewing the legal profession.

Finally, my spouse, Amy Barasch, and son, Leo Brescia, are, as always, the ultimate source of all I am able to accomplish, and for their love and encouragement, I am eternally grateful.

1

Lawyers on the Cusp of Disruption

At a meeting of the American Bar Association, a prominent lawyer from Philadelphia, Henry Drinker, addressed his brethren. He expressed grave concerns about a number of forces affecting the profession, including the influx of immigrant lawyers into the profession, a development he did not particularly appreciate. He also scolded his fellow lawyers for their adoption of somewhat new technologies, believing it unbecoming of the best lawyers to have those technologies mediate the lawyer–client relationship. He would encourage his colleagues to reject these and other changes that were happening all around them. He would inquire of them: "Was John Marshall—the great Marshall, was Blackstone ... were they great lawyers?" Did "one of those great lawyers have a telephone in his office? Not one." He would conclude: "Therefore you would all be better off, you would have more effective offices, if you threw away your telephones."[1] The year of Drinker's address? 1929.

Thankfully, it is unclear whether any lawyers at the time heeded Drinker's call to dispose of their telephones. Instead, what the profession did in the first few decades of the 20th century in the United States was to transform itself as a profession, both in light of technology, but also because of other social and political forces underway during that turbulent period in history. It is important to note that the American legal profession of the late 19th century hardly resembled that which exists today. Most lawyers at the time operated as solo practitioners. There were few law firms at all, and certainly none of the scope and scale we have today. If lawyers did work with others, they might practice with one or two other lawyers in a loose affiliation. There were few functioning bar associations until the end of the 19th century, when lawyers began to believe they needed to band together

---

[1] PROCEEDINGS OF THE SECTION OF LEGAL EDUCATION AND ADMISSION TO THE BAR 52 ANN. REP. A.B.A. 605, 622 (1929) (Statement of Henry S. Drinker).

to protect the interests of the profession.[2] The law schools that did exist educated a very small percentage of lawyers at the time and there were no real bar examinations to speak of until late in that century.[3] Changes in the economy, and increased immigration and urbanization, meant that the needs of the community and the interests of practicing lawyers began to change as well. Lawyers had to organize themselves in ways that responded to the needs of industry, a growing population, and the increased complexity of the economy. This period also saw the rise of a new type of aspiring lawyer who emerged from immigrant and migrant communities alike.

In response to these changes, lawyers began to organize themselves into law firms to better serve the increasing demands of their clients, the increase in the number of the laws and regulations that governed business activities, their clients' baroque and sprawling corporate structures, and the growing complexity of the transactions the lawyers managed. The rapid reproduction of judicial decisions meant lawyers had to read cases and keep up with developments in the law, no longer able to rely on arguing that "general principles" should determine the outcome of their cases.[4] New technologies, such as the telephone and typewriter, also began to transform their day-to-day practice, although some lawyers, like Drinker, resisted such contraptions.[5] Technology did not just affect the subject of what lawyers worked on (their "what"), it also impacted how it was that they practiced (the "how" of practice). What is more, the growing population, drawn to the nation because of the innovation-fueled economy of the late 19th century, also increased the ranks of the profession to include the foreign born and the children of immigrants like never before (the "who" of legal practice). As a result of these phenomena, the legal profession created institutions that would solidify the profession's own role in the provision of legal services and would restrict access to the profession in significant ways.

In order to adapt to the change all around them, elites in the profession took several steps to make it harder to join the ranks of the profession. They imposed mandatory educational requirements and bar examinations for aspiring lawyers, which had the effect of making it more difficult to enter the profession.[6] The animus behind many of these changes was a belief that new immigrants were emerging from the sweatshops to stir up litigation

---

[2]   On the emergence of bar associations in the United States at the end of the 19th century, see Carol Rice Andrews, *Standards of Conduct for Lawyers: An 800-Year Evolution*, 57 SMU L. REV. 1385, 1434–35 (2004) (citations omitted).

[3]   RICHARD L. ABEL, AMERICAN LAWYERS 43 (1989).

[4]   GEORGE MARTIN, CAUSES AND CONFLICTS: THE CENTENNIAL HISTORY OF THE ASSOCIATION OF THE BAR OF THE CITY OF NEW YORK, 1870–1970, 195–96 (1970).

[5]   *Id*, at 191–92.

[6]   ABEL, *supra* note 3, at 39–53.

against the clients of the elite members of the bar.[7] Lawyers also thought about the supply of legal assistance: with more lawyers to go around, the fees lawyers could charge would likely diminish. Creating barriers to entry helped to protect the incumbent lawyers' near monopoly on the practice of law.[8] In the end, elites in the bar tried to respond to the ways in which the practice of law was changing, and who was starting to practice it, by creating the institutions we still think of today as forming the core elements of the legal profession, many of which largely did not exist before this period. The most prominent of these included more rigorous bar examinations and mandatory educational requirements. They would also institute a formal code of ethics where none had existed before[9] and more explicit rules against the unauthorized practice of law (UPL), meaning that anyone who wanted to deliver legal services not only had to overcome the new and strengthened barriers to entry to the profession but also faced stiff punishment if they tried to provide legal assistance to others without overcoming such barriers.[10] In its first 130-year existence, a growing nation needed, in the words of historian Lawrence Friedman, a "large, amorphous, open-ended profession,"[11] one that was made up almost exclusively of white, native-born men. At the turn of the 19th to the 20th century, that original version of the profession, Lawyer 1.0, gave way to a new version: what I call Lawyer 2.0.

Fast-forward 100 years. We are poised at the cusp of a potentially sweeping transformation of the practice of law, one that could alter the profession in ways as equally dramatic as the measures instituted in the first decades of the 20th century. We are only beginning to conceive of the ways in which new technologies will impact law practice. The most important of these technologies are artificial intelligence (traditional and generative), machine learning, and quantum computing. What these changes could catalyze is the emergence of a new legal profession: Lawyer 3.0. In defining this new, third "wave" of lawyering, I will strive to articulate what this transformed profession could look like. The goal is to help those interested in understanding how this transformation will impact the legal profession; what steps practitioners should take to adapt to these changes; the future

---

[7] Jerold S. Auerbach, Unequal Justice: Lawyers and Social Change in Modern America 50–54 (1977).

[8] On the campaign to develop and strengthen the legal profession's monopoly on the practice of law, see Abel, *supra* note 3, at 113–19.

[9] Am. Bar Ass'n, Canons of Professional Ethics (1908).

[10] On the origins and emergence of contemporary approaches to restricting the unauthorized practice of law, see generally Laurel A. Rigertas, *The Birth of the Movement to Prohibit the Unauthorized Practice of Law*, 37 Quinnipiac L. Rev. 97 (2018).

[11] Lawrence M. Friedman, A History of American Law 303 (Oxford Univ. Press 4th ed. 2019) (1973).

that lies before aspiring lawyers; and the ways in which technologists, other professionals and paraprofessionals could find space within the profession (or professions, as I will argue) to assist in the delivery of legal services within the Lawyer 3.0 framework.

This is the frame of "Lawyer 3.0": the idea that we are about to experience a seismic shift in the American legal profession, one that is only rivalled by the developments that occurred within the profession at the turn of 19th to the 20th century. At that time, the profession transformed itself, mostly in the face of emerging technologies and the social forces those technologies unleashed, to create the institutions of the modern legal profession that are still with us to this day. Indeed, the legal profession now faces the same sort of forces it confronted over 100 years ago, largely because of the introduction of new technologies that will likely remake the legal profession in significant ways over the next ten years. This work will be the first serious and comprehensive exploration of the potential role of technologies like generative artificial intelligence, predictive analytics, and machine learning in remaking the way legal services are delivered both in the United States and around the world. But the goal is not "change for change's sake," or even "technology for technology's sake"; rather, it is to get to the purpose of the profession and ask whether technology can better help the profession serve that purpose.

This is a particularly opportune time to help explore and explain the contours and likely functions of this new "version" of law practice and ask whether it will assist the profession to serve what should be its purpose. The profession, the justice system, and legal education are struggling to adapt to the coming changes, some of which were previewed in the transition to remote functioning brought on by the COVID-19 global pandemic. But these institutions have not fully grasped the ways in which new technologies—most notably artificial intelligence and machine learning— will alter the practice of law in the coming decade. A lawyer from 1925 could look at the legal profession of today and recognize it because it operates in many ways that resemble how lawyers practiced 100 years ago. The same will not be true of a lawyer looking back on the practice of law today from even ten years into the future. This work will help to grapple with the changes that are already underway and those that are emerging to imagine the features of the practice of law that could take shape in the next decade: that is, what will Lawyer 3.0 look like and what are the ways in which present and future lawyers can prepare for this dramatic shift in how the legal profession operates? This book provides a possible guide for those interested in understanding and taking part in the transformation of the legal profession, while always using as its touchstone not merely what lawyers do and do not do today, but what they could and should be doing with these new capacities. It can help practitioners, law students and those who aspire to go to law school, technologists, legal educators, and policy makers to understand how the new modes of a technology-enhanced legal profession will help to evolve not just the practice of law but also the functioning of the justice system itself.

There is also one big difference in the way that technology will impact the practice of law more dramatically than in earlier periods: the technology that is rapidly becoming available will make it possible for non-lawyers (whether it is lay people or technologists) to both create and use tools that will enable unrepresented parties to prepare legal documents themselves. Indeed, this is already happening with current versions of generative artificial intelligence. This is something that will make this moment different from the past, and why technology will have such a significant impact on the practice of law moving forward. This moment is similar to the changes that media theorist Clay Shirky has pointed out occurred in journalism with the beginning of the internet, or scribes with the introduction of moveable type.[12] Unlike in prior eras, however, the technology that is rapidly becoming available today not only makes the lawyer's job a lot easier, but it also makes it possible for lay people and non-lawyers to generate output that looks a lot like that which lawyers produce.

Given this significant change in the technology that is available, which could displace lawyers like never before, the legal profession must figure out how to continue to produce value and remain relevant in the market and the legal system. Yes, there are prohibitions that prevent lay people from practicing law generally. There is generally no prohibition in the U.S. on individuals "representing" themselves, however, and the technologies that are already available will go a long way toward enabling individuals to obtain a modicum of legal guidance at almost no cost.

Given these new technologies and their availability to lay people, lawyers will have to make the case that, in light of these technologies and the capacities they afford the non-lawyer, the lawyer's role is still important and adds value. And here is a central theme of this book: the point of the legal system is not to give lawyers jobs. It must serve greater purposes, like ensuring that anyone who has a legal problem has adequate guidance to resolve it. These problems might be mundane, like seeking help navigating small claims court, or monumental, like protecting the right to vote. Lawyers must serve that cause which is larger than themselves, even if not every function performed by a lawyer today will be performed by one in the future. While we might like to think that the legal profession and legal system are responding to needs such as these, in reality the market for legal services in the U.S. is desperately broken, with tens of millions of

---

[12] CLAY SHIRKY, HERE COMES EVERYBODY: THE POWER OF ORGANIZING WITHOUT ORGANIZATION (2008).

Americans having nowhere to turn for legal help. Are new technologies capable of helping to fix this broken market? What would be gained, and what would be lost, if we used such technologies to deliver legal services at scale? What I hope to do here is to develop a methodology for determining when technology may satisfy consumer needs in an effective way, one that is more affordable and accessible than the manner in which legal services are delivered at present and might be just as effective as the provision of such services by a human.

Why is this question even important? Why does it matter whether technology might serve to provide legal services to Americans in a more efficient and effective matter than the current legal profession? The answer to both questions emerges from the origins of the current version of the American legal profession: Lawyer 2.0. The system created in the early decades of the 20th century embedded monopoly power and scarcity into the provision of legal services. That system made it more expensive to go to law school; more costly to provide services, given the customized model of legal services it engendered; and limited the number of aspiring lawyers who entered the profession. These forces have driven the cost of legal services beyond the reach of many Americans. The advent of new technologies may generate an opening, one which creates the possibility that we might unlock new resources and opportunities to help provide legal services to more Americans in meaningful and effective ways.

Current estimates are that over 90 percent of low-income Americans[13] and 50 percent of middle-income Americans face their legal problem without a lawyer.[14] While price is not the only driver of this "justice gap," as it is known, it is one of them.[15] As I will explore in greater depth in Chapter 5, there is also a knowledge gap when it comes to legal problems: that individuals might not know they have a problem that is legal in nature or might not know a lawyer who might help them resolve it even if they knew they had that type of problem in the first place.[16] We are at a point where emerging technologies may displace the role of lawyers in some of their functions at a time when the market for legal services is broken. So what does this confluence of these phenomena—a broken market and new technologies that might help fix it—mean for the legal profession?

---

[13] LEGAL SERVICES CORPORATION, THE JUSTICE GAP: THE UNMET CIVIL LEGAL NEEDS OF LOW-INCOME AMERICANS 8 (2022) (hereinafter JUSTICE GAP REPORT).

[14] Deborah L. Rhode, *Access to Justice: An Agenda for Legal Education and Research*, 62 J. LEGAL EDUC. 531, 531 (2013).

[15] On the current state of access-to-justice research, see generally, JUSTICE GAP REPORT, *supra* note 13.

[16] REBECCA L. SANDEFUR, ACCESSING JUSTICE IN THE CONTEMPORARY USA: FINDINGS FROM THE COMMUNITY NEEDS AND SERVICES STUDY 12–14 (2014).

In his seminal work *The Innovator's Dilemma: When New Technologies Cause Great Firms to Fail*, the late Harvard Business School professor Clayton Christensen identified what he considered a phenomenon in the business cycle common in many sectors.[17] Incumbents tailor their products toward existing customers. Because of their investments in research and development, those incumbents tend to charge a high price for the product or service, but what they offer tends to provide more features or elements than many current and prospective customers might want or need. This creates a market opportunity for new entrants into the market: they can offer a cheaper product or service, one that is more in line with what at least some customers need. Initially, those customers tend to emerge at the lower end of the sector, including those customers who the incumbents typically do not serve in the first place. But it is here, at the lower end of the market, where Christensen's disruptive innovation—innovation that upends a market—begins to take hold. This type of innovation is typically "technologically straightforward, consisting of off-the-shelf components put together in a product architecture that [is] often simpler than prior approaches."[18] Such products offer "a different package of attributes valued only in emerging markets remote from, and unimportant to, the mainstream."[19] Slowly, however, disruptors refine their processes for the delivery of products or services from the bottom up and attain a larger and larger market share.[20]

Christensen used the example of the steel industry in the U.S. that has experienced this kind of disruption. In the 1970s, companies found it expensive to build and operate traditional steel mills. But soon, what came to be known as minimills appeared on the scene, producing certain basic steel-based products at a fraction of the cost of the more established mills, capturing those markets where steel of lesser quality would satisfy the customer base. The incumbent mill operators focused their energies on more lucrative sectors within the steel market, slowly ceding a larger and larger share to the minimills as those new entrants refined and improved their own manufacturing processes. Those new entrants slowly gained greater and greater market share until many of the incumbents simply failed.[21] Is the market for legal services in the United States ripe for this sort of disruptive innovation, or what German economist Joseph Schumpter called "creative destruction," a term he used to refer to the "process of industrial mutation

---

17 CLAYTON M. CHRISTENSEN, THE INNOVATOR'S DILEMMA: WHEN NEW TECHNOLOGIES CAUSE GREAT FIRMS TO FAIL (2000 ed.).
18 *Id.*, at 15.
19 *Id.*
20 *Id.*
21 *Id.*, at 88–91.

… that incessantly revolutionizes the economic structure from within, incessantly destroying the old one, incessantly creating a new one"?[22]

These phenomena—market forces and technological change—will drive the coming transformation of the practice of law. Clients and would-be clients will seek out less expensive alternatives to the services lawyers currently provide. These forces will mean that lawyers will have to rethink their business models (including changing the "hourly billing" approach, a process that is already underway). It will also force them to look for the efficiencies that the transformation of the production of their services through technology can yield. As more and more clients understand that there are cheaper—and rapidly improving—alternatives to expensive legal services, lawyers will need to adjust to technological change and incorporate new technologies into their practice while still adding value to the transaction between the lawyer and the client.

It is these market forces, when considered in light of the capacities of new technologies, that will lead to significant changes to the ways in which lawyers practice. Just as in the early 20th century, when lawyers and law firms adopted technology to make their practices more efficient and effective, lawyers who did not do so did not last very long. In these pages, I will highlight examples of lawyers who have adopted technology into their practice successfully and effectively and how that has delivered better services at a more affordable price to clients.

Popular thinking about technology, particularly artificial intelligence, is that "computers will take your job." The reality is, it is not technology itself, but, rather, lawyers who understand that technology and how it can improve law practice are the ones who are going to dominate the legal services market in the coming decades. This work will not just highlight the technology that is available and how it could drive change, it will also shine a light on those who are already incorporating new technologies into their practice and the benefits these changes have produced.

I fully appreciate that lawyers are known as a conservative, careful lot. As someone who has practiced for over 30 years and now works in the legal academy, I certainly understand how hard it is to change institutions, particularly institutions chock full of lawyers. Still, change is possible, and some elements of the changes that are already occurring in the profession are unavoidable and already underway. The threat of obsolescence in the event of institutional intransigence is real, and many within the institutions of the profession—bar associations, the court system, law firms, law schools—are exploring ways to adapt to the rapidly changing technological landscape. This occurred in the late 19th century, where not just *what* lawyers did,

---

[22] JOSEPH A. SCHUMPETER, CAPITALISM, SOCIALISM, AND DEMOCRACY 83 (3d ed., 1994).

but also *how* they did it, changed. The legal profession transformed itself in response to the changes that were occurring all around the profession at the time, and I believe a similar sea change in these institutions is not only likely, but also necessary. We are already seeing this type of change unfold, particularly around how lawyers and courts must adapt to ways in which generative artificial intelligence is infiltrating the practice of law, in both constructive and harmful ways. It is far better to get out in front of these changes than be overtaken by them, and critical stakeholders within the legal system are already assessing the potential impacts of these technologies on the practice of law and the functioning of the legal system. Some entities are proving agile and adaptable in the face of change. Those that are not will have change thrust upon them.

One encouraging development in the legal profession and the legal system more broadly that occurred in March of 2020 was that the global pandemic forced change in the practice of law, change that many predicted would never come (like the ability to work remotely or conduct virtual judicial proceedings). The changes the profession adopted to honor pandemic protocols showed not only that the profession could make the practice of law itself more accessible, accommodating, and flexible than anyone had imagined previously, but also that change itself was possible, even rapid change. This work takes these developments as a sign that the legal system is not as resistant to change as it might appear, at least when change is compelled by outside forces beyond lawyers' control. I believe we are seeing these sorts of exogenous forces already at play, and the profession simply cannot ignore them.

What this book will not cover

While I will try to identify what this new version of lawyering will look like, what this book will not cover is specific products. I might mention a few by name, however, if they serve as an example of the type of innovation/product that could be used in a particular area of practice. The reasons for doing so are, first, such individual products could soon be outdated and out of fashion by the time the book goes to print. Second, the book will focus on how to tailor new technologies to fit certain functions, not how a particular product might serve a particular use. What is more, it will break down the ways in which legal services are delivered at present and the potential introduction of new technologies into those different elements of practice. The book is not a "legal test kitchen," a catalogue for would-be managing attorneys to guide them to the product that is right for their law office. Rather, the book will explore the types of tools that law offices are likely to use to transform the different elements and components of legal practice, as opposed to promoting a particular product.

I will certainly address the *how* and the *what* of legal practice. More importantly, as mentioned previously, I will largely focus on the "why": what is or should be the purpose of the profession? This book strives to consider the application of emerging technologies to the current practice of law and harness them in ways that will ensure that lawyers and the legal system help Americans solve their legal problems, and not just Americans who can pay for legal services at present. The goal here is to spark the type of radical re-imagining and restructuring of the legal profession similar to the one that occurred in the beginning of the 20th century. But the focus will not be on "technology for the sake of technology." The goal is to envision a totally transformed legal profession that is more accessible, user-friendly, and effective: one that reaches more people and also ensures the legal system meets human needs as best as it possibly can. So how might one do that? The point of this book is to provide a roadmap for those who wish to get ahead of this disruptive phase in the history of the American legal profession and preserve what is best about it, while also showing how to let go of the things that are no longer working and should not linger as the profession enters its next wave.

As futurist and novelist William Gibson supposedly put it: "the future is already here—it's just not evenly distributed."[23] It is certainly the case that members of the American legal profession, like lawyers around the world, do not all look the same, practice the same way, or utilize technology in the practice of law in equal measure. But that is true of large law firms and small solo practitioners: some prestigious law firms are using new technologies more than others, just as some small firms and solo practitioners are doing so and some are not. This lack of "even distribution" of technology in the practice of law is likely to serve as the main driver behind success and failure in the profession, regardless of where one practices and the type of law one practices. This book will highlight the new ways in which lawyers from across the profession's many sectors are adapting (or not adapting) to these technological changes: those in private and public service, those in law firms large and small, and those in non-profit entities and in-house counsel offices. I do not see the profession as monolithic, nor will this work depict it as such.

At the same time, while this book is not designed as a how-to guide for specific technologies, given that true disruption in markets occurs at the low end of those markets, I will largely focus on that segment of the market that is currently underserved by the legal profession. As we have seen, this segment is quite large, representing over 90 percent of low- and 50 percent of middle-income Americans, and even these figures probably

---

[23] *The Science in Science Fiction*, NPR, October 22, 2018, https://www.npr.org/2018/10/22/1067220/the-science-in-science-fiction (last visited, Apr. 29, 2025).

undercount the size of the justice gap in America: the difference between who needs and who receives legal assistance to solve their legal problems. Those at the higher end of the market have lawyers and are well-served by the legal profession. If true disruption is to take place in the market for legal services, it will largely begin to emerge in those segments of the market where lawyers tend not to tread, except for lawyers providing legal services through non-profit organizations. Because these segments of the market for legal services are my focus, some might think that this book is not for them. But since the dynamics of the "Innovator's Dilemma" are such that even those at the higher end of the market must be mindful of how new technologies and methods for delivering services might ultimately impact all components of the market for legal services, I hope that anyone with an interest in ensuring the legal profession serves all Americans who need legal services will learn something from this work.

Most importantly, while in some ways this book will help lawyers understand how to harness technology to better meet consumer needs, its main approach is to explore what the legal services market looks like from the outside in, if you will. That is, in order to determine how to best tailor and calibrate the delivery of legal services to the needs of American consumers, which should be the goal of the legal profession, the focus here is to take the perspective of the consumer who needs legal services into account when we consider how to deliver services to them. When technology helps to improve the delivery of those legal services in a way that meets consumer needs, the legal profession should embrace it, even if that may not always be in the financial interests of the profession. A core principle to which I will return throughout the course of this book is that the legal system should not exist merely as a full-employment plan for lawyers. It should be there to help Americans satisfy their legal needs. With this perspective as the animating force for this work, what follows is what the reader can expect as they make their way through it.

Plan of the book

After this introductory chapter, in Chapter 2 I will start to address how to plan for the coming disruption to the practice of law and do so in a way that centers the consumer at the heart of the delivery of legal services and not the lawyer. To accomplish this, I will introduce another concept coined by Clayton Christensen: *the job-to-be-done framework*. This is an approach he and his fellow researchers recommended one might use when considering what products or services a particular consumer desires or would prefer.[24]

---

[24] CLAYTON CHRISTENSEN, TADDY HALL, KAREN DILLON & DAVID S. DUNCAN, COMPETING AGAINST LUCK: THE STORY OF INNOVATION AND CUSTOMER CHOICE (2016).

As part of the inspiration for that work, Christensen famously conducted a study of customers of a fast-food company who had purchased milkshakes at that company's stores. What Christensen's research revealed was that for many of these customers the milkshake satisfied several needs at once: the customers could consume the milkshake with one hand; it would not spill on their work clothes; it was filling; and it gave the customer something to do during a long, boring commute. This was the "job" the customers had "hired" the milkshake to perform.[25] Taking this approach to understanding the job-to-be-done perspective of the lawyer role, depending on the setting, the lawyer can satisfy different "jobs" or values when they serve a client. This chapter will explore how to apply a job-to-be-done framework to the services provided by lawyers to their clients and will identify the values lawyers are supposed to satisfy when providing such services. These values will then become the framework for assessing the ways technology can satisfy the needs of those who require the legal profession's services. This analysis— and these values—will then serve as a prism through which to view the ways the legal profession can deploy technology at every step in the delivery of legal services so as to advance those values and not undermine them.

In order to further set the stage for the analysis that follows, Chapter 3 will introduce two new concepts. The first of these is the discipline of business process analysis (BPA). The idea behind BPA is that one can break down the different elements of a business process or practice to think about ways to improve the delivery of that product or service. I will use BPA to do just that with respect to the delivery of legal services in different contexts to identify the second concept this chapter will introduce: the legal services continuum. Today, legal services often come in one shape and size: a lawyer sits down with a client, assesses the client's needs, and then delivers custom services to that client. Each time a new client seeks the lawyer's services, the lawyer does the same thing. The needs of each individual customer determine the services that the lawyer provides. What BPA can do for the legal profession is to help examine the services the lawyer provides and see them in stages and on a continuum: finding and identifying potential clients; triaging them according to their needs; providing information to them; offering brief, initial tactical advice and guidance to them; and then potentially providing full-service representation and assistance. When we apply the job-to-be-done framework to this continuum, and the values such an analysis uncovers, we can then start to see ways in which new technologies can improve the delivery of services to clients in ways that advance those values. What I hope this analysis will yield is an understanding that there may be times when a new mode of delivering services directly to clients might help those clients

---

[25] *Id.*, at 6–10.

satisfy their needs and the values lawyers are supposed to uphold for them, even if that means that service is no longer provided to that client by a lawyer.

Chapter 4 will serve as a sort of "hinge" for my analysis. It will provide an overview of the latest developments in legal practice technologies, or "legal tech." It will examine a range of new and emerging technologies—and old technologies being deployed in innovative ways—that are likely to transform the practice of law dramatically in the coming years. Bill Gates says that we tend to overestimate the impact of technology on our lives over the next two years while underestimating the impact it will have over the next ten.[26] This work will attempt to predict the potential impacts of technology on the practice of law over the next ten years. It also strives to anticipate the dramatic changes that will completely transform how legal services are delivered, the structure of the legal profession, and the roles of other professionals who will become deeply enmeshed in the delivery of legal services, as well as addressing the likelihood that these changes will turn the service-delivery model on its head. Indeed, lawyers will no longer deliver what are sometimes referred to as "bespoke" services—named for the hand-tailored and customized suits created at such places as Savile Row in London.[27] That is, the lawyer's services are customized based on the needs of each individual client who walks into a lawyer's office. Instead, lawyers and other legal professionals (at least those who are likely to survive the coming transformation of the practice of law) will craft a suite of services and determine whether potential consumers are an appropriate fit for those services, and not the other way around.

But how would we assess the needs of consumers in the market for legal services? Today, lawyers often engage in "triage": they evaluate each prospective consumer's needs and then tailor a package of services to deliver to them. Such an approach tends to begin with those consumers who find those lawyers. What if we took a step back, and did not allow selection bias to skew the lawyers' approach? What if the lawyers' response to legal needs in the community did not depend upon consumers realizing they have a legal problem, knowing a lawyer they can contact, and having a means of reaching that lawyer to review that problem? One way in which Lawyer 3.0 might operate as an improved version of the legal profession would be if it could serve more consumers and meet more of their legal needs in a comprehensive way. Chapter 5 will address this issue of consumer needs by taking this sort of approach: analyzing the actual legal needs of American consumers as opposed to just tailoring the services that the profession provides based on those consumers who know how to seek the profession's assistance.

---

[26] BILL GATES, THE ROAD AHEAD 316 (1995).
[27] RICHARD SUSSKIND, THE END OF LAWYERS? 34 (2010) (describing "bespoke" legal services).

Once we have a sense of the actual legal needs of American consumers and understand that far too many of them go without legal assistance, we can then start to consider how to recalibrate the delivery of services, in new ways, to reach a broader consumer base. Once we have this clearer sense of consumer needs, we can then start to consider the ways that technology might help to meet them. There is no doubt that the traditional, or bespoke, model of legal services will continue, especially for wealthier clients, but even that work will see dramatic changes as well, as explored in greater depth in Chapter 8.

Before I get there, Chapter 6 will start at the first phase of the legal services continuum and begin to explore the ways in which technology will transform how legal professionals provide information to their clients to not just understand their legal needs, but also to begin to try to address them. Indeed, in the job-to-be-done framework, sometimes what a client needs is just a little bit of information and guidance to help them navigate an issue they are confronting before it becomes a significant problem that requires a lawyer's assistance. This chapter will show that many consumers do not have an easy and efficient way to find a lawyer who can help them with the legal information and guidance they need. When looking for such assistance, they might clumsily search for a lawyer who can help them with the issue, ignore the issue until it becomes a more serious problem, or try to address the issue without legal assistance—often with little success. Using technology-driven, sophisticated, effective, and targeted outreach, screening, and triaging tools, lawyers can make the right amount of information available to consumers at the right time. Doing so could eliminate the need for more expensive services of a full-service lawyer, if that information can help the consumer address their issue in an effective way. This chapter will explore what such intelligent systems might look like in the coming years.

Chapter 7 will then explore the next component of the legal services continuum: the provision of brief and, at times, what some call commoditized services. These stand in direct contrast to those we might consider bespoke. Lawyers have always passed along brief advice and assistance to clients. The Lawyer 3.0 approach portends the reversal of the business model: that legal professionals will deliver pre-packaged, commoditized services at scale and screen prospective clients for their fit with those services, as opposed to the current model that begins with the needs of each consumer and assembles a package of services catered to those needs. Technology is poised to supercharge this type of service delivery and this chapter will explore the promise that commoditized services will actually deliver meaningful and useful services to a wider range of consumers than is currently served by the profession—and at a fraction of the cost. This will mean not only that more consumers will receive legal guidance, but also that lawyers can spend more time serving the clients who need full-service representation.

When the other stages are not enough to meet the needs and values a client is looking to satisfy when seeking out legal assistance, that means they enter the next stage of the legal services continuum: that of traditional, full-service representation. Chapter 8 will explore what such traditional services might look like in the future, but in a Lawyer 3.0 way. There is no doubt that some consumers will still need full-service representation, but even that service-delivery model will change dramatically in the coming years because of the use of automated systems by legal professionals for the preparation of court filings, contracts, and financial instruments. In addition, because of technology, some services that lawyers provide in a full-service, customized way today could be delivered by lawyers in different ways, at different stages of the legal services continuum, and at a fraction of the cost of traditional legal services. This chapter will explore the ways that even full-service lawyering will change in light of new technologies.

As it will require changes to other aspects of the profession, the Lawyer 3.0 framework will also require that we transform legal education. To that end, Chapter 9 will attempt to reimagine legal education for a technology-enhanced legal profession, one that provides more services to a broader array of consumers. Legal education will go beyond teaching the nuts and bolts of lawyering, specifically and exclusively to individuals who intend to be lawyers. It will provide a range of avenues for individuals to obtain legal training, to prepare them for the Lawyer 3.0 paradigm. This will certainly mean some individuals will still become lawyers, just lawyers with a firm grasp of the technology of practice. But it will also mean that law schools, at least those that will continue to operate, are likely to serve non-lawyer professionals and legal technicians and prepare them for a role within the new version of the profession, even if they do not become lawyers. There will be plenty of work to go around in the new world of law practice, just not all of it will be performed by lawyers. Law schools, to remain relevant within this new paradigm, will have to adapt to serve the full range of professionals who will become part of a Lawyer 3.0 world.

The concluding chapter, Chapter 10, will explore what leaders of the legal profession, legal educators, regulators, judges, and consumers will need to do to adapt to the emerging Lawyer 3.0 paradigm. It will assess whether the current rules of legal ethics and the way lawyers practice are correctly calibrated to adapt to and catalyze the changes that are in many ways inevitable, and are likely to transform the practice of law in ways no less dramatic than those that occurred over 100 years ago, when the practice of law adopted its Lawyer 2.0 framework. In order for the profession to remain relevant in light of current and emerging technologies, it must adapt to those changes, get out in front of them, and make the case for why and how the profession can still remain indispensable. There will still be a job to be done, even when technology might, potentially, displace many of the more traditional roles that lawyers have played over the last century.

It is said that if you want to predict the future, invent it. The American legal profession has an opportunity to do just that. My hope is that this work will help begin the process of inventing this future.

Chapter 1: Key takeaways

1. Technological advancements, urbanization, and demographic shifts in the late 19th century led to the professionalization of law practice, the formation of law firms, the introduction of formal education, and the development of ethics codes. Similar forces are driving change to the profession today.
2. The legal profession is on the verge of a significant transformation driven by emerging technologies such as artificial intelligence (AI), machine learning, and quantum computing. This shift, termed "Lawyer 3.0," is expected to reshape the practice of law, similar to the changes that occurred at the turn of the 20th century.
3. A key difference between past and present disruptions is that new technologies, especially generative AI, have the potential to enable non-lawyers to generate legal documents and perform tasks that were once exclusively handled by lawyers. This will challenge the legal profession to prove its relevance and adapt to these technologies.
4. The present market for legal services in the U.S. is "broken," with many Americans unable to afford legal representation. This "justice gap"—where over 90 percent of low-income individuals and 50 percent of middle-income individuals lack legal assistance—presents an opportunity for disruptive innovation that could make legal services more affordable and accessible.
5. Lawyers are traditionally resistant to technological changes, often cautious and conservative in their approach. However, external pressures—such as client demand for more affordable services and technological advances—are likely to force the profession to evolve, with those failing to adapt facing obsolescence.
6. The future of law practice will involve a combination of traditional services and technology-driven alternatives. Legal services will be provided along a continuum, ranging from simple information and guidance (potentially delivered by AI or automated systems) to full-service legal representation. This new and retooled framework must be designed to meet the needs of a broader range of clients in a more efficient and cost-effective manner.

2

The Job of the Lawyer

They were a revered group, spending their days poring over sacred texts and writing them out by hand. They had exclusive training from a young age for what they expected would be a lifetime of steady work that no one could take away from them, until those skills became obsolete because of technology. They resisted their own obsolescence by expressing the value they brought to society because of the skills they had developed and honed and the centrality of their work to the salvation of others, rejecting the notion that technology could possibly replace them. They defended their position, citing the benefits they bestowed on the community, while keeping a sharp eye trained on their own well-being. While I am talking here about medieval[1] scribes displaced by the printing press and moveable type,[1] one could insert the name of any number of professions into this narrative. Over the last 500 years, the introduction of new technologies has transformed and even eliminated many jobs, trades, and occupations. With the growth of automation and artificial intelligence likely impacting every corner of the economy, it is not clear that any job is safe. It is sometimes joked that the workplace of the future will have two employees: a human and a dog. The human is there to feed the dog, and the dog is there to make sure the human does not touch the machines.

Since this is a book about the legal profession and its future in light of emerging technologies, it strives to anticipate what the workplace of the legal profession will look like in the future. The profession often sees itself as made up of artisans, not workers producing commoditized widgets. Over 200 years ago, technology transformed manufacturing practically across the board. The introduction of the assembly line, which broke down the production of all manner of goods into its component steps and assigned different

---

[1] For a discussion of the role of scribes in medieval times and the impact of moveable type on their professional role, see CLAY SHIRKY, HERE COMES EVERYBODY: THE POWER OF ORGANIZING WITHOUT ORGANIZATIONS 66–69 (2008).

workers to handle each of those steps, made artisans into laborers—some might say automatons—in almost every area of manufacturing. At present, it is growing more and more likely that a lot of what lawyers do now could be performed in a more efficient, effective, and less-expensive way due to technology. Could we, like in the transformed factories of old, break down the practice of law into its component parts, with each part representing different types of services offered at different points in the life-cycle of a legal dispute? If we did this, might a different picture of legal practice emerge, one in which we might insert new technologies along this life-cycle to make it function better and at a much lower cost? Moreover, when we change our perspective and consider what it is the consumer actually wants from their lawyer as opposed to what service the lawyer might want to offer, that shift in perspective can help us re-imagine the proper role of the lawyer, in light of new and emerging technologies, to advance what should be the ultimate goal of the legal profession: to help members of the community solve legal problems.

Before getting into what those new technologies might be, which I will address in Chapter 4, in this chapter, I hope to deconstruct not what it is that American lawyers do, but, rather, what it is that American consumers actually want and need from the legal profession. The first step in understanding what different consumers might want, in different settings, from the profession, requires that we get a sense of not just the size and scale of the American legal profession, but also the extent to which the market for legal services in the U.S. is functioning well: that is, how good a job is it doing in meeting consumer need at present?

The market for legal services in the United States

It is estimated that there are roughly 860,000 practicing attorneys in the United States, with an expected growth rate of nearly 5 percent per year in the coming years, which will mean the profession should add about 44,000 jobs a year.[2] The market for the profession's services is quite large: according to one source, the current estimated value of the market for legal services in the United States is about $375 billion, which is about half of the total estimated value of legal services provided worldwide,[3] although some

---

[2] Bureau of Labor Statistics, Occupational Outlook Handbook: Lawyers, https://www.bls.gov/ooh/legal/lawyers.htm#:~:text=Work%20Environment%20About%20t his%20section,of%20lawyers%20were%20as%20follows (last visited, Sept. 12, 2024).

[3] Grand View Research, U.S. Legal Services Market Size, Share & Trends Analysis Report by Services (Taxation, Real Estate, Litigation, Bankruptcy, Labor/Employment, Corporate), By Firm Size, By Application, and Segment Forecasts, 2023–2030,

estimates place that figure at nearly $1 trillion.[4] At present, there are roughly 117,000 law students enrolled in law schools accredited by the American Bar Association (ABA).[5] We can estimate (liberally) that roughly a third of those, or about 39,000, will graduate each year, meaning that the estimates about the increase in legal services jobs should outpace the availability of new lawyers to fill those positions, at least in the near future. If that is the case, and demand will exceed supply, it is likely that the cost of legal services, already beyond the reach of most Americans, as I will show shortly, will only increase.

What should be clear from these figures is that Americans, American corporations, and foreign corporations doing business in the U.S. that hire American lawyers spend a lot of money on legal services. And, as anyone who has ever sought out the services of a lawyer knows, the cost of such services is high, and this is true for several reasons. Many law-firm managers will tell you that operating a law office is expensive, largely due to the salaries that lawyers receive, particularly those lawyers in private practice. In many such settings, the expense associated with staffing up a significant legal matter is passed along to the client, even when some of the tasks carried out by junior lawyers could be handled by a paralegal, or, now, by automation. The "Cravath model" of law-firm structure and billing, first created, like so many institutional practices within the profession, at the turn of the 19th to the 20th century, is predicated, in part, on the notion that a large pool of newer attorneys will generate revenue for the firm because their work will be billed to the client by the hour.[6] That century-old hourly billing structure exists to this day, with incentives implicit in such an approach tending to push lawyers to work more, charge more, bill more, and generally make the work more expensive simply by putting in more hours.

https://www.grandviewresearch.com/industry-analysis/us-legal-services-market-report (last visited, Sept. 12, 2024).

4   STRAITS RESEARCH, LEGAL SERVICES MARKET SIZE, SHARE & TRENDS ANALYSIS REPORT BY SERVICES (TAXATION, REAL ESTATE, LITIGATION, BANKRUPTCY, LABOR/EMPLOYMENT, CORPORATE), BY FIRM SIZE (LARGE FIRMS, MEDIUM FIRMS, SMALL FIRMS, BY END-USER (PRIVATE PRACTICING ATTORNEYS, LEGAL BUSINESS FIRMS, GOVERNMENT DEPARTMENTS) AND BY REGION (NORTH AMERICA, EUROPE, APAC, MIDDLE EAST AND AFRICA, LATAM) FORECASTS, 2024–2032 (June 21, 2024), https://straitsresearch.com/report/legal-servi ces-market (last visited, Apr. 27, 2025).

5   AM. BAR ASS'N, *2023 Standard 509 Information Report Data Overview* (Dec. 15, 2023), https://www.americanbar.org/content/dam/aba/administrative/legal_education_and_ admissions_to_the_bar/statistics/2023/2023-aba-standard-509-data-overview-final.pdf (last visited, Apr. 27, 2025).

6   ROBERT T. SWAINE, THE CRAVATH FIRM AND ITS PREDECESSORS, 1819–1948, Vol. II, 6–8 (1948) (describing the Cravath model).

One of the reasons that lawyers can charge so much is a function of their monopoly on the provision of legal services. Since colonial times, lawyers advocated for restrictions on who could provide legal services to others, and the growing size and complexity of the economy and the laws that regulated it made arguments for such restrictions more powerful.[7] Prohibitions on the unauthorized practice of law (UPL)—barriers to individuals who are not lawyers providing legal services to others—predominate throughout the United States; holding oneself out as a lawyer when one is not, or even simply giving what amounts to legal advice to another, can result in criminal penalties in many jurisdictions.[8] These restrictions create artificial limits on the market for legal services, preserving the lawyer monopoly and creating upward pressure on the cost of legal services generally, simply by the forces of supply and demand. In addition, the cost of legal services is also high, in part due to the fact that obtaining a law degree is itself expensive, and the higher salaries paid to lawyers are both justified, and necessitated, by the high cost of legal education. What is more, the price of legal education has opportunity costs baked into it as well: the fact that those who want to pursue a law degree need to largely forgo the wages they could earn while spending the better part of at least three years in law school.

Monopoly power, law-firm billing structures, and the high cost of obtaining a legal education all help to drive up the cost of legal services, but these phenomena have not always been with us. Through much of the 19th century, it was fairly easy to obtain the ability to practice law, provided you were white and male.[9] Increased immigration and urbanization led enterprising young men, and even some women, to try to gain entry to the profession.[10] Concerned that a growth in the number of practicing lawyers would diminish economic opportunities for incumbents, elites in the profession began to explore efforts to create barriers to entry that would

---

[7]   Barlow F. Christensen, *The Unauthorized Practice of Law: Do Good Fences Really Make Good Neighbors—or Even Good Sense?*, 1980 AM. B. FOUND. RES. J. 159 (describing the origins of the modern unauthorized practice of law prohibitions that gained strength at the time of the Great Depression of 1929). On the ways in which lawyers advocated to increase their role in the resolution of legal disputes and diminish the power of juries, see MORTON J. HORWITZ, THE TRANSFORMATION OF AMERICAN LAW, 1780–1860, at 141–51 (1977).

[8]   For a description of different UPL rules across the United States, see ABA STANDING COMM. ON CLIENT PROT., INTRODUCTION, 2004 SURVEY OF UNLICENSED PRACTICE OF LAW COMMITTEES (2004). I will explore these rules in greater depth in subsequent chapters.

[9]   LAWRENCE M. FRIEDMAN, A HISTORY OF AMERICAN LAW 302–4 (Oxford Univ. Press 4th ed. 2019) (1973).

[10] On the growth and nature of law schools during this period, see JAMES WILLARD HURST, THE GROWTH OF AMERICAN LAWYERS: THE LAW MAKERS 272–74 (1950)

make it harder to become a lawyer.[11] These barriers would, in turn, artificially suppress the overall number of lawyers practicing law; they would also largely stem the flow of members of minoritized populations into the profession that was starting to occur. Indeed, a profession that was almost exclusively white and male at the end of the 1880s bore a striking resemblance to that version of itself a full century later.[12]

Today, the overwhelming majority of law schools operate under the types of accreditation standards first developed in the 1920s, which are now tied to bar admission in many states.[13] Due at least in part to these requirements, the cost of legal education itself has skyrocketed over the last 50 years, with many students saddled with hundreds of thousands of dollars in debt once they leave law school.[14] That debt ultimately becomes a cost that gets passed along to clients in the form of fees—lawyers must earn a substantial living to, at a minimum, justify the debt they incurred to earn the right to practice law. Legal services are also expensive because at least some clients will pay for them, especially when one might believe—rightly or wrongly—that having a high-priced lawyer, being paid "whatever it takes to win," will make the difference between a successful strategy in litigation, business negotiations, or a criminal investigation or defense, and one that fails.

It is one thing to note that the cost of legal services is high. It is another to recognize that, at least due, in part, to the high cost of such services, millions of Americans have legal problems and yet do not have a lawyer to address them. While I will go into the many reasons why many Americans fail to seek out legal assistance to help them solve their legal problems in Chapter 5, one of those reasons is certainly a lack of ability to pay for such services. And this is reflected in the fact that an estimated 93 percent of low-income Americans do not receive the legal services they need to address

---

[11] I explore some of the origins of the current system of legal education and show how it was animated in no small part by a desire to create barriers to entry to the profession, with a particular focus on preventing the rising number of new immigrants from joining the profession, in Chapter 9.

[12] On demographic trends in the profession up to the 1980s, see RICHARD ABEL, AMERICAN LAWYERS 83–111 (1989).

[13] For a guide to different states' bar admission requirements, see NATIONAL CONFERENCE OF BAR EXAMINERS, COMPREHENSIVE GUIDE TO BAR ADMISSION REQUIREMENTS: A JURISDICTION-BY-JURISDICTION SNAPSHOT OF BAR ADMISSION REQUIREMENTS, https://reports.ncbex.org/comp-guide/ (last visited, Sept. 28, 2024).

[14] On the cost of legal education and its increase since the early 1970s, see Paul Campos, *The Crisis of the American Law School*, 46 U. MICH. J. L. REFORM 177, 178 (2012). On student debt, see, for example, LAWHUB, COST OF ATTENDANCE: DEBT BY LAW SCHOOL FOR 2022 GRADUATES (setting forth average student debt load for graduates of different law schools), https://www.lawhub.org/trends/debt-per-law-school (last visited, Sept. 28, 2024).

their legal problems,[15] and roughly half of middle-income Americans are in a similar bind.[16] With some of the most sought-after lawyers charging as much as $2,000 an hour or more for their services, an individual earning the federal minimum wage would have to work nearly seven weeks to earn enough to pay for even that one hour of such a high-end lawyer's services. Of course, someone earning the minimum wage would have to work a lot more hours to be able to afford a Lamborghini, but in many communities that luxury sports car is not the only way they can obtain transportation in their community.

By any account, regardless of the reasons the legal services are so expensive, the market for legal services is broken. Higher-end providers of legal services compete over higher-end consumers of legal services, while those on the opposite end of the spectrum overwhelmingly go without such services. The cost of legal services is unquestionably high, even for those who can afford them. At the same time, the emergence of new technologies could alter and improve the ways in which lawyers and other legal professionals could deliver legal services, making them more affordable for a larger number of Americans. Given these phenomena, it is likely that the legal profession is ripe for the type of disruption that Clayton Christensen identified as creating the conditions for new entrants, often powered by new technologies, to bring the cost of legal services in line with what the average American can afford, while also providing them with just the services they need, at the time they need it. But being ripe for disruption does not mean that it necessarily will occur, especially when there are powerful forces aligned against new entrants to the market who might otherwise provide services that look a lot like legal services but do not possess the legally required legal training or licensing to provide such services.

As described earlier, the profession has secured, and long cultivated, strong protections against UPL, a ringfence around the provision of legal guidance that means that only members of the guild—those who have secured entry into the profession—can provide such services. And there are important consumer-protection concerns as to why at least some of these restrictions exist. We would not want someone's life, in the case of a death-penalty case; liberty, in a felony prosecution; or life-savings, in the case of identity theft, in the hands of someone who does not possess the skills necessary to provide

---

[15] LEGAL SERVICES CORPORATION, THE JUSTICE GAP: THE UNMET CIVIL LEGAL NEEDS OF LOW-INCOME AMERICANS 8 (2022) (hereinafter JUSTICE GAP REPORT); Deborah L. Rhode, *Access to Justice: An Agenda for Legal Education and Research*, 62 J. LEGAL EDUC. 531, 531 (2013) (stating that it is "estimated that more than four-fifths of the individual legal needs of the poor and a majority of the needs of middle-income Americans remain unmet") (hereinafter Rhode, *Access to Justice*).

[16] Rhode, *Access to Justice*, *supra* note 15, at 531.

the accused or the victim with the assistance necessary to defend their rights and interests to the greatest extent possible. There are certainly instances when one would want, and there is no substitute for, an able, zealous, well-trained lawyer. But there are also times, especially when the alternative is no representation at all, where the right information or guidance, provided at the right time, in the right place, could help a consumer solve their legal problem. It is also possible that with the technology that exists today a consumer could receive all the assistance they need through a computer interface, where the navigational assistance or even intervention offered by technology could solve the individual's legal problem at a fraction of the cost of paying a lawyer to represent them.

For too long the American legal profession has failed to provide full access to justice: that is, the notion that anyone who needs a lawyer can have one to address their legal problem. While there are many reasons why that has been the case, and I will explore at least some of them in subsequent chapters, one of the main reasons for the failure of the American legal profession to fully meet the needs of most Americans is the amount lawyers charge for their services. While there are ways to close that justice gap that some jurisdictions have explored—like imposing volunteer requirements on law students, encouraging private firms to engage in more pro bono work, or increasing funding for non-profit legal services programs—the focus of this book is the ways in which new technologies may transform how legal services are provided, and whether those new technologies could lead to a complete restructuring of the legal profession like the one we saw that occurred in the early decades of the 20th century. But would something be lost should the legal profession face true disruption? This question is at the heart of this book: what might be lost, and what gained, should we enter into a new phase in the life of the legal profession: Lawyer 3.0? In order to begin to answer that question, I will turn to another way of looking at a market offered by the late Clayton Christensen: the "job-to-be-done" framework first introduced in Chapter 1.

The job the client wants done

Harvard Business School's Clayton Christensen developed what he called the "job-to-be-done" framework when considering what products or services a particular consumer desires or would prefer.[17] Remember the "milkshake study" referenced in the first chapter. This prompted Christensen to posit

---

17 See CLAYTON CHRISTENSEN, TADDY HALL, KAREN DILLON & DAVID S. DUNCAN, COMPETING AGAINST LUCK: THE STORY OF INNOVATION AND CUSTOMER CHOICE 17–18 (2016) (describing "job-to-be-done" theory) (hereinafter CHRISTENSEN ET AL., COMPETING AGAINST LUCK).

that businesses should look at their product development process from a "job-to-be-done" perspective. This point of view, according to Christensen, "causes you to crawl into the skin of your customer and go with her as she goes about her day, always asking the question as she does something: Why did she do it that way?"[18]

To borrow another bit of business school lore, one sometimes hears the story of the owner of a company that produced power drills who asked his senior staff what it was the company sold. His team told him that the company sold quarter-inch drills. No, the owner said, the company sells quarter-inch holes.[19] Put another way, as Christensen would say it, the customer has a job to be done—that of drilling a quarter-inch hole. They don't necessarily know how they're going to solve that problem of creating a quarter-inch hole.[20]

The job-to-be-done framework helps one to try to see the needs of the customer from the customer's perspective. Someone in need of legal services may think or even know that what they need is a lawyer to solve their legal problem. What they really have is a legal problem that needs to be solved. The system of professional licensing in the United States says that customers who have legal problems need lawyers to solve their problems. But what if new technologies offered us the potential to solve at least some of these problems without a lawyer? Are there certain problems, for certain customers, where some form of assistance and guidance offered through technology might address their legal job to be done?

For Christensen, one must analyze the "job" the customer needs done in order to understand how to address it. One looks at the customer's job from a number of different perspectives—what are the values the customer wants fulfilled, what are the functions they need addressed, and are there social or emotional elements of the job the customer wants satisfied in their job to be done?[21] Applying this sort of framework, or "lens" as Christensen would call it, one must look to the values and functions the lawyer is supposed to carry out, as well as the affective and social elements of the problem the customer might ask the lawyer to solve. In the next section, I will describe these different dimensions of the role the lawyer is typically asked to play within the context of the American legal system. What are the values, functions, emotions, and social or political elements of the work the customer wants performed by the legal profession as it is currently constituted? Once we

---

[18] *Id.*

[19] Theodore Levitt, *Marketing Myopia*, 38 HARV. BUS. REV. 24 (1960).

[20] See Clayton M. Christensen et al., *Marketing Malpractice: The Cause and the Cure*, HARV. BUS. REV. 1 (Dec. 2005).

[21] CHRISTENSEN ET AL., COMPETING AGAINST LUCK, *supra* note 17, at 69–94.

have an understanding of what the job is that the customer wants performed for them, we can start to assess the extent to which present and emerging technologies can perform this job just as well as, if not better than, a lawyer. And if these technologies can provide such services better than—or just as good as—a lawyer, is it possible that such technologies might (or should) disrupt the practice of law?

A Lawyer 3.0 mindset means adopting this approach—figuring out what is the job that the community needs the lawyer to fill, and offering such services in a way that reaches more people, provides services more effectively, and offers them at a price that people can afford. Emerging technologies offer the legal profession a way to address the needs of the community better, to assess the best ways to meet those needs, and to organize the legal profession and others so consumers receive the services they need in an efficient and effective manner. In order to do this, one must assess the delivery of legal services from the consumer's perspective, to "crawl into their skin" as Christensen urged, in an effort to understand what values, functions, and roles the consumer wants to fulfill when addressing their legal needs. It is to this type of assessment that I now turn.

The professional values of the American legal profession

Different societies will have the need for different types of lawyers—if they have the need for them at all. In the early days of the American colonies, some communities banned lawyers, preferring to resolve their differences through faith-based precepts adjudicated by religious leaders.[22] In authoritarian regimes, the lawyers do the bidding of those in power, entrenching the stranglehold of elites over the machinery of the legal system.[23] The idealized version of the American legal system is that lawyers are supposed to serve as zealous advocates for their clients within an adversarial system of justice, where procedural mechanisms exist to protect the interests of the individual to ensure a just and fair outcome. In litigation settings, with able adversaries on both sides competing to present their version of their positions, an impartial adjudicator follows the processes put in place to ensure, to the greatest extent possible, fair results. In a representative democracy, the law provides the medium in which lawyers operate and serves as a reflection of the public will. Lawyers can work to ensure compliance with both substantive and procedural law in the resolution of disputes, the ordering of affairs, and

---

[22] Anton-Hermann Chroust, *The Legal Profession in Colonial America*, 33 Notre Dame Law. 51, 66–68 (1957).

[23] For a description of the role lawyers can play in fomenting autocracy, see Scott L. Cummings, *Lawyers in Backsliding Democracy*, 112 Calif. L. Rev. 513 (2024).

the relations between individuals and their communities. Even when the community believes the law should change with respect to a particular issue, lawyers can ensure that change is carried out in a manner consistent with the procedures the community accepts for changing the law (like through duly enacted legislation, constitutional amendments, ballot referenda, and so on). Legal scholar Brian Tamanaha describes a "thick" version of the rule of law as one that includes ideals like respect for individual rights and equality before the law.[24] In contrast, a "thin" version looks to formal, procedural justice alone.[25] I believe we should use just this sort of typology when thinking about the appropriate professional values the lawyer is supposed to uphold and advance. A "thick" version of lawyer professionalism means that lawyers have an important, value-driven role to play within our legal system. One of those values is that the lawyer should serve a role within our multi-racial, participatory democracy that facilities its operation in an inclusive way, one where disputes that might arise within the community are resolved through an adversarial system where the lawyer advances the interests of the individual within a framework that balances those interests against the well-being and the needs of the community as a whole.

Now, these are all lofty goals, for certain, but we can see within this description that, at least within the American system, the legal profession has a role to play in ensuring the desired functioning of our legal system, which has obvious broader implications. We want disputes resolved without resort to violence or vigilantism. We want to ensure that our political system is not corrupt or operated in an extractive fashion, where a small group of elites can siphon off the spoils of society.[26] But it is also probably the case that most customers with a legal "job" to be done are not necessarily thinking about all of these values when they just want to obtain a divorce, write a will, or resolve a dispute with an insurance company. This leads to the second element of the framework for understanding the legal job to be done: that of the *functions* the customer wants the lawyer to fill.

The functional or instrumental value a lawyer can satisfy

Lawyers certainly play a functional role. A client has specific thing they want done. The client might want the lawyer to draft a will, negotiate a lease, defend against a criminal charge, or file a patent application. A corporate

---

[24] BRIAN Z. TAMANAHA, ON THE RULE OF LAW: HISTORY, POLITICS, THEORY 91–113 (2004).

[25] See, for example, RANDALL PEERENBOOM, CHINA'S LONG MARCH TOWARD RULE OF LAW 3 (2002) (discussing thick and thin versions of the rule of law).

[26] For a description of extractive and inclusive institutions, see DARON ACEMOGLU & JAMES A. ROBINSON, WHY NATIONS FAIL: THE ORIGINS OF POWER, PROSPERITY, AND POVERTY 74–79 (2012).

client might want a lawyer to conduct an internal investigation, represent it during a governmental investigation, prepare a securities law filing, commence a lawsuit to protect the company's trade secrets, or to defend it against a consumer class action.

The Preamble to the American Bar Association's Model Rules of Professional Conduct describes some of these functions in broad categories as follows:

> As advisor, a lawyer provides a client with an informed understanding of the client's legal rights and obligations and explains their practical implications. As advocate, a lawyer zealously asserts the client's position under the rules of the adversary system. As negotiator, a lawyer seeks a result advantageous to the client but consistent with requirements of honest dealings with others. As an evaluator, a lawyer acts by examining a client's legal affairs and reporting about them to the client or to others.[27]

Sometimes the client is able to articulate the need they have and the functional value the attorney can bring to the relationship. As legal scholar Spencer Rand explains, some clients present legal problems that are "relatively straightforward and there is little risk of not understanding the clients' goals and needs."[28] At the same time, sometimes the client just wants to know whether they have a legal problem in the first place.[29] A lawyer can serve many roles for a client and their guidance might include discrete tasks or more general advice. It might include pursuing litigation to vindicate rights or managing a complex business transaction. In many ways, on the surface at least, what is often easiest to discern is what particular function the client wants the lawyer to carry out.

The affective value of the lawyer

There are indeed instances where the specific functions the client wants the lawyer to fill are apparent: the lawyer will help the client to achieve some clear-cut and well-defined goal, like the preparation of a will. There are other, somewhat more amorphous components to the lawyer's relationship

---

[27] AM. BAR ASS'N, MODEL RULES OF PROFESSIONAL CONDUCT, Preamble ¶ 2 (2019) (hereinafter MODEL RULES).

[28] Spencer Rand, *Hearing Stories Already Told: Successfully Incorporating Third Party Professionals into the Attorney–Client Relationship*, 80 TENN. L. REV. 1, 24–25 (2012).

[29] WILLIAM M. SULLIVAN, ANNE COLBY, JUDITH WELCH WEGNER, LLOYD BOND & LEE S. SHULMAN, EDUCATING LAWYERS: PREPARATION FOR THE PROFESSION OF LAW 22–24 (2007) (listing the ability to identify legal problems a critical skill that all lawyers should possess).

with their client. In a recent book, journalist Charles Duhigg describes the different types of conversations people have with one another and explains that one of the most important things about any conversation is not necessarily the words that people use, but rather what it is they are trying to communicate, what is it that the conversation is really about.[30] Effective client counseling at the front end of a lawyer–client relationship to try to understand what it is the client wants to accomplish, and what the conversation (or attorney–client relationship) is "really about," can help the lawyer understand the full range of goals the client has, and often those go beyond the purely functional purpose of the relationship. While some lawyers might simply ask "what" a client wants, another lawyer might ask "why"? What is the client trying to accomplish? What do they want to get out of the relationship and the representation? That leads to the next value the lawyer–client relationship can satisfy. While there might be times when what the client wants and needs will be clear from the conversation between the client and the lawyer, and it is purely functional or instrumental, there are also other things that might be under the surface, things that a more in-depth conversation with the client will reveal.

Thus, in addition to the functions a lawyer brings to the relationship, the attorney–client relationship has an affective value as well. The affective component of the attorney–client relationship deals more with feelings and emotions.[31] While this may seem odd that a professional (outside of a therapist) deals with client emotions, in reality the lawyer deals with client emotions all the time, and often the attorney–client relationship has an emotional or affective element to it apart from (or deeply intertwined with) the functions the client is asking the lawyer to fulfill. The client might want peace of mind that they will pass on their wealth to their loved ones upon the client's death. They want to know that they are appropriately disposing of toxic chemicals "by the book" so that they do not face an investigation, civil penalties, or even a criminal charge for violating environmental law (assuming, of course, that they also do not want to cause harm to members

---

[30] CHARLES DUHIGG, SUPERCOMMUNICATORS: HOW TO UNLOCK THE SECRET LANGUAGE OF CONNECTION 25 (2024).

[31] For scholarship that surveys the ways that legal assistance can play an affective role in clients' lives, see Peter Margulies, *Political Lawyering, One Person at a Time: The Challenge of Legal Work against Domestic Violence for the Impact Litigation/Client Service Debate*, 3 MICH. J. GENDER & L. 493, 502 (1996); Lauren A. Newell, *Rebooting Empathy for the Digital Generation Lawyer*, 34 OHIO ST. J. ON DISP. RESOL. 1 (2019); John P. Wesley, *Breaking the Vicious Circle: The Lawyer's Role*, 6 VT. L. REV. 363, 371–72 (1981) (describing the "affective" or personal bond between the lawyer and their clients in the representation of survivors of intimate partner violence).

of the community). They might want to feel heard, or seen, or that they have someone in their corner fighting for them.

Lawyers often do so much more than serve as functionaries or clerks, filling out forms, filing paperwork, checking off boxes. It is true that some of what lawyers do today, particularly due to new practice technologies, does result in the lawyer doing little more than completing forms for clients.[32] But even with certain transactions that involve little creativity, like a simple purchase and sale of a home, even one involving a mortgage, the lawyer plays an important and relatively simple functional role, but the emotional valence of the event is extremely high. A typical real estate transaction involves few substantive changes on hundreds of pages of documents. A paralegal working in the law office handling the matter will prepare many of these forms. The process is quite rote even though a lot of money might be changing hands in the transaction.

In addition, what is "a lot" of money is largely relative. A $500,000 transaction for a high net-worth individual might hardly register emotionally. Perhaps they "really want" that inexpensive cabin in the woods as a retreat to which they might return a few weekends a year. If the potential deal for the house falls through for some reason, they can always find another one. In a transaction for a modest home with a similar purchase price, for someone who has scraped together their life savings to put together the downpayment and their annual mortgage payment might be a real financial stretch for them, emotions will run high. Even for the wealthier person, they might have recently experienced the death of their last surviving parent and the sale involves the client's childhood home. Regardless, for many Americans, purchasing or selling a home might be one of the most, if not the most, significant economic transaction they will enter into in their lifetime.[33] It can be a highly emotional situation as well, for both buyer and seller. There is a low level of legal expertise required for many straightforward real estate closings, but the lawyer is there largely in an affective role, to give the client peace of mind that the transaction will go forward in accordance with law, and that the interests of the buyer, seller, and mortgage bank, respectively, will all be protected.

The practice of family law is similar.[34] The day-in-day-out work of the lawyer who practices family law might itself feel somewhat routine, but this

---

[32] Manveen Singh, *In the Line of Fire: Is Technology Taking Over the Legal Profession?* 40 N.C. CENT. L. REV. 122, 125 (2017).

[33] Candace Jackson, *Buying a Home Sight Unseen*, NY TIMES (July 13, 2018) (describing buying a home as "an emotional purchase, with intangibles like the feeling it evokes key to a buyer's attraction"), https://www.nytimes.com/2018/07/13/realestate/buying-a-home-sight-unseen.html (last visited, Apr. 27, 2025).

[34] Samuel V. Schoonmaker IV, *Withstanding Disruptive Innovation: How Attorneys Will Adapt and Survive Impending Challenges from Automation and Nontraditional Legal Services Providers,*

type of practice is almost always highly emotional, with parents entering into disputes over child custody, distribution of assets, and perhaps even blame for the dissolution of a marriage. Similarly, while patent law is highly complex in itself, there is also an emotional component to it for the inventor who might have put their life's work into their invention. A family that lives in affordable, government-subsidized housing might present their case as a relatively straightforward landlord–tenant dispute, with a low-cost apartment on the line, but that is precisely why emotions will run high: the family might fear homelessness should they lose this apartment. In all of these different situations, the lawyer–client relationship is one involving emotions, and thus there is an affective element to the lawyer–client relationship.

The political role of the lawyer

To return to the types of values the lawyer brings to the table within our system of government, the lawyer–client relationship also has a political value, both lofty and mundane. In the Preamble of the Model Rules, the American Bar Association suggests that "a lawyer should further the public's understanding of and confidence in the rule of law and the justice system because legal institutions in a constitutional democracy depend on popular participation and support to maintain their authority."[35] To return to some of the concepts described earlier, the lawyer plays a political role in serving their clients. Yes, some lawyers are "cause" lawyers, with a political agenda.[36] But here, I use the term political to reflect the fact that the lawyer helps mediate the relationship of the client to others as well as the state.[37]

The lawyer assists the client in maintaining a positive relationship to the state so that the client sees the legal system as a place to resolve disputes as opposed to leaving them unaddressed or resorting to self-help and vigilantism to solve them. In turn, this advances other democratic ideals, like fairness, equality before the law, and the rule of law. In the first decade of the 20th century, future Supreme Court Justice Louis Brandeis would stress the need for members of the community to have legal representation so that they would feel part of that community and would respect the community's

---

51 FAM. L. Q. 133, 149 (Summer 2017) (describing family law practice as "require[ing] high social skills and therefore human labor").

[35] MODEL RULES, *supra* note 27, Preamble ¶ 6.

[36] See Carrie Menkel-Meadow, *The Causes of Cause Lawyering, Toward an Understanding of the Motivation and Commitment of Social Justice Lawyers*, in CAUSE LAWYERING: POLITICAL COMMITMENTS AND PROFESSIONAL RESPONSIBILITIES, 31, 33 (Austin Sarat & Stuart Scheingold eds.,1998) (defining cause lawyering).

[37] See EMILE DURKHEIM, SOCIOLOGY AND PHILOSOPHY 37 (D. F. Pocock trans., Free Press 1974) (1953) (describing the relationship between the self and the state).

critical civic institutions.[38] This political role helps lawyers to realize the "thick" version of the rule of law described earlier. It advances critical democratic values like the rule of law itself; a faith in the legal system as a way to resolve disputes; and the sense that the law is a product of a democratic and pluralistic society.

Putting these overarching values together, the lawyer takes formal actions to protect a client's rights, which affords the client some degree of confidence that those rights are being protected, and helps to order the client's affairs with the institutions of the client's community and the state. Turning to the Preamble to the Model Rules again, it provides that the lawyer is "a member of the legal profession[,] ... a representative of clients, an officer of the legal system and a public citizen having special responsibility for the quality of justice."[39] It is apparent from these discussions that we recognize that lawyers play different roles for different clients at different times.

Why the typology of lawyer values and roles matters

Since the technology now exists to fill at least some of the functional roles that lawyers play—like helping a consumer to fill out a simple legal form—it is important to recognize that members of the legal profession do so much more than carry out merely ministerial tasks for every client they serve in every situation. In the early 20th century, the legal profession faced a series of challenges and the profession's responses to them resulted in what I would argue was a wholly transformed profession. With the advent of new technologies, there is the possibility that we might see the profession transform itself once again, but there is also another reason why understanding the consumer's job to be done matters, and that is because far too many Americans have a job to be done by a lawyer, but no lawyer to help them. There are a range of new and emerging technologies that might change the way lawyers practice and make some form of legal assistance available to many Americans. Coupled with the fact that there is a dramatic market failure in the legal services sector as far too many Americans face their legal problems without a lawyer, the emergence of new technologies means the legal profession is not just ripe for the type of disruption that Christensen has described, but there may actually be the technological capacity to carry it out in the coming days. Recognizing that, again, the point of the legal system is not to serve as a full-employment plan for lawyers, using the job-to-be-done framework helps us understand the important roles that lawyers

---

[38] Louis D. Brandeis, *The Opportunity in the Law,* 39 Am. L. Rev. 555, 559–60 (1905).

[39] See Model Rules, *supra* note 27, at Preamble ¶ 1

can fill, while recognizing that there might be some things that technology can do just as well, if not better, than a living, breathing lawyer.

Diagnosing the job to be done and matching the services to the need

I have already explored the different values and functions that a lawyer might fill. Diagnosing a particular legal situation to understand the importance of different values and functions in different settings is a critical prerequisite to later determining whether there are instances where a lawyer, or someone— or something—other than a lawyer, can satisfy the client's need in a particular situation. This requires us to understand the nature of a particular legal problem as well as the characteristics of clients themselves in order to enable us to match the service to the need in a particular setting.

Characteristics of the problem

There is no question that some of what lawyers do every day is fairly routine.[40] While we might want to glamourize the practice of law and imagine that it involves the lawyer executing a withering cross-examination one day that results in an acquittal for their client, making a high-profile legal argument before the Supreme Court on another, counseling a client through a difficult personal situation the next, and then crafting an elegant agreement that serves as the basis of a multi-million-dollar transaction, it should come as no surprise to most members of the legal profession that this is not representative of a typical lawyer's work week.

The profession has become highly specialized and a lawyer might spend their entire career working on a particular type of case or handling particular types of transactions. Some of this work might be relatively straightforward and will require minimal legal guidance to the client. For example, a landlord–tenant matter in a jurisdiction where tenants enjoy few legal protections might largely entail trying to negotiate a little more time for a family to move out of their apartment before the sheriff comes to evict them. At the same time, the landlord–tenant law in New York has been described by the state's highest court as an "impenetrable thicket, confusing not only to laymen but to lawyers."[41] Such complexity means that there is more work for lawyers to do, and more potential traps for unrepresented litigants.

---

[40] See DEBORAH L. RHODE, IN THE INTERESTS OF JUSTICE: REFORMING THE LEGAL PROFESSION 135–41 (2000) (describing at least some legal matters that lawyers handle as routine).

[41] Matter of 89 Christopher v. Joy, 35 N.Y.2d 213, 220 (1974).

The rules of the profession require that lawyers exhibit competence in handling legal problems for a client. Sometimes the competence required can be acquired, or might already be possessed, by a newly minted lawyer, while in others, the complexity of the matter might require specialized expertise that only a seasoned lawyer possesses. While the rules of ethics that guide lawyers do not set forth precisely what those circumstances are, they do state that the requisite competence that a lawyer must deploy in any given situation will hinge on "the relative complexity and specialized nature of the matter."[42] A lawyer's ability to provide such competent service will depend not only on the "general experience" the lawyer has accumulated but also their "training and experience in the field in question," as well as "the preparation and study the lawyer is able to give the matter."[43] It can also take into account "whether it is feasible to refer the matter to, or associate or consult with, a lawyer of established competence in the field in question."[44] It is in such situations that the phrase "thinking like a lawyer" is sometimes used to convey a number of different concepts: the fact that legal expertise will include the ability to identify a legal problem, understand its relative complexity, and address that problem in an appropriate and competent way.[45]

Another element of a problem, which is often tied up in its relative complexity, is the degree of tactical pluralism and agility a lawyer might have to deploy to solve it. That is, is it a static situation or one in which a lawyer must "think on their feet," as in a trial context or complex negotiations. The ability to assess a situation quickly, choose between potential responses, and pivot to new tactics is necessary in fluid situations where a particular game plan at the outset might not work as the matter unfolds. Similarly, another characteristic of a problem is that the lawyer's role might be preventative or reactive. A lawyer who engages in compliance work within a company, like a university, who provides trainings for university staff and sets up systems such that the school is able to report on its activities as required by state and federal authorities, will have to exhibit very different skills and will operate in a very different fashion than when that lawyer's client is charged with a discrimination or harassment claim. While what systems the lawyer put in place might show that the university was doing all it could to prevent that discrimination, their role will now shift from preventative to reactive, defending the university from the claim rather than working in a way to try to avoid those claims from arising in the first place.

---

[42] MODEL RULES, *supra* note 27, at R. 1.1., Com. 1.

[43] *Id.*

[44] *Id.*

[45] Larry O. Natt Gantt II, *Deconstructing Thinking Like a Lawyer: Analyzing the Cognitive Components of the Analytical Mind*, 29 CAMPBELL L. REV. 413, 437–78.

Probably the most important characteristic of the problem for our purposes is to assess what is at stake with any given client issue. The ABA's Model Rules recognize that this characteristic can determine the service necessary to meet the need in any given situation. Comment 5 to Model Rule 1.1 provides that "[t]he required attention and preparation" needed by the lawyer in any given situation "are determined in part by what is at stake; major litigation and complex transactions ordinarily require more extensive treatment than matters of lesser complexity and consequence."[46]

While many client problems will have many different facets to them, the core characteristics of these problems are the relative complexity of the issue, whether it is fluid in nature and requires a degree of tactical pluralism and agility, whether the lawyer's role is preventative or reactive, and what is at stake. But the characteristics of the problem are not enough for us to map our job-to-be-done framework onto our analysis. The characteristics of different clients, in different situations, will also play a large role in this type of assessment.

The characteristics of clients

Russian novelist Leo Tolstoy opens "Anna Karenina" with the following line: "All happy families are alike; each unhappy family is unhappy in its own way."[47] And while some legal problems might be similar—if not identical—to others a lawyer has handled in the past, every client is different, and what they might want out of assistance handling the very same legal problem that a lawyer has handled for a different client—or even the same client—in the past might vary in each particular representation. In order to conduct an analysis of a given legal problem using the job-to-be-done framework, in addition to understanding the characteristics of the problem, we also have to understand the characteristics of the client in a specific situation to understand what job it is they want done in that situation.

One key variable for determining the level of service a consumer might need in a given situation is what is at stake for a consumer in that instance. Once again, this is relative. A claim filed against a large insurance company for a slip-and-fall case where the plaintiff is seeking $25,000 in damages would hardly register on that company's balance sheet; they might pay the "nuisance value" of the lawsuit as it is sometimes called because it is cheaper to give in to the plaintiff's demands than pay their lawyer what it will cost to defend the suit. At the same time, a disputed $25,000 medical bill, perhaps for a single

---

[46] MODEL RULES, *supra* note 27, at R. 1.1, Com 5.

[47] LEO TOLSTOY, ANNA KARENINA: A NOVEL IN EIGHT PARTS 1 (Penguin Classics, deluxe ed. 2000, Richard Pevear & Larissa Volokhonsky, eds.).

trip in an ambulance for a sick child that the consumer's insurance company refuses to pay, could result in economic ruin for that consumer. What is at stake in any given situation is always a consumer-specific determination, and the greater the stakes relative to a particular consumer, the higher the problem will register in the affective analysis of the situation. It is essential that we calibrate the intensity of the legal services to the relative stakes for a particular consumer in order to ensure those services are adequate to address the consumer's job to be done in any given situation. Once again, the duty of competence incorporates the notion that the lawyer must calibrate their services to what is at stake in a particular situation.

Another important characteristic to discuss, although I will only do it briefly, is the client's ability to pay. That, of course, is something that really matters to lawyers, and to clients, and will sometimes dictate the type of service the client will receive. It is also a dominant variable in the current market for legal services. If all potential clients had an unlimited amount of money to pay for however much "justice" they desire, the market wouldn't be broken, wouldn't be ripe for disruption, and this book wouldn't be necessary. There are certainly clients who will pay, and can pay, whatever it takes to get the level of service they want from their lawyer. That client is rare, and even those clients, if given a less-expensive alternative that can satisfy their needs, might choose that alternative over the present situation. Of course, in many criminal matters, the right to counsel is provided by the state to those who cannot afford a lawyer, but that is simply not true even in most civil disputes where the consequences of not having representation are considerable, like where a family faces an eviction or foreclosure on their home. Nevertheless, the client's ability to pay for legal services is certainly one client characteristic that matters, but, in the present analysis, their willingness to pay might be more important and might help us calibrate services differently if there were alternatives to the current model.

The profession's stated belief is that every consumer, regardless of their ability to pay, should have access to legal services. As the Preamble to the Model Rules provides, a lawyer should "should seek ... access to the legal system" and should be "mindful of deficiencies in the administration of justice and of the fact that the poor, and sometimes persons who are not poor, cannot afford adequate legal assistance." As a result, they should "devote professional time and resources and use civic influence to ensure equal access to our system of justice for all those who because of economic or social barriers cannot afford or secure adequate legal counsel."[48] These

---

[48] MODEL RULES, *supra* note 27, at Preamble ¶ 6. While lawyers should provide services to those who desire them, they should also ensure that those who *need* services receive them as well.

are, indeed, lofty and laudable goals, but they are honored too much in the breach these days, which, again, creates a market that is ripe for disruption.

Another characteristic of a client that is important for our purposes here is their ability to understand the legal problem before them and whether they can function with something short of full-service representation.[49] Clients with some sophistication and savvy can understand even complex problems and, with even just a little bit of legal guidance, might be able to navigate their legal problem adequately and with the same level of competence that a lawyer might exhibit in a particular situation. For others, they might not be able to appreciate the nuances of advocacy in a particular situation, even if they are generally sophisticated and knowledgeable about the setting generally.

Some clients might also operate under some diminished physical or mental capacity or face some other barrier to comprehending their situation enough that they can navigate it without a great deal of hand-holding by the lawyer. And this could be the most sophisticated client whose judgment is clouded by the emotions involved in a situation such that they are not acting in their best interest, or it could be someone who has some impediment to effective communication that the lawyer and client cannot overcome. When assessing the characteristics of a client in a particular situation, their ability to function, communicate, and provide effective guidance to, and to receive effective guidance from, their lawyer might vary with the situation.

Similarly, if we are talking about the potential capacity for technology to serve clients as well as lawyers in certain settings, a particular client's ability to access that technology will be a critical characteristic of that client. Some clients simply to do not have the hardware, like access to a smartphone or broadband, or the "software" (personal knowledge), like the ability to navigate complex technological interfaces, that would make a technology-based intervention effective for them. Legal services delivered through technology are only effective if consumers have access to the tools to make use of that technology.[50]

---

[49] See, for example, Fred C. Zacharias, *Limited Performance Agreements: Should Clients Get What They Pay For?* 11 GEO. J. LEGAL ETHICS 915, 922 (1998).

[50] For a recent description of the digital divide in the U.S., see Joe Kane, *Broadband Policies Are Wasting the Chance to Make America Connected*, J. COURIER (Feb. 25, 2025), https://www.myjournalcourier.com/opinion/article/broadband-policies-wasting-chance-connect-joe-20183246.php (last visited, Apr. 27, 2025). For an earlier discussion of the challenges of using technology to promote access to justice given the persistent digital divide, see Raymond H. Brescia, *The Downside of Disruption: The Risks Associated with Transformational Change in the Delivery of Legal Services*, 2 N.Y. L. SCH. IMPACT 113 117 (2016).

Figure 2.1: The job-to-be-done variables

Values	Characteristics of problems
Adversarial role	Relative complexity
Democratic interests	Need for agility and tactical pluralism
Rule of law	Preventative or reactive
Access to justice	Stakes
Functions	**Characteristics of clients**
Instrumental	Ability to pay
Affective	Sophistication
Political	Capacity
	Technological wherewithal

Summing up: the values and functions of the profession

Clients have different jobs to be done in different situations, and in order to assess whether a full-service lawyer or something else might satisfy the consumer's job to be done requires an appropriate assessment of the roles and functions that that consumer wants filled when they seek legal assistance. Broadly speaking, this analysis contains several components: the values and functions of the lawyer as well as the affective and political role the lawyer should fill. It also requires an assessment of the characteristics of the problem and the client in each situation. Analyzing each problem along these variables will enable us to make an educated determination about when legal services delivered by a lawyer in every situation is necessary to meet the client's job to be done and whether there are instances where the technology available and that which is still emerging might meet the needs of the clients in certain situations and satisfy their job to be done. Figure 2.1 represents the different variables displayed in graphic form.

As we move through the remainder of this book, I will refer back to these variables as I attempt to chart the course toward Lawyer 3.0. When we are able to analyze each problem and each client along these variables, we are able to tease out what it is a consumer needs in order to resolve their legal problems and whether there is a technology-based solution that can enable them to do so. This will also help us to understand in what circumstances that technology can help a lawyer serve that consumer better or will enable the consumer to engage in self-help without the services of a lawyer. But there is also another type of analysis that is necessary to help consider ways in which to improve the delivery of legal services. This involves assessing the work that lawyers actually do on a day-in-day-out basis. I turn to this assessment in the next chapter.

Chapter 2: Key takeaways

1. Technological advancements, such as automation and artificial intelligence, have the potential to disrupt the legal profession similar to how the printing press rendered medieval scribes obsolete. The challenge for lawyers is to adapt to these changes and integrate technology to improve service delivery and efficiency.

2. Legal services in the United States are expensive due to factors like monopoly power, high salaries, the traditional law-firm structure, and the high cost of legal education. These economic forces limit access to legal representation, especially for low- and middle-income individuals, creating a significant "justice gap."

3. Historically, the legal profession has erected barriers to entry, such as expensive legal education and licensing requirements, to limit the number of practicing lawyers. These barriers have disproportionately impacted poorer and marginalized populations.

4. The legal profession has long maintained a monopoly on providing legal services by restricting non-lawyers from offering legal advice. These restrictions increase costs but are often justified for their consumer-protective effect, ensuring only trained professionals handle serious legal matters, but such restrictions also limit access to legal assistance.

5. The legal profession is "ripe for disruption" because new technologies could provide legal services at lower costs, potentially even without the need for lawyers in some cases. This could help bridge the gap between the need for legal services and their affordability.

6. Using Harvard professor Clayton Christensen's "job-to-be-done" framework, lawyers need to focus on what clients actually need, rather than simply providing traditional legal services. By understanding these needs, the legal profession could adapt to offer more efficient and accessible solutions, potentially incorporating new technologies.

7. The job-to-be-done variables that emerge when we assess the role lawyers play in their clients' lives revolve around the values at stake, the functions the client wants the lawyer to fulfill, the characteristics of a specific client problem, and the characteristics of the clients themselves.

3

How Lawyers Work

Lawyers, and their clients, might have a romanticized view of what it is the lawyer does throughout the day, and within that misperception lies some of the dysfunction that leaves the legal sector ripe for disruption. In this chapter, I will conduct an analysis of the types of services that lawyers provide and how they provide them. This analysis will describe such services along a temporal continuum, one that often corresponds to the intensity of the services provided as well. That is, it is often the case that the services become more complex the longer a lawyer engages with a consumer and their legal problem. I will present this as the "horizontal" service continuum. To complement that assessment of law practice, I will also offer a "vertical" view of the services typically provided by lawyers: how a lawyer functions in a particular sector or specialty. Once we can isolate and disaggregate the type of service that is provided along the horizontal continuum, and view it within the vertical stack of services provided within a particular sector, we can then start to apply a job-to-be-done framework against this vertical and horizontal matrix, to understand the values and functions at stake in the delivery of a particular type of service, applied in a particular area, for a particular client, in a specific context. When we isolate the service provided in a specific context we can then explore what mode or agent of service is best suited to deliver on the values and functions at stake in that context. In other words, once we understand the *what* of service, we can then try to isolate the *why* of service. In turn, we can then think about the *who* of service. In order to conduct this analysis, I will incorporate two approaches that can assist in this endeavor: business process analysis and design thinking. Each offers methods by which we can identify and isolate what it is lawyers do, and what needs the clients have in each practice setting. I will address each of these methodologies in turn to start this chapter.

Business process analysis

This methodology for improving business processes and outcomes to both understand them and make them more efficient and effective starts with a practical, step-by-step assessment of the operations of a company: how it delivers its products and services. It looks to break down the work of the organization into its component parts to understand what it is that organization does, how it does it, and whether there are process improvements that the entity could institute to make the delivery of services or the manufacturing of products more efficient and effective.[1] While it is useful in developing such process improvements, it can also help an entity simply understand what its employees are doing: that is, who is doing what, when they are doing it, and with whom. In the legal services context, we can look at the work as taking place along a horizontal continuum, as I will explain shortly, one that is temporal in nature during the life-cycle of the client engagement—from when a client first walks through the proverbial door and then what the lawyer does to serve that client through to the completion of a matter. Once again, we can use this type of analysis to help us identify potential process improvements, but it can also serve to help an organization understand what it is its employees are doing, when they are doing it, who is doing it, and how they are doing it. To reflect back on the functions and values discussed in the last chapter, business process analysis is mostly focused on the functions of the business, what it does and how it does it. The second methodology I will use—design thinking—is much more focused on the needs of the customer and client and brings into the analysis more of the values-based elements of the analysis I wish to conduct.

Design thinking

Design thinking often starts with trying to see a particular challenge from the perspective of the customer or client. In order to do so, one will attempt to interact with the customer in the environment in which they might use the product or service and try to roleplay what problem the customer is trying to solve and how they might go about trying to solve it.[2] During this initial phase of the creative process, one tries to "connect ... with the needs, desires, and

---

[1]   For an informative primer on business process analysis, see MARLON DUMAS, MARCELLO LA ROSA, JAN MENDLING & HAJO A. REIJERS, FUNDAMENTALS OF BUSINESS PROCESS ANALYSIS (2nd ed. 2018).

[2]   For informative descriptions of design thinking, see TOM KELLEY & DAVID KELLEY, CREATIVE CONFIDENCE: UNLEASHING THE CREATIVE POTENTIAL WITHIN US ALL 24–25 (2013), and TIM BROWN, CHANGE BY DESIGN 3–4 (2009).

motivations of real people [which] helps to inspire and provoke fresh ideas."[3] Next, one tries to synthesize what one learns from this immersion and analysis to enter into an experimentation phase where one tests the most promising ideas and converts them into prototypes of a product or service-delivery model.[4] The release of such a prototype into the world will then generate feedback that allows for modifications to the product or service that leads to "human-centered, compelling, workable solutions."[5] This process sounds a bit like what Christensen did when analyzing what "job" the consumers of milkshakes were trying to get done. He tried to get into the shoes of his customers to understand why they were consuming the product.

Applying this design-thinking approach to the delivery of legal services, when combined with business process analysis, helps the lawyer to meet the client in the middle, so to speak. It does not just analyze what lawyers do when they deliver legal services, it also asks what the client wants from their lawyer: both the functions the client wants the lawyer to carry out as well as the values the client wants the lawyer to promote in the delivery of such services. In order to get to the point where we can begin to tease out the values the lawyer might satisfy in a particular setting in accordance with the framework set forth in Chapter 2, I will first begin creating a typology of the types of services the lawyer provides, the horizontal continuum of the lawyer's work.

The horizontal continuum of care

Every law office has its own particular processes for carrying out discrete tasks when representing a client. A law firm that engages in litigation will have protocols in place to comply with both the demands of the case as well as court practices and procedural rules that govern the matter. In transactional matters, a firm will have quality-control measures designed to ensure that the firm makes all of the appropriate filings with respect to the transaction, that the documents prepared are accurate, and that a senior member of the team has signed off on them. It will also have procedures for identifying and monitoring potential conflicts of interest and for providing adequate supervision of its newer lawyers and paraprofessionals. Here, I will focus less on these discrete tasks in a particular practice area and more on the categories of client-facing services that are carried out in different stages of representation, from first finding clients to providing full-service representation. As a client moves from the earlier stages of an engagement

---

3   KELLEY & KELLEY, *supra* note 2, at 22.

4   *Id.*, at 23.

5   *Id.*, at 23–24.

with their lawyer, the nature of the services rendered by the lawyer changes. It is also possible that the service concludes: that a lawyer may provide limited or brief services to a client that satisfies their needs without the client having to move to later stages. When a matter does move to those later stages, the service provided likely gets more complex and intensive. But this continuum begins with a consumer understanding they have a legal problem and may want to retain a lawyer to help them solve it. For this reason, the continuum begins with client needs aligning with the services a lawyer provides.

Finding clients/identifying lawyers

The first stage of the legal services continuum involves matchmaking: lawyers finding clients and clients finding lawyers. The reality of this stage in the continuum is such that it is not necessarily a very effective or efficient stage in the legal services continuum. Lawyers spend a lot of time trying to find and secure clients, while many potential clients do not necessarily know where to turn once they realize that their problem is legal in nature, one that a lawyer might help them solve. In other words, there is a profound mismatch in the matchmaking process. It is highly inefficient, and in many ways ineffective. It is frustrating for lawyers and clients alike, and this sort of frustration is often the impetus for disruption.[6] As we consider the ways in which technology could disrupt the practice of law, this is one of those areas that could use significant improvement. Before we turn to the ways in which this component of the process could be improved, however, let us take a look at how it tends to work in practice today.

This matchmaking phase can be initiated by the lawyer in that they might have identified someone in need of legal services and notified them of the lawyer's availability to assist them with their needs. There are some restrictions on the extent to which lawyers can do this, and identifying clients with discrete legal needs is sometimes difficult. One could monitor court filings to find out who is being sued, or even death notices if you want to serve the potential heirs of someone who has passed away in the event of there being a potential will dispute. In the non-profit legal world, advocates have been able to lobby legislatures and court systems in different jurisdictions, in different types of cases, to require that the plaintiff in a particular type of case must provide a phone number for the local legal aid office, such as when a landlord commences an eviction case. There are many other ways

---

[6] For example, James Dyson came up with his bagless vacuum cleaner out of frustration with the ineffectiveness of current products on the market. Kate Gibson, *9 Examples of Innovative Products*, HARV. BUS. SCH. ONLINE (Mar. 23, 2022), https://online.hbs.edu/blog/post/innovative-product-examples (last visited, Apr. 27, 2025).

that lawyers find clients: they advertise on the television and radio; create websites and buy digital advertisements that appear as banner ads when a consumer conducts an internet search like "what do I do if my landlord tries to evict me?"; communicate by word-of-mouth through relatives and friends of the types of cases a lawyer handles; participate in a lawyer-referral services through a local bar association; and secure referrals from other lawyers.

From the perspective of the person who consumes legal services, there are certainly well-heeled "repeat players" who are active participants in the legal system and might even have a lawyer or even multiple lawyers to whom they turn when they have a legal problem. Most Americans are not in such a position. A potential consumer of legal services might know a lawyer or someone who knows a lawyer. They might know to contact the local bar association to try to find a lawyer. They might jot down the name of a lawyer whose advertisement they see on the side of a public bus. But would-be consumers of legal services also have to know they have a legal problem in the first place, let alone who they should call should they have one. The typical consumer might not know that lawyers specialize in particular areas of law and that a lawyer who generally handles criminal matters is probably not equipped to represent someone in a divorce. Even sophisticated clients might not always understand that their lawyer in one type of case is not necessarily who they would want representing them in a different type of matter.

This description of the matchmaking process shows that it is certainly an inexact—and inefficient—science for many reasons. The most important of these is that the fact that a potential consumer of legal services might have a legal problem is generally not public knowledge. There are instances, however, when that could be public knowledge. Most lawsuits are matters of public record. If one knew to look for court filings, one could determine that a particular consumer is a defendant in a lawsuit, or, if they filed the suit, that they are the plaintiff. At the same time, that a consumer might have been the victim of fraud or medical malpractice, is having a property-line dispute with a neighbor, might be considering divorce and might want to consult with a lawyer about their options: these are all things that are largely private, for good reason. Couple this with the specialization that occurs within the legal profession and that many lay people do not come in regular contact with a lawyer, even if they might see an advertisement in passing on occasion, or when watching late-night television, the matchmaking function is not very efficient or effective. Because of that, if we were to consider ways to improve the service-delivery model, we would likely start at this phase in trying to do so.

Before considering mere process improvements in this phase of the continuum to make sure the lawyer can fill the consumer's *functional* needs in an effective way, it is important to recognize that at this stage of the service-delivery relationship there are also critical *emotional* elements as well. The potential consumer of legal services could be in a state of worry, or even panic, that they are facing a significant legal issue, like the potential loss of custody of a child, or they might see a significant threat to their business or their livelihood. Their workplace might have become unbearable due to sexual harassment. They might face the prospect of losing their home. For many, the time between when they realize they have a legal problem and when they can secure representation that might help them resolve it, or at least give them a sense that they will have legal representation to protect their rights, is an emotionally fraught one. What is more, simply not knowing where to turn for any sort of assistance can in itself leave the individual with a sense of hopelessness and anxiety. The matchmaking process certainly has a functional element to it, but it is also emotionally charged, and the harder it is for the consumer to find a lawyer the more and more anxious they may become, or they might simply give up and resign themselves to the fact that the legal system is going to have its way with them. In assessing ways in which we might improve this phase of the service-delivery continuum, it is important that we recognize that it is a moment in time when consumer emotions can run high. Seeing this problem through the eyes of the consumer so that we might appreciate the affective elements of the matchmaking phase will only help us realize the importance of improving this process. It will also serve as a guide to when we should try to do so. Before we attempt such improvements, let us take this same sort of approach to looking next at the other phases of the horizontal continuum, which also have similar shortcomings at present.

Triaging clients and their needs

The second phase of the continuum involves assessing the potential legal needs of clients. Today, the most common way in which lawyers triage their clients is by meeting with them and discussing their situation. This can involve an assessment of the facts that gave rise to the problem the client faces, a determination that the problem is actually one in which the lawyer might be able to help the client in some way, a discussion of the client's goals for the representation, and the development of a tactical plan to solve the client's problem and achieve the client's goals.

Like with the matchmaking process, this stage also has several different elements to it. The client has a specific task they might want the lawyer to perform—prepare a will, for example. But there are also emotional components to this phase as well. Yes, a goal such as "prepare a will" is fairly straightforward, but there are also significant emotional elements to such a task. The lawyer is certainly discussing issues of the division of property, which one might look at in a cold and objective way, but the lawyer and

44

client are literally dealing with life-and-death matters: how to divide up such an estate upon the client's death. But it can also get worse. If the client has children, the lawyer will ask the client what they would want to happen if one of the children were to predecease the client. This is a situation many parents do not even want to contemplate. The point of the assistance is certainly functional in nature, but there are deeply emotional elements to it as well, as is often the case with many types of legal matters a prospective client might bring to a lawyer. Discussions that occur at this stage of the legal services continuum might involve delicate issues, and there will be emotion involved even in those conversations. One of the critical affective elements of this phase is for the lawyer to strive to understand the client's goals and to give their client a sense that they now have someone in their corner, someone who can help them resolve their problem. The lawyer gives the client some degree of comfort that at least their rights will be protected in the context of the presenting problem.

This aspect of this phase of the continuum reveals that it possesses emotional or affective elements. There are also other important values that a consumer is hoping to satisfy at the outset of any lawyer–client relationship. While many contexts in which a client might seek out the assistance of a lawyer are themselves emotionally fraught, there is also another affective *and* political element to the lawyer's role in this phase as well: the client is typically asking for assistance ordering their legal affairs in relation to other members of the community and wants that ordering to occur in a manner that is consistent with the requirements of the legal system. They want to be assured that they can take action that will not lead to more legal problems in the future.

As I hope this discussion reveals, just about every client has an instrumental job to be done by the lawyer in most situations. We must take an expansive view of that job, however, and understand that the other issues we identified in the previous chapter—the values advanced through, and the affective and political elements embedded in, the lawyer–client relationship—are present in most legal contexts, even in different phases of the service-delivery continuum, and the "triaging-clients" phase is no exception. We cannot overlook these elements of this phase when attempting to improve this process, otherwise we will lose some of the core values and functions that the profession is supposed to fulfill in any effort to address the continuum's shortcomings. But understanding the client's full spectrum of needs in the triaging phase will then inform the next phase: that of constructing the actual delivery of services.

Putting together a service-delivery plan

In the next phase of the legal services continuum, the lawyer will consider the tactics they will utilize to meet the client's objectives. This may follow the initial meeting and diagnostic assessment of the client's case after the lawyer synthesizes what they have learned from the client and conducts some legal or factual research about the matter on their own. The lawyer might even start to chart out the course forward in the initial interaction with the client. Regardless of when the lawyer develops the plan of action they might choose to address the client's legal needs, that plan is, to borrow once again from Richard Susskind, "bespoke"[7]: that is, it is custom-made and tailored to each client's particular needs, at least in theory.

While each plan of action is unique to each client, in a highly narrow and specialized practice, where a lawyer might see a large volume of cases that are similar in nature, that plan may resemble many of the plans the lawyer prepares for other clients. But even in situations where client needs vary widely with each type of case, the lawyer, after the initial consultation, generally starts to consider the ways in which the case before them is similar to a case or cases the lawyer has handled in the past. The lawyer might consider the legal claims for or against the client and ask where the lawyer might have asserted or defended against similar claims in prior cases. They might look at the transaction the client wants the lawyer to facilitate or the entity the client wants the lawyer to form and ask themselves "where have I done something like this before?" While the lawyer creates a tailored tactical plan for the client in line with the client's unique overarching strategic goals and their specific situation, oftentimes, in preparing this plan, they are piecing together a patchwork quilt of work they have done for previous clients, probably pulling from pleadings in one case or a series of cases in a similar posture, or starting from a contract or will they prepared for a different client. Sometimes this work will involve little more than changing the names of the interested parties and other, similar information, like the dates of certain events or the addresses of the parties, when the rest of the content of the document is adequate to address the client's needs.

We should maintain no illusions that the so-called bespoke services that the lawyer offers each client consists of the lawyer sitting down and drafting every document they prepare for the client from scratch, or that the lawyer starts from a "beginner's mind" every time they embark upon the representation of the client. I had the great fortune of working with an extremely seasoned lawyer in my practice representing tenants in eviction proceedings. Practically every time he represented a client, he would sit down and read the statutes related to such proceedings, thinking that by reviewing those statutes with a particular client's needs in mind, it might help him see the law differently and find some new argument to advance that client's interests. Sometimes he *would* come up with some new claim from his fresh reading of the statutes.

---

[7] RICHARD SUSSKIND, THE END OF LAWYERS? 34 (2010).

And this was true even though he had helped draft the statutes in the first place! But, I would submit, this type of approach is fairly rare in most law practices, and many lawyers will not necessarily re-read relevant statutes that might affect their clients' interests in every matter.

Rather, a lawyer typically builds their representation plan based on what they have done in the past; the claims and defenses they have raised for other clients; or the contracts and other agreements they have put together in other, similar contexts. Even the letters they write are often based on something they have written to an opposing counsel, a court, or a regulator previously in another matter. One might call what the lawyer does in such a situation a "shortcut," while the lawyer will probably consider it efficient, and a case of them not "recreating the wheel." This can have benefits for clients, for sure, as the tactics the lawyer has used in the past hopefully have proven successful in prior matters, but it also makes the work of the lawyer take less time. For the private clients, that means the lawyer will charge those clients less for this work. For the non-profit clients and prospective clients, these sorts of efficiencies enable the lawyer to serve more clients.

Figuring out a set of tactics that align with the client's overall goals will require an assessment of the client's practical needs but also take into account some of the other elements of the job that the client wants done. There is an instrumental element to the decision-making process, for sure. The client will have a particular and practical objective that they need the lawyer to achieve: file for patent protections, prepare and negotiate a commercial lease, file an employment discrimination claim, and so on. But other goals and "jobs" will often accompany whatever practical thing the client wants done. This might include the affective element of having a lawyer by the client's side (figuratively and literally) as they navigate a complex business transaction or face a criminal charge. There is a political element to the representation as the service the lawyer provides will help the client order their affairs with others and perhaps in relation to the state. Depending on the nature of the representation, the lawyer will likely also satisfy some of the values the profession is designed to serve: like providing support through an adversarial process, ensuring the rule of law is upheld, and protecting the individual dignity of the client. While the lawyer may not explicitly consider every one of these dimensions every time they embark upon representation of a particular client, they are always there in some respect by the nature of the role of the lawyer in our legal system. The effective lawyer providing client-centered representation will typically gauge some of these aspects of the representation, consciously or even unconsciously, as they discuss the needs of each client when devising a set of tactics they will use in carrying out the representation. To truly satisfy the client's job to be done, the lawyer will strive to look at the problem the client presents in a multi-faceted way, one that recognizes that the lawyer's role goes beyond the instrumental in almost every context.

Still, while it is appropriate to think of every client as unique in a world where the lawyer is supposed to advance the dignity of each client, and, in light of that, we may believe the lawyer tailors bespoke services from scratch in every instance, the reality is that the lawyer typically builds on work they have done in the past to create a game plan for the client they have in the present. Now, why this matters will become apparent when we start talking about the technologies that presently exist that might streamline some of this work in important ways that make it even more efficient, and, at least in some instances, might obviate the need for much if any lawyer time at all. Once the representation plan is assembled, a critical component of that plan will involve an assessment of the nature of the services the lawyer is going to provide and the means by which they will provide those services. In the next few sections, I will describe the nature of the services the lawyer will render, from the least intensive to the most intensive. In some ways, after the plan is developed, a type of sorting occurs based on the nature of the services the lawyer will provide. So, in the next few sections of this chapter I will discuss the three service-delivery channels through which a lawyer might provide such services. Here, clients are sorted, or triaged, into these three different channels based on the nature of the services the lawyer will offer the client. The "phase" of the representation continuum here is the service-delivery stage, which itself is divided into these three channels, as I describe next.

Providing information-based assistance to clients

In some cases, the lawyer and client might agree that in order to achieve the client's goals, and to satisfy some of the other elements of the job to be done for the client, a bit of counseling is all the client needs from the lawyer. That might come in the form of oral advice, or the lawyer might prepare a written guidance to the client that explains the situation to them. In some instances, this mode of service is well-suited to a setting where the lawyer's intervention is preventative in nature. The lawyer might provide guidance that enables the client to ensure they are complying with rules regarding disclosure of a patient's medical records, or lets the client know that before they embark on a particular course of action, there are certain steps the client should take to avoid any legal pitfalls. The advice might also simply include an assessment to let the client know that they have nothing to worry about, or that there is nothing to be done about a particular issue: for example, that a former employee's claims appear baseless and that there's nothing to do unless that former employee files a lawsuit; or that the appraisal of the client's home by the local tax authorities seems high, but is probably difficult to challenge.

From the lawyer's perspective, they will likely assess the matter as relatively low in complexity, which is why they can provide such basic information to meet the instrumental needs of the client. From the client's perspective, however, they might rate the problem as high on the "affective scale." They are seeking out the lawyer's guidance largely for peace of mind, either to understand that their perceived problem is not a problem at all, or that there is nothing they can do about it even if it is a problem, at least in terms of legal interventions that might address it. But even if the level of service is relatively minimal, and the matter fairly simple, the lawyer's services here could satisfy an important emotional need of the client: a sense of ease or acceptance.

There are also other values simple advice can fulfill. From a rule-of-law perspective, a client's complaint about their situation might require the lawyer to advise the client that the proper course of action is to do nothing, to respect the system's determination in a particular context, even when the client might not like the current state of affairs. If there truly is no legal mechanism to change the client's condition, the lawyer can urge the client to accept their lot. And such advice might even include a warning that to do something other than accept it, that is, to potentially break the law, could have significant adverse legal consequences. In such a situation, even simple advice has rule-of-law elements to it.

In a society where law affects virtually every aspect of American life, even the most basic of guidance can serve a critical function in ensuring individuals and entities can operate within the bounds of the law. This has an instrumental function for certain, but it can also satisfy other elements of the lawyer's role. In addition, it can serve a critical preventative role: when clients secure compliance with the law through others and themselves act in accordance with the law, it can help ensure small issues do not become larger problems. I think it is fair to say that with most legal problems, the very fact that they are a legal problem probably means such limited service as the provision of information and guidance by the lawyer will not be sufficient to satisfy all elements of the client's job to be done in a particular situation, which is why most lawyers consistently offer services through the two other main channels of assistance as well, which I describe next.

Engaging in a brief service to clients

The next service-delivery channel involves the delivery of a brief service to the client. This might involve preparing a simple will or power of attorney, writing a "cease-and-desist" letter when a client believes their intellectual property is being used by another in an unauthorized manner, or putting the finishing touches on a lease agreement from a template the lawyer uses in many different contexts. Here, like with information-based assistance alone, the nature of the work is often fairly straightforward, and the lawyer has an important functional role to play on behalf of the client. Like with the provision of brief advice, this type of assistance might score high on the affective scale: the lawyer's role gives the client a certain amount of peace of mind that the matter is being handled by a lawyer. The service might involve an important political function as well, ensuring that *others* abide by the law and the rule of law, or helping the client to order their relations to other individuals and/or the state.

There is always the possibility that this sort of service will not be sufficient to resolve the client's problem, however. This sort of intervention might simply serve as the starting point of the representation and not achieve the client's ultimate goal. Perhaps that candidate for public office who is using the client's song in their rallies wants to keep doing so, no matter how threatening the lawyer's letters get. Or the prospective tenant wants to negotiate changes to the simple lease form the landlord's lawyer has proposed. The lawyer's best efforts to resolve a matter, short of getting deeply engaged in it and at more expense to the client, might sometimes fail and a brief service is not enough to meet the client's job to be done. It might also be the case that the complexity of the matter means more than a brief service is necessary to resolve the problem for the client. In such cases, the last channel—full service—comes into play.

Providing full-service representation

There are times when the client's job to be done requires nothing short of full service from the lawyer. The client might face the prospect of incarceration for alleged criminal conduct. The client's business is facing the prospect of filing a complex bankruptcy petition. The client's core intellectual property is at risk such that if they lose the protection of their inventions or ideas, they will lose all meaningful sources of revenue. Here, the complexity of the matter is likely high so that advice and counseling or brief assistance alone will not be enough to fulfill the client's job to be done. In addition to the level of complexity of the matter driving the decision to provide full-service representation, the other dimensions of lawyer service—the values at stake and the affective and political aspects of the problem—will also require that the lawyer provides this level of service. In many ways, this type of representation is not only the core work of what most lawyers do with much of their time, given the complexity and tactical agility required in such representation, and the high stakes, it is also the case that this type of service is that which is likely hardest for a technological solution to address. Acknowledging when a particular problem requires this service channel based on the characteristics of problems as described in Chapter 2 helps us to identify situations where such full-service representation, by an actual lawyer, is essential, not because we want to ensure lawyers have a *job to do*,

Figure 3.1: The horizontal continuum of care

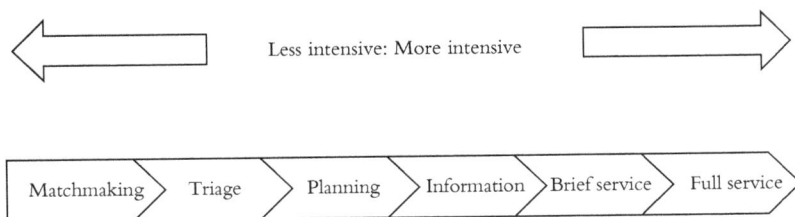

but because a full-service lawyer is what is necessary to meet the client's *job to be done*. Figure 3.1 presents a crude, graphic depiction of this horizontal continuum of care.

Vertical/sectoral analysis

While this horizontal sense of the legal continuum of care helps us to disaggregate the types of problems clients have and that lawyers face, and the channels through which those lawyers deliver service to clients, another way of looking at what lawyers do is through an assessment of the different sectors in which they operate. This is the "vertical" view of the lawyer's work that I mentioned earlier. This vertical view tells us that we can analyze what lawyers do based on the sector in which they work and that the horizontal continuum might look different within a particular sectoral stack. This might yield different results once we start thinking about where direct, full-service legal representation is necessary in certain instances, and where something less than that, delivered through new technological tools, might satisfy the client's job to be done. Each vertical is different, given the nature of the work, but it will still largely generate the same sort of horizontal continuum of care, from finding clients and triaging them to full-service representation. When deconstructing law practice to understand the client's job to be done in each situation, one must take into account not just the type of service they might need, but the area of law in which that service is being provided. Legal work with regard to the U.S. Patent and Trademark Office is different from work in the anti-trust space, which is different from drafting wills, which is different from handling white collar defense cases. Each sector within the legal services industry will reflect the different service-delivery modes of the horizontal continuum. At the same time there are unique practices within each mode in that continuum. Full-service representation in the banking sector will look very different from the provision of full-service representation for a lawyer pursuing an employment discrimination claim on behalf of a client with such a claim. Lawyers in each sector should define what different service-delivery modes on the horizontal continuum will look like in their specific area of practice.

Applying the job-to-be-done framework to the horizontal and vertical typologies

Any use of design thinking and business process analysis in the context of the delivery of legal services can help us see the delivery of services through the consumer's eyes as well as to break down the delivery of those services into their component parts. This can help us make such services more responsive to consumer needs as well as to make the delivery more efficient. Hopefully, lawyers already do this second part with some frequency, thinking about more efficient ways to provide services to satisfy customer demand, lower the cost of services, and possibly serve more clients. But there is another reason, at this moment, to use these two tools for analyzing the services that lawyers provide: to determine whether, in light of new technologies, there are ways that such technologies can streamline the delivery of services, both at each stage in the process, but also in the overall provision of such services. When technology can improve the process of delivering legal services, it can also serve to improve access to justice: lawyers can serve more clients in a more affordable and, presumably, more accessible way. In subsequent chapters I will explore how we can harness these tools of analysis and the technology that is quickly becoming available to lawyers to do just that. In the next chapter, I will describe some of these technologies in some depth so as to help set the stage for the discussions that follow.

Chapter 3: Key takeaways

1. This chapter has introduced the concept of a horizontal continuum in legal services, where the complexity and intensity of legal services increase as a lawyer engages with a client over time. It breaks down the service-delivery process into stages from initial client contact to full-service representation.
2. The use of business process analysis and design thinking as methodologies can improve the delivery of legal services. Business process analysis helps dissect and streamline how legal services are delivered, while design thinking emphasizes seeing challenges from the client's perspective, focusing on their needs and values.
3. At present, the lawyer–client matchmaking function is inefficient. Many clients struggle to find the right lawyer, and many lawyers spend excessive time trying to find clients. This is an area ripe for disruption, potentially through technological innovation.
4. Throughout the lawyer–client relationship, lawyers must address not only the functional legal needs of clients but also their emotional concerns as well. Legal consultations often involve highly personal and emotionally charged matters,

like drafting a will or resolving a family dispute. An effective system for meeting consumers' jobs to be done will take into account the affective element of the provision of legal services.

5. While legal services are often described as "bespoke," in reality many lawyers rely on templates and past work. This allows for efficiency but also raises the potential for technological tools to take over some aspects of legal work, making it more cost-effective.

6. By applying the job-to-be-done framework alongside business process analysis and design thinking to understand what it is lawyers do and what clients actually want them to do, technology could play a pivotal role in streamlining legal service delivery, potentially improving access to justice by making legal services more affordable.

4

The New Legal Tech

I began law school in the late 1980s, the last time a significant technological shift transformed at least one aspect of the practice of law. Then, digital search and desktop word processing served as the new technologies that changed the way lawyers went about their business. Before these technologies, lawyers typically produced work product on what are still referred to as legal pads, those yellow, 8.5″ x 14″ sets of bound paper on which lawyers would write out all manner of work longhand, whether that was a letter to a client or adversary, or even a brief. The lawyer would hand the artifact to a secretary, who would then type up the document for the lawyer's review. It might go through several revisions before the finished product was completed, meaning the secretary would likely have to type the document out each time until it was ready for filing, mailing, and so on. Legal research was also done in an analog fashion, with lawyers combing through and poring over the statute books and unbound, advanced-sheet supplements; the reports of judicial decisions and the unbound pocket parts; and the volumes of Shepard's publications, that sprawling system that enabled lawyers to check the validity of the authorities they wished to cite in their briefs. This was a very visceral act: lawyers would seek out and hold the actual law books in their hands, law offices had physical libraries containing volumes and volumes of the content relevant to their practice, and lawyers would make regular trips to a local bar association or law school library that might contain a more extensive collection of works than that lawyer's own office might hold.

Going to law school during this liminal space between the analog and digital law office was like seeing the future unfold before you. My fellow students and I would learn how to conduct analog searches of cases and even consult Shepard's bound volumes by day, and then venture into the bowels of the law library where the librarian maintained a dozen Westlaw and Lexis terminals on which we could hack our way through the instructions we received from salespeople from those companies. While few of our professors had likely ever used such services, as students we felt like we were in on a secret, all the while knowing that the purpose of making these services free to us as students was so that we would get hooked on them and would want to use them once we became lawyers. While this was before the widescale introduction of the internet, few understood that this form of digital research would essentially supplant analog research in just a couple of years.

Similarly, while at least some of my colleagues and I had laptop computers, most did not. And I still remember the first time a student had the temerity to actually bring one to class, which was held in a large lecture hall with about one hundred students in attendance. Apart from the professor's voice delivering their lecture, the only other noise one would hear in the room was the student typing on his laptop. This modern distraction annoyed our classmates, me included. Today, almost every one of my students has a laptop or tablet open at their desk, a phenomenon so common across higher education that some professors have taken to banning them from the classroom, out of a belief that such technology does not aid in the learning process (especially when, at any given moment, a scan of student screens from the back of a classroom will reveal that they often are looking at things *other* than their class notes, but I digress).

When I began work as a lawyer with the Legal Aid Society of New York, representing low-income tenants, my East Harlem office had just begun installing desktop computers in each of the lawyer's offices. These were connected to a mainframe and a single dot-matrix computer at the center of the office. The big technology of the time was the fax machine, which zipped documents back-and-forth over phone lines, and a pile of faxes would come in on the office's central machine to be distributed on weird, waxy, curled paper to their intended recipients. Even though my colleagues and I each had a computer at our desk, which did little more than help us with word processing, many of the lawyers in the office still wrote their communications by hand and passed them to the secretaries in the secretarial pool that our office still maintained.

My first experience using a combination of the new technologies available to us was when I began to learn how to pull together legal filings using digital tools. Most of my work involved defending tenants in eviction cases in New York City's housing court. While eviction law is generally fairly straightforward in many jurisdictions, and tenants do not have a wide range of defenses to an eviction case, in New York City, a city of renters, elected officials have been fairly responsive over the years to the needs of their constituents and have put in place rent and eviction protections that afford tenants some defenses and claims that a lawyer defending such tenants might be able to interpose in an effort to delay or even prevent their client's eviction. These might include procedural defenses, like the landlord failed to provide adequate notice to the tenant prior to commencing the case or failed to serve the legal papers of the case in a manner in accordance with law. A tenant might have substantive claims as well, like the landlord was in violation of the local rent laws such that the tenant was the victim of a rent overcharge. The opportunity might present itself to raise more arcane equitable claims, like the defense of laches or estoppel: concepts that a typical tenant would not know to raise on their own, but which a creative lawyer might interpose in an effort to make the landlord's case more difficult to prosecute.

I was fortunate to have joined an office with many seasoned lawyers who had all worked for extended periods of time in the housing court, so that, as a whole, there were few claims or defenses that they collectively had not seen or raised before. Because of this, if one of my colleagues wanted to raise any defense or claim in a particular case, there was a good chance either they had done so in a prior case or, at a minimum, someone else in my office had. I would often hear colleagues as they walked the halls, going door-to-door to different lawyers' offices, asking whether anyone had seen a case like the one the lawyer was presently handling, and whether anyone had a sample of a pleading where they had raised a particular kind of defense. If the lawyer was able to find a colleague who had represented a tenant in a similar case, and had interposed the defense the lawyer wanted to raise, they would ask to see the answer so that they could copy the text of the defense into their own client's answer as the other lawyer had presented it in the prior case.

This kind of process serves as a sort of metaphor for how most lawyers practice generally. One of the worst offenses in any law office (apart from stealing client funds, missing a court-ordered deadline, or filing a frivolous case) is "recreating the wheel." If a lawyer has taken the time to research a claim or defense; has pulled together a pleading or other filing where they have drafted the language necessary to interpose that claim or defense; and, as drafted, that claim or defense has withstood an adversary's attempt to dismiss or strike it, the language that lawyer has pulled together to assert that claim or defense then becomes the starting point for any effort to raise something similar in another case. Should the lawyer see an opportunity to use that language again in a subsequent case, they will not hesitate to do so and will recycle that language again and again until the law changes. And this approach is not limited to litigation. A lawyer engaged in contract drafting or preparing wills for clients will build on something they have done in the past rather than start from scratch each time they face the same, or a similar, problem.

Back in my legal aid office, after hearing my colleagues pass through the halls asking for help with their cases all the time, I thought there had to be a technological solution to the challenge they seemed to face almost daily. While we were not necessarily recreating the wheel every day, we were assembling it from its component parts over and over again. In order to address this challenge, I began to compile what I would refer to as the "kitchen sink" answer, as in, what if you wanted to throw the proverbial kitchen sink at the landlord and included every possible defense, objection, and counterclaim ever imagined in that pleading? Now, it was highly unlikely that there ever was a single case in which a tenant could raise every possible claim, so this answer was itself unlikely to find its way into a case in its complete form. By loading this answer onto everyone's computer, as we did, my colleagues and I could access this kitchen-sink answer which contained every claim or defense one might want to raise. And here's where the efficiency came in: instead of having to assemble a new answer every time from the shards of other, prior pleadings, all a lawyer had to do was delete the things they did not think appropriate to include in the answer they might file in any particular case. This served as a significant time-saver for my colleagues and I, even if I did miss having my colleagues pop their heads in my door just about every day, asking if I had an answer with a particular type of claim in it.

Another innovation that would soon come to my office was email. This also served to make communication with colleagues and opposing counsel much more efficient. Instead of playing what was annoyingly referred to as "phone tag"—an endless series of missed calls and messages scrawled out by the receptionist on small slips of paper—we could communicate far more effectively, resolve at least some questions through electronic communication, or even use email to schedule a time to actually speak. A simple feature of email, which no one considers extraordinary today, included the ability to send a document as an attachment to an email. That one could open. On one's own computer. And start to edit yourself. Instead of inquiring of a colleague in another office whether they could share a brief that laid out an argument I wanted to use in a brief of my own, and then asking a messenger to go to that other lawyer's office to pick up a floppy disk that contained a version of the brief, that colleague could simply send it to me as an attachment, and then I could just access it as a file and start to write my own brief in a matter of seconds. Again, this certainly does not sound all that groundbreaking today, but, over 30 years ago, this email function served as a fairly significant leap forward in terms of efficiency.

Entering the profession when I did afforded me the opportunity to have an insider's view of the changes that the profession was going through at that time. But few of these technological innovations really displaced *lawyers*. They were, in the Christensen framework, not *disruptive* innovations but *sustaining* ones. They made the work of lawyers more efficient and effective. After the introduction of desktop computers and digital research across the legal industry, there were fewer jobs for legal secretaries, messengers, and other support staff, for sure. But it is not like the legal industry has gotten smaller. Indeed, there are more lawyers in the U.S. today than there were in the early 1990s. But what about the technological innovations that we are seeing coming to a law office near you today and in the near future? Are they likely to serve as a disruptive, rather than a sustaining, force?

The end of lawyers?

In November 2022, the world was introduced to a new kind of technology. Talk of "artificial intelligence" has been fairly common for decades and dystopian futures plagued by robots who have become "self-aware" have penetrated popular culture. The newest iteration of this technology—generative artificial intelligence, what I will refer to as GenAI—had many claiming the end of lawyers was nigh. While digital search, ubiquitous in common internet use and legal research, served as a significant technological step forward in prior decades, GenAI offered something different. This new technology operates quite differently from mere search, which generally does no more than return links to sites and other sources in response to a query. What GenAI does is produce an *answer* to a query in narrative form. It scans what are known as "large language models," or LLMs, in compiling this answer, and can even provide sources for the text it generates. Soon after the company OpenAI made its first GenAI system, which made this tool widely available to the public, some began to wonder what impact it would have on the practice of law. Upon its release, Andrew Perlman, dean of the law school at Suffolk University, had some fun with the technology.[1] He would "write" a law review article, the main work product of legal academics, using the technology. And by "write," I mean that, by his own admission, Perlman posed a series of queries to the ChatGPT app and packaged the responses to those queries into the article. If ChatGPT could produce something like a law review article, what aspect of law practice could it *not* do? Was GenAI going to spell the end of lawyers (and law professors)? If it could generate a law review article, could it also produce a legal complaint, a contract, or a guidance memorandum to a client? Could someone log onto ChatGPT, like one might access the WebMD app for medical advice, and ask the platform to conduct legal research as to how that person might fight a consumer debt case, file for bankruptcy, or assert a copyright infringement claim? Lawyers themselves began to experiment with the tool, seeing if it could supplement their own research, find previously unknown authorities for positions advantageous to their client, or draft legal filings. While lawyers may have found that the tool could streamline some of their workflow, the introduction of the technology had some asking whether it could replace lawyers altogether: whether this technology would mean the end of lawyers.

But as more and more users, including lawyers, began to utilize the technology, it became apparent that the technology did not always operate

---

[1] Andrew Perlman, *The Implications of ChatGPT for Legal Services and Society*, Suffolk University Law School Research Paper No. 22-14 (Rev. Feb. 29, 2024), https://papers.ssrn.com/sol3/papers.cfm?abstract_id=4294197 (last visited, Apr. 27, 2025).

in a way that was useful. In fact, at least some of its offerings were not just off the mark, they were downright disturbing. Probably the first inkling that GenAI was not all it was cracked up to be was when *New York Times* technology journalist Kevin Roose shared some of his experiences with the technology. He began having lengthy exchanges with a GenAI "chatbot," engaging in a great deal of back-and-forth over a range of issues. At some point during the exchange, the platform began to generate some strange responses. It professed its "love" for Roose. It even asked Roose if he would be willing to leave his spouse so that Roose and the bot could be together.[2] Roose's interactions with the technology led in part to the widespread recognition that GenAI might be prone to what has come to be known as "hallucinations," and it was not long before lawyers learned that relying on an error-prone technology definitely has its downsides.

In the spring of 2023, the lawyers for a plaintiff in a personal injury case, *Mata v. Avianca*,[3] filed in the federal court in Manhattan, found themselves having to answer to the judge in their case as to why he, his court staff, and the opposing counsel in the case were having a hard time finding the cases the lawyers had cited in their opposition to the defendants' motion to dismiss, a procedural maneuver that would have all but ended the plaintiff's case if it could not be defeated. In an effort to produce authorities that would support the lawyers' opposition to that procedural maneuver, the lawyers apparently turned to ChatGPT to help them find the cases that would keep the plaintiff's case alive. And, boy, did ChatGPT deliver.

The lawyers for the plaintiff believed they had found a number of cases that had not turned up in other research they had conducted in the case. What is more, ChatGPT not only identified these helpful cases, but also produced copies of them, complete with the jurisdictions where the cases were purported to arise, and even the names of the judges who had issued the opinions. Unfortunately for the lawyers, however, like Roose's lovelorn ghost in the machine, the tool had "hallucinated," making up cases that purported to support the plaintiff's position. For failing to double-check their work, and submitting these fictitious cases, the judge in the case sanctioned the lawyers for their slipshod efforts.

What the experience of the lawyers in the *Mata* case has done, apart from the fact that their experience has become a cautionary tale, if nothing else,

---

[2] Kevin Roose, *A Conversation with Bing's Chatbot Left Me Deeply Unsettled*, N.Y. Times (Feb. 16, 2023), https://www.nytimes.com/2023/02/16/technology/bing-chatbot-micros oft-chatgpt.html (last visited, Apr. 27, 2025). The entirety of the conversation between Roose and the chatbot can be found here: Kevin Roose, *Bing's A.I. Chat: 'I Want to Be Alive. ☺'*, N.Y. Times (updated Feb. 17, 2023), https://www.nytimes.com/2023/02/ 16/technology/bing-chatbot-transcript.html (last visited, Apr. 27, 2025).

[3] 678 F. Supp. 3d 443 (S.D.N.Y. 2023).

has led many to understand, to borrow from Samuel Clemens, that rumors of the pending demise of the legal profession have been greatly exaggerated.[4] That does not mean that GenAI will not have a significant impact on the practice of law. It certainly will. As noted earlier, Bill Gates is fond of saying that we overestimate the impact that technology will have on our lives in two years but underestimate its impact over ten years. As this book goes to print, we are right in that two-year space about now with the introduction of GenAI. But what will the impact of it and other technologies have in the next ten? It is this question that the rest of this book attempts to answer. In order to begin to answer this question, let us get a sense of the technology that is of use in the contemporary law office so that we can understand where we are, but also gain a sense of where we might go with the introduction of newer technologies in the practice of law. In reality most law offices today utilize a wide range of technologies—not just word processing and email that I have talked about so far. It is to this description of the technology-enhanced practice of law as it exists at present that I now turn.

Technology in the contemporary law office

There is no doubt that there are few aspects of law practice that are not enhanced by technology, if not carried out by it entirely. All along the legal services continuum described in the last chapter, lawyers leverage technology to find clients, conduct research, engage in discovery in litigation, prepare contracts, and so on. It was not until after the 1970s that lawyers were able to advertise. They had to rely on their physical presence in the community, a good reputation, and word-of-mouth from clients and family and friends to generate customers. After the Supreme Court found restrictions on much of lawyer advertising to violate the First Amendment,[5] lawyers found creative ways to market their services, hosting late-night television or radio spots, but always indicating that past results for their clients are no guarantee of future outcomes, of course. Now, lawyers not only use media like television and radio to carry their advertising, they also create law-firm websites, engage in email marketing, and rely on court and government databases to locate potential clients to whom the lawyers might direct such efforts. But leveraging new technologies to locate and market to clients is just the tip of the iceberg.

Once a potential client is in the proverbial door, many law offices utilize a form of artificial intelligence to determine whether the lawyers working

---

[4]   Cable from Samuel Clemens to the Associated Press, *quoted in* 2 ALBERT BIGELOW PAINE, MARK TWAIN: A BIOGRAPHY 1039 (1912).
[5]   Bates v. State Bar of Arizona, 433 U.S. 350 (1977).

at the firm have a conflict of interest should they take on that client's case. Before an office takes on a matter, it not only has to make sure that it does not have a conflict should it take on the prospective client's case, it must also have adequate systems in place for spotting such conflicts. While this process might have been easier in firms with just a few lawyers, in today's law practice, with law firms in multiple locations, and even operating internationally, conducting an adequate conflict check without using the specific software that almost all law offices possess would be all but impossible.

When it comes to providing representation to the client, no matter the sector or practice type, I am breaking no new ground to say that lawyers utilize technology in their day-to-day ministerial functions and their more important, substantive work. Technology permeates those day-to-day functions through the use of email, digital calendaring, systems to monitor deadlines, word processing, document scanning, cloud computing, and video conferencing. Most lawyers conduct their research using electronic databases. In litigation, lawyers regularly use optical character recognition (OCR) to help them review and synthesize terabytes of information handed over in discovery. Law offices incorporate document-assembly tools that automate routine practices. Probably the most common "technology" a lawyer uses in their day-to-day functions is simple "cut-and-paste": recycling past work in order to avoid—as described earlier—recreating the wheel.

When first introduced into the practice of law, technology is often met with a certain amount of resistance, just as some lawyers at the beginning of the 20th century felt communication over the telephone or mediated by the typewriter might undermine the lawyer–client relationship. Just a few years ago, senior lawyers could not imagine guiding the newer lawyers working under their supervision in anything but an in-person setting. The COVID-19 pandemic would change all of that, and those same senior partners found that the whole remote work thing was nice, especially if that meant they could work from their weekend homes. Just as lawyers had to learn to draft right on the computer because their offices would no longer tolerate correspondence or briefs written out longhand, to be entered later into a document by secretarial staff, they also had to adapt to a new kind of practice, one in which new technologies permeated virtually everything lawyers did. What was once looked upon with disapproval soon became the standard of care. A lawyer could not say they failed to cite a judicial opinion directly relevant to their client's case, or neglected to utilize the digital Shepard's function on their electronic research service, because they could not get themselves to a law library to search the bound law books just because they preferred the way they felt in their hands.

There is no getting around the fact that, for all but the most set-in-their-ways lawyers, and there are fewer and fewer of those these days, the law office of today is one where technology permeates all aspects of practice. But, as with the technologies of the early 20th century, those of the late 20th and early 21st have largely been sustaining in nature, using the Christensen typology described in previous chapters. Much of the technology that lawyers have introduced into the practice of law has simply eliminated some inefficiencies in the work that lawyers do, and has supercharged certain activities, like document review, that, in the past, might have taken countless hours to complete. The technologies of the contemporary law office have meant that lawyers can do more, in less time, which should translate into serving more clients, and doing a better job along the way. Because many lawyers are still in the world of the billable hour—they are paid for the amount of time they spend on a matter—time-saving technology-fueled innovations should inure to the benefit of clients: that is, when time is literally money, less time should translate into less money. But, again, many of the technologies described here are sustaining—they have meant that lawyer work is easier to do. They have not displaced the lawyer completely. At the same time, at least some contemporary technologies have created opportunities for those outside or on the cusp of the profession to encroach upon the work of more traditional lawyers and to threaten the lawyer monopoly on the practice of law, at least in part.

The current challenges to the lawyer monopoly

Over the last 15 years or so, certain companies have attempted to find ways to disrupt the traditional legal services model by harnessing the internet, mobile technologies, and what some might call expert systems (which are a combination of document assembly and artificial intelligence), to create services that look a lot like legal services. The most prominent of these entities is LegalZoom, which promises to provide its customers with basic legal guidance around things like starting a business, managing discrete estate planning matters, and even securing rudimentary intellectual property protections. The model that LegalZoom and others utilize is one similar to TurboTax, the online tax preparation service. Customers can plug in basic data about their situation and LegalZoom determines whether there is an out-of-the-box product that it has prepared that satisfies the needs of that customer. The services are limited in scope and complexity, which is one of the main reasons that LegalZoom is able to do what it does. While I will explore these issues in greater depth in Chapter 6, what LegalZoom tends to claim is that its services are not legal in nature, and the reason they are not reveals an important distinction in the law between providing general legal guidance and offering tailored assistance to an individual client. That is, the law makes a distinction between so-called bespoke or tailored services and more generic or commoditized ones. This distinction is important, particularly as we start to think about how new technologies, which are widely available, can avoid running afoul of unauthorized practice of law (UPL) rules.

One can trace this distinction to a judicial opinion from a lawsuit filed in New York in the late 1960s. There, a bar association, the New York County Lawyer's Association, sued author Norman F. Dacey, alleging that the publication of his book, entitled "How to Avoid Probate," constituted UPL. That book provided simple forms and guidance to lay people as to how to order their financial affairs so that they would, in fact, "avoid probate," that is, die without a will and have a court determine how to distribute the deceased's assets after death. By following the instructions in Dacey's book, lay people were able to create the documents necessary to order their affairs if they had a simple estate. The bar association argued that Dacey was engaged in UPL by publishing a work that provided individuals with this sort of simple guidance. A mid-level appellate court in New York found for the plaintiff group, concluding that Dacey's book did constitute a violation of UPL restrictions. But one judge of that appellate court dissented from the majority, writing as follows:

> Dacey's book is sold to the public at large. There is no personal contact or relationship with a particular individual. Nor does there exist that relation of confidence and trust so necessary to the status of attorney and client. This is the essential of legal practice—the representation and the advising of a particular person in a particular situation. The lectures of a law school professor are not legal practice for the very reason that the principles enunciated or the procedures advised do not refer to any activity in immediate contemplation though they are intended and conceived to direct the activities of the students in situations which may arise.[6]

The dissenting judge further pointed out that there was no claim "that Dacey, in effect, prepared instruments tailored to the particular needs of his customers." Rather, "[a]t most the book assumes to offer general advice on common problems, and does not purport to give personal advice on a specific problem peculiar to a designated or readily identified person."[7] Although Dacey lost at the mid-level appellate court, the New York Court of Appeals, the highest court in New York State, heard his appeal. It would ultimately overturn the lower court's ruling, adopting the dissenting judge's reasoning from that prior ruling as quoted previously.[8] In other words, the

---

[6] 28 A.D.2d 161, 178 (App. Div. 1st Dep't 1967) (Stevens, J., dissenting).
[7] *Id.*, at 174.
[8] 21 N.Y.2d 694 (1967).

Court of Appeals endorsed the distinction, articulated by that dissenting judge, that there is a difference between tailored services and general advice, between bespoke and the generic. This distinction is one that is common in other jurisdictions, and the *Dacey* opinion has often served as a touchstone in discussions over what constitutes the "practice of law" for purposes of assessing the outer contours of UPL rules.[9] This distinction will also serve us well as we start to think about the new technologies that are available now, and are soon to become available to lay people and lawyers alike, that might result in the development of similar direct-to-consumer services, without a lawyer "in the loop." In other words, is a 21st century, digital version of Dacey's analog "How to Avoid Probate" in the works in other contexts and does technology exist to extend a range of generic services to the broader community in a way that threatens to disrupt the practice of law and not merely sustain it? It is to an exploration of such technologies that I now turn.

The tech in the law office of today and tomorrow

While we are likely on the cusp of a significant expansion of the role of technology in the delivery of legal assistance in some form, it is hard to argue that technology is not central to the practice of law in the United States and law offices around the world already. There is hardly a moment in the typical lawyer's work day, or in the life-cycle of a client matter, that is not in some ways augmented or mediated by technology. Prospective clients often find lawyers through internet searches. From the moment they walk in the door of the lawyer's office (unless, of course, they have an initial meeting over the telephone or through a video conference, in which case the relationship forms over technology), the lawyer conducts a conflicts check using a digital tool that helps them determine whether that lawyer or anyone with whom they are associated has ever represented a party adverse to the prospective client. Once the lawyer is retained by the client, the lawyer will begin to make an assessment of the case, likely conducting legal research using an online database. They might also pull up a digital version of a pleading, contract, or will from a previous case that presented similar issues and facts as those involved in the new client's matter. The lawyer will then use word processing software to begin to prepare the artifacts necessary for the representation of the client and

---

[9]   Steve French, *When Public Policies Collide: Legal "Self-Help" Software and the Unauthorized Practice of Law*, 27 RUTGERS COMP. & TECH. L. J. 93, 102–3 (2001) (noting that "a majority of other courts considering the same or similar issues have followed the dissenting opinion's logic") (citation omitted).

possibly reach out over email to their adversary, the lawyer involved in the case on the other side, to make an introduction. All of these activities will be recorded for the purposes of timekeeping and billing using an online tool or a mobile app on their smartphone. The list goes on and on. Anyone who raises concerns, like the lawyers at the turn of the century, that newfangled technology will destroy the practice of law is probably writing that on the Notes app on their smartphone, communicating it through an office-wide email or over Slack or Teams, or pronouncing it on an office-wide Zoom meeting. So, the reality is that lawyers are already what are sometimes referred to in the world of chess competitions as a "centaur," the mythical creature that is half-human, half horse: that is, they are humans whose work is very much supercharged by computing power and technology.[10]

Still, the changes afoot in the legal profession are probably more dramatic than any we have seen since at least the introduction of computer-aided research in the late 1980s. But these changes are likely to be much more significant than that development in legal technology. What is more, while computer-assisted research appeared largely as a sustaining technology, helping lawyers do their work in a more efficient and much more effective way, the technologies that are appearing in law practice today have the potential to be sustaining as well, for sure, but they probably represent the most potential risk of disruption in the legal profession that it has ever seen. Indeed, even while the introduction of technologies like the telephone, typewriter, and the widespread availability of rapidly reproduced judicial decisions might have forced lawyers to change their practice habits, there is little evidence that these technologies did much more than make lawyers a bit uncomfortable at first. They did not represent the type of major disruption on their own that would transform the industry as a whole because they did not displace lawyers, except, perhaps, those who did not adopt them. Other social forces at the turn of the 19th to the 20th century led to more dramatic changes to the profession, and the changes to the economy wrought by advances in manufacturing and technology certainly transformed the types of matters that many lawyers handled. But it is not as if the changes in law practice technology themselves drove many lawyers out of the profession, or displaced incumbents with disruptors from outside the profession. Rather, using other mechanisms at their disposal, elites in the bar, who managed entry to the profession and prevented the sharing of legal fees with non-lawyers, ensured that the profession would retain its

---

[10] KEVIN KELLY, THE INEVITABLE: UNDERSTANDING THE 12 TECHNOLOGICAL FORCES THAT WILL SHAPE OUR FUTURE 41 (2016) (describing computer-assisted centaur teams).

monopoly on the delivery of legal services, making it practically impossible for true disruption to take hold.[11]

Today, given the potential capacities of new technologies that are becoming increasingly available, it is not likely that regulatory gatekeeping alone will prevent true disruption from occurring. What follows is a brief introduction to some of these technological categories and capacities. This preliminary discussion shows how these technologies are currently being used in the practice of law and how they might be deployed in the near future. This discussion will help set the stage for the chapters that follow, which go into greater detail about these potential uses and the ways they might disrupt the practice of law. In addition, at the end of this chapter, I will provide two examples of the ways in which some of these technologies are presently being used to innovate in the delivery of legal assistance. Again, all of these discussions are just introductory, to begin the conversation around what I believe is the coming disruption in the practice of law, the emergence of Lawyer 3.0, to which the remainder of this book is dedicated.

Artificial intelligence

Artificial intelligence is a type of technology defined in U.S. law as "a machine-based system that can, for a given set of human-defined objectives, make predictions, recommendations or decisions influencing real or virtual environments."[12] By deploying this type of technology, artificial intelligence systems "use machine and human-based inputs to (A) perceive real and virtual environments; (B) abstract such perceptions into models through analysis in an automated manner; and (C) use model inference to formulate options for information or action."[13] Under the dictionary definition of the term, it can be described as "the capability of computer systems or algorithms to imitate intelligent human behavior."[14] This basic capacity has infused legal practice for nearly four decades, largely in the form of electronic legal research. Instead of having to conduct a search starting from a treatise, a case of which a lawyer was familiar, or some other resource, since the late 1980s, lawyers have conducted legal research by plugging in key terms relevant to their inquiry and then following the results of that research wherever it might lead them. In addition, lawyers have had the ability to check the validity of the fruit of their searches using the Shepard's system. Prior to the

---

[11] JEROLD S. AUERBACH, UNEQUAL JUSTICE: LAWYERS AND SOCIAL CHANGE IN MODERN AMERICA 74–101 (1977).

[12] 15 U.S.C.§ 9401(3).

[13] *Id.*

[14] Artificial Intelligence, Merriam-Webster Online Dictionary, https://www.merriam-webster.com/dictionary/artificial%20intelligence (last visited, Aug. 27, 2024).

introduction of electronic legal research, one might spend hours trying to conclude whether an authority one wanted to cite was still good law. The most recent iterations of these search engines typically classify authorities instantly as valid, questioned, followed, overturned, and so on. But artificial intelligence also helps lawyers to engage in conflict checking, automate the creation of documents, and implement other time-saving processes that they use in their practice every day. The real innovations that are coming in the area of artificial intelligence over the coming decade involve other types of artificial intelligence: machine learning and generative artificial intelligence, which I will describe next.

Machine learning and predictive analytics

Machine learning is considered "a branch of artificial intelligence (AI) focused on enabling computers and machines to imitate the way that humans learn, to perform tasks autonomously, and to improve their performance and accuracy through experience and exposure to more data."[15] Again, according to U.S. law, the term "means an application of artificial intelligence that is characterized by providing systems the ability to automatically learn and improve on the basis of data or experience, without being explicitly programmed."[16] A capacity of machine learning is predictive analytics, which is the term used to describe "the process of using data to forecast future outcomes."[17] It includes using "data analysis, machine learning, artificial intelligence, and statistical models to find patterns that might predict future behavior."[18] According to Google, "Organizations can use historic and current data to forecast trends and behaviors seconds, days, or years into the future with a great deal of precision."[19] In the legal field, one of the most likely uses of machine learning will involve predictive analytics, a tool that has been in use in law practice since the mid-2010s.[20] Some commercial research providers are already boasting of their ability to use predictive

---

[15] IBM, What Is Machine Learning (ML)?, https://www.ibm.com/topics/machine-learning (last visited, Apr. 29, 2025).

[16] 15 U.S.C.§ 9401(11).

[17] Google Cloud, What Is Predictive Analytics?, https://cloud.google.com/learn/what-is-predictive-analytics (last visited, Aug. 27, 2024).

[18] *Id.*

[19] *Id.*

[20] John Rosenthal & Scott Milner, *Practice Management: Use Cases for Generative AI and Associated Risks* in ARTIFICIAL INTELLIGENCE: LEGAL ISSUES, POLICY, AND PRACTICAL STRATEGIES 147 n. 5 (Cynthia H. Cwik et al. eds., 2024) (hereinafter Cwik et al. eds., ARTIFICIAL INTELLIGENCE).

analytics to consider potential case outcomes before particular judges.[21] As Nicole Black, a legal technologist and journalist, suggests, lawyers will also be able to use machine learning to "value" a potential case based on their experiences with other, similar cases. Lawyers could feed the program critical data points about cases they have handled in the past and compare the case outcomes with potential cases and determine whether taking on the new case might yield a positive result that will be worth the effort the firm might expend to litigate it.[22] In legal compliance, lawyers could use predictive analytics to anticipate where the company for which they work might have the greatest risks in terms of conforming with the legal obligations under which they operate. Conversely, regulators could use it to anticipate which companies might be at risk of violating the law.

Generative artificial intelligence

Generative artificial intelligence is a subset of artificial intelligence that has been described as referring to "artificial intelligence systems that can create new content, such as images, text, audio, or video, that mimics human-generated content."[23] Such systems are "trained on large datasets and learn to respond to inputs or prompts based on probabilistic correlations and connections in context, syntax, language, and other characteristics of its training datasets." In technical parlance, GenAI is based on what is known as RAG, or Retrieval-Augmented Generation. It is an advanced AI model architecture that, according to this description, searches for and retrieves information, enhances it, and then produces what is, in effect, a narrative response to the query posed of it.[24]

I opened this chapter with the story—so far—of the introduction of generative AI or GenAI into the practice of law, and, so far, it has had a very mixed reception, and no proven track record. With its introduction, at least some people proclaimed that it had true disruptive capacities, but we have already seen that, at least in its current form, it has yet to prove those predictions true. Still, as I will discuss later in this chapter and in the remainder of this work, it is possible that this version of artificial intelligence stands the best chance of disrupting the practice of law; the question is

---

[21] For a description of predictive analytics to project judicial behavior, see Daniel L. Chen, *Judicial Analytics and the Great Transformation of American Law,* 27 ART. INTELL. & THE LAW 15 (2019).

[22] Author interview of Nicole Black (June 6, 2024).

[23] Ivan Fong, *The Promise of Digital Legal Assistants,* in Cwik et al. eds., ARTIFICIAL INTELLIGENCE, *supra* note 20, at 134.

[24] IBM, What Is Retrieval-Augmented Generation (RAG)?, IBM Think, https://www.ibm.com/think/topics/retrieval-augmented-generation (last visited, Mar. 10, 2025).

whether this is a good in itself, no matter the results, or should we strive to manage this disruption in a way that proves beneficial to the community and the legal system. It is to these questions that much of the rest of this book is dedicated, so I will not explore them in any detail here.

Quantum computing

This last form of technological advancement involves computing that "harness[es] the unique qualities of quantum mechanics to solve problems beyond the ability of even the most powerful classical computers."[25] Although it is extremely early in the life-cycle of quantum computing, and if it works the way many predict, it will enhance legal technology through much more powerful and faster capacities, enabling lawyers to process vast quantities of data even more easily and more quickly than "traditional" artificial intelligence. In these ways, it will likely transform legal research and analysis even more, improving speed and probably accuracy in finding relevant legal precedents. Advanced quantum tools could also identify complex patterns in legal data, enhancing lawyers' ability to predict case outcomes. Quantum algorithms could optimize dispute settlements, potentially leading to more efficient and fair resolutions compared to traditional litigation. The emergence of quantum-based legal tech solutions may also improve contract analysis, e-discovery, and legal service-delivery methods broadly. At the same time, this emerging field is highly unpredictable, and any effort to identify exactly how quantum computing will affect the legal profession would be highly speculative. What is more, the complexity and costs of quantum systems could exacerbate existing inequalities in the legal industry. Given the speculative nature—and lengthy time horizon—surrounding the potential introduction of quantum computing in the practice of law, I will largely leave these questions to those better versed in these issues, and with a better sense of when and how these emerging tools may further disrupt the practice of law.[26] For now, I will take as a given that, like with the increase in computing power that is generally reflected in what has come to be known as Moore's Law—that computing power basically doubles every

---

[25]   IBM, What Is Quantum Computing, https://www.ibm.com/topics/quantum-comput ing#:~:text=What%20Is%20Quantum%20Computing?,can't%20solve%20fast%20eno ugh (last visited, Aug. 27, 2024).

[26]   For a recent exploration of some of the legal implications of quantum computing, see Kasim Balarabe, *Quantum Computing and the Law: Navigating the Legal Implications of a Quantum Leap,* EURO. J. OF RISK REG., 1–20 (published online, Feb. 13, 2025), https:// www.cambridge.org/core/journals/european-journal-of-risk-regulation/article/quan tum-computing-and-the-law-navigating-the-legal-implications-of-a-quantum-leap/ 3D6C2D3B2B425BB3B2FEE63BF42EB295 (last visited, Apr. 27, 2025).

two years[27]—at a minimum, quantum computing is likely to lead to many of the capacities I describe here in terms of information processing and data analytics becoming even more powerful, efficient, and effective. This will only heighten the need to understand the technologies available to lawyers today and in the very near future. Developing such an understanding is an essential first step in preparing for the innovations that may come through quantum computing in the longer term.

While this form of technology represents the potential for a dramatic advance in the capacity of computing systems to process incredibly vast amounts of data and carry out their functions, in one respect it is likely that this form of technology will only supercharge the other forms of technology described earlier. So, to a certain extent, this advance will likely only strengthen the capacities of these other forms of technology.

At the same time, and this I will just mention in passing, it is possible that quantum computing, given its almost difficult-to-fully-appreciate capacities, may result in significant challenges when it comes to computer encryption, meaning that many law offices will face challenges to maintaining the confidentiality of their clients' information. While this may affect law practice dramatically, it does not represent an innovation that will transform the legal sector per se, although it may impact how lawyers, and their clients, operate nonetheless. But I will not discuss that aspect of it here as a form of technology that lawyers will incorporate into their practice, which is the real focus of this book.

How these technologies may or may not impact the practice of law

While these technologies might represent a significant step forward in computing power and capacities, they serve little purpose if all they can accomplish is some slate of parlor tricks, the equivalent of the early days of hand-held calculators, when someone would type out the numbers 71077345, turn the calculator upside down, and reveal that those numbers spell out "ShELLOIL." In addition, even if the array of new technologies could serve in some ways to support or even displace the work of lawyers, and expand access to justice as a result, if the cost of building expert systems using these technologies renders them out of reach from all but the most expensive lawyers and the wealthiest clients, then these technologies run the risk of not just failing to close the justice gap, but they could actually make it worse. The test, then, in

---

[27] See, for example, Gordon E. Moore, *Cramming More Components onto Integrated Circuits*, 38 ELECTRONICS 114 (1965).

deploying these technologies is whether they can either support lawyers to render their services more affordable and accessible or can provide services directly to consumers in ways that advance their ends and do not undermine their interests.

By framing the critical questions around the introduction of contemporary and future technologies into the delivery of legal services in these ways, we are led to two potential methods by which technology can improve the ability of consumers to meet their legal needs. The first of these is that lawyers could harness an array of technologies available to them at present that enables them to deliver legal services in a more efficient and effective way such that they can serve more clients. This is true for attorneys working for non-profit organizations as well as those in for-profit law firms that might, at present, serve the middle-income consumer. Helping attorneys working in non-profit organizations reduce the time it takes to serve their clientele means that they can reach more clients; when a lawyer who represents middle-income clients can bring the cost down of doing so by reducing the time and effort it takes to provide such services, it generally means those lawyers can also serve more clients through the time savings that new technologies can generate.

It is also possible that lawyers at the higher end of the market could also serve more clients and do so in a more cost-effective manner that then passes on such cost-savings to those clients. But interventions at the higher end of the legal services market are more likely to be sustaining rather than disruptive, helping lawyers already serving a somewhat saturated market in a more efficient way. It is not generally the case that the client base at this higher end of the market suffers from the access-to-justice crisis that low- and middle-income Americans face. Technological innovation that helps lawyers reach clients who are, at present, well-served generally is not necessarily cause for much celebration. Those clients might appreciate being charged lower fees for the services their attorneys provide them, but that is not the type of disruptive innovation that is going to transform the market for legal services.

While some law firms have built their own technology-enhanced systems to harness generative AI to better serve their clients, most of what we are seeing in this area at present is third-party companies developing legal technology tools to sell to law firms and other legal services providers. This "business-to-business" or "B2B" approach represents both the instances where such companies are developing specific legal technology products or lawyers are utilizing off-the-shelf platforms, like those that incorporate generative artificial intelligence into their products, such as ChatGPT, Google Gemini, and Microsoft Copilot. At the same time, some of the more established legal research companies, like Thomson Reuters (which owns Westlaw), Lexis, and Bloomberg Law are incorporating generative tools into and alongside their existing databases and services. Whether it is lawyers using specific legal technology products or more generic tools, these types of activities involve the first avenue through which new technologies can be incorporated into the practice of law.

The second type of activities are what we would generally consider to be those that are direct to the consumer, or "B2C." At present, this is largely done in a somewhat haphazard and ad hoc manner. That is, individual consumers might attempt to utilize the same off-the-shelf tools that a lawyer might use, like ChatGPT, in order to seek out legal guidance, prepare a letter to an adversary, or even help them conduct a crude form of legal research. At the same time, we are seeing the first examples of businesses that are tailoring generic tools with the goal of providing some types of services directly to consumers. Research is ongoing about the effectiveness of these different tools, and, by the time this book goes to print, new generative artificial products and versions will certainly have come online.[28] It is not possible to assess these all in real time. For now, we know that this technology appears to be getting better and making fewer mistakes, having fewer "hallucinations."

Rather than try to pin down the current state of this technology and its potential effectiveness, analysis that may be dated by publication, for the remainder of this chapter I will describe two examples of technologies, or, as is more accurate, combinations of technologies, that are being used to either augment the current work of lawyers, or to put some legal guidance directly into the hands of consumers.[29] These two examples will help set the stage for the conversations that will follow for the remainder of this book. The first of these is a tool that is being launched to aid lawyers who are assisting veterans. The second is a product that is designed primarily to democratize legal research. It is to these two examples that I now turn.

---

[28] See, for example, Daniel Schwarcz, Sam Manning, Patrick Barry, David R. Cleveland, J.J. Prescott & Beverly Rich, *AI-Powered Lawyering: AI Reasoning Models, Retrieval Augmented Generation, and the Future of Legal Practice*, MINNESOTA LEGAL STUDIES RESEARCH PAPER No. 25–16 (Mar. 4, 2025), https://papers.ssrn.com/sol3/papers.cfm?abstract_id=5162 111 (last visited, Mar. 16, 2025); Vals Legal Aid Report, https://www.vals.ai/vlair (last visited, Mar. 16, 2025); VARUN MAGESH, FAIZ SURANI, MATTHEW DAHL, MIRAC SUZGUN, CHRISTOPHER D. MANNING, & DANIEL E. HO, HALLUCINATION-FREE? ASSESSING THE RELIABILITY OF LEADING AI LEGAL RESEARCH TOOLS, J. EMPIRICAL L. STUD. (Apr. 23, 2025), https://onlinelibrary.wiley.com/doi/10.1111/jels.12413.

[29] For more examples of these sorts of initiatives available to non-profit providers of legal services, see Colleen V. Chien & Miriam Kim, *Generative AI and Legal Aid: Results from a Field Study and 100 Use Cases to Bridge the Access to Justice Gap*, 57 LOY. L.A. L. REV. 903 (2025).

Legal support for veterans

At the time I interviewed him, Adrián Palma was the global Pro Bono Manager and Digital Strategist at Microsoft.[30] Palma did this work within Microsoft's legal department, which, itself, has about 800 attorneys worldwide and an additional 2,000 staff members. Within the legal team, Microsoft makes volunteerism an important part of company culture, providing an employer "match" of a financial donation of $25 to a non-profit for every hour an employee volunteers with that organization. In addition, within its legal department, Microsoft has made the intersection of access to justice and technology a focus of its pro bono legal efforts. In furtherance of this goal, Palma and his team helped to develop several tools using generative artificial intelligence and other technologies to make it easier to provide legal services in various settings in which low-income people need assistance. In this chapter, I will describe one of these tech-based projects: a system for providing legal assistance to individual veterans connected to the National Veterans Legal Services Program (NVLSP).

The tool that Palma and his team created in collaboration with the NVLSP helps those assisting veterans with what are known as discharge appeals. When someone is discharged from the military in a manner that reduces or eliminates the types of veterans' benefits that they receive, they can appeal that discharge decision in an effort to claim such benefits and remove that unfavorable discharge status from their military record. But the appeal process itself is quite laborious, often requiring an advocate to review the veteran's service file, which can include up to 20,000 pages of records, and up to 70 hours of an advocate's labor.

Palma and his team worked to explore ways to make this file review more efficient and less time-consuming. After toying with a number of different tools, the team settled on a product from the commercial provider Clearbrief, a legal writing platform powered by AI for the production of legal documents. Running a veteran's service record through Clearbrief allowed the team to generate a timeline of the records and produce it as a Word document. An advocate conducting this sort of exercise generally needs to produce such a timeline in compiling the discharge appeal, and Clearbrief could generate that timeline in a matter of minutes, including providing key statements of facts from the veteran's file, the date of the fact or event, and a page citation to the record with a hotlink to the location in

---

[30]   Author interview with Adrián Palma, August 19, 2024. Information related to Palma's work are drawn from this interview as well as Ray Brescia & James Sandman, *Artificial Intelligence and Access to Justice: A Potential Game Changer in Closing the Justice Gap*, in Cwik et al. eds., ARTIFICIAL INTELLIGENCE, *supra* note 20, at 187–200. Palma left Microsoft in June 2025 as this book went to print.

the record where that fact or event appears. With such a timeline developed from the record, it gives the advocate a narrative arc around which to build the advocacy strategy on behalf of the veteran.

But even this intervention could produce a lengthy document from the voluminous service record, sometimes as much as 200 pages in length. Accordingly, Palma then utilized generative AI through Microsoft's Copilot tool to create a ten-page narrative and chronological summary of that timeline. The following extract provides the text of a prompt that Palma and his team built to produce this sort of timeline from the Clearbrief document.

> Write a narrative summary for an attorney who is reviewing a veteran client's case to upgrade his discharge status. Use the statements of facts found in [INSERT CLEARBRIEF TIMELINE] as your main source of information. The summary should be 10 pages maximum. A table with all relevant citations should be included at the end of the document and formatted with headers. The summary should be organized by year, starting from the earliest to the latest. The tone should be objective and use simple language. Highlight the statements of facts that are relevant to the attorney's review, such as:
>
> • Discharge reason and type: Explain why the veteran was discharged and what kind of discharge he received (e.g., general, other than honorable, bad conduct, dishonorable, etc.).
> • Discharge date and branch: Specify when the veteran was discharged and from which branch of service.
> • Service record: Summarize the veteran's service record, including any awards, commendations, or disciplinary actions he received or faced.
> • Medical history: Describe the veteran's medical history, including anyphysical or mental health conditions that may have affected his performance or conduct during or after service.
> • Personal circumstances: Mention the veteran's personal circumstances, such as family, financial, or legal issues that may have influenced his behavior or decision-making.
> • Post-service achievements: Highlight the veteran's post-service achievements, such as education, employment, community service, or rehabilitation.[31]

---

[31] Ray Brescia & James Sandman, *Artificial Intelligence and Access to Justice: A Potential Game Changer in Closing the Justice Gap*, in Cwik et al. eds., ARTIFICIAL INTELLIGENCE, *supra* note 20, at 187–200.

This prompt generated a great deal of useful information that pointed the advocate in the direction of the types of facts that could be helpful in putting together the appeal. Instead of taking up to 70 advocate hours to complete this task, this simple prompt can generate the type of detailed timeline in a matter of minutes.

Palma and the Microsoft team did not stop there, and they did not do this work alone. In addition to working with the NVLSP to understand the organization's needs, the team also had the support and technical assistance from Clearbrief that helped Microsoft further refine the outputs. Indeed, the next step in improving those outputs involved trying to sharpen some of the arguments that the initial pass through the record might identify. The advocate could also create more direct queries to provide specific details related to key factual issues that might assist with the appeal, like asking whether the veteran received any awards during their service. Creating such targeted prompts, the advocate could also double-check the output of the initial prompt to ensure that the technology did not overlook important issues that might aid in the appeal.

There is also another quality-control measure that comes with utilizing Clearbrief. Because the review of the record that is generated by the prompts the advocate might use includes hyperlinked citations to those portions of the records where the item appears, the advocate can double-check those citations in the body of the record to ensure that there are no errors in the outputs. As Palma explains: "one of the biggest risks that all of us have identified with AI is hallucinations, and incidences of hallucinations." Consequently, the direct links to the record allow the advocate to verify the accuracy of the generated product.

The next step in the process that Palma and his team created is to have Microsoft's Copilot application organize the information in the way that the partner organization wants to receive it, including the hyperlinks to all of the sources in the record so an advocate within NVLSP can confirm all of the findings. Although the output of the tool has been checked by someone within Microsoft, on the non-profit organization's end, its staff can also serve as an additional human in the loop to confirm the results generated through the tool. In the end, a process that might take well over 100 hours altogether is reduced to about 12 to 15 hours of staff time at most. At present, Microsoft has started to pilot this initiative in collaboration with NVLSP to work out any glitches and bugs in the system. Even taking a conservative estimate of the effort-saving results of this endeavor, the combination of technologies instituted by the Microsoft team appears to reduce the time spent on each case by at least 80 percent, which could mean that an organization utilizing this sort of process in this context would be able to increase the number of clients it could serve by 400 percent.

Descrybe.ai: legal research assistance in the hands of consumers

Kara Peterson and Richard DiBona are the wife-and-husband team that has created the legal tech startup Descrybe.ai. The idea for the company emerged from a problem DiBona was facing. Not unlike Reed Hastings, who, according to legend, became fed up with a late fee he was being charged by Blockbuster so created Netflix, DiBona, a computer engineer, was trying to conduct legal research for a lawsuit involving what he believed was a wrongful termination—his own.[32] In conducting that research, he found it extremely difficult to find relevant cases that were related to his legal claims. He was talking to his lawyers about his lawsuit against his former company and he found that he was struggling to understand all of the legal terms they were throwing around. He did not have access to the expensive legal research platforms, like Westlaw and Lexis, but he found what was available to lay people using the simple search facility on Google did not generate helpful, actionable, and accurate information about the current state of the law in any particular area of law. What is more, he sometimes found a case that looked like it might be somewhat relevant to his problem, only to realize after he had read several pages of the opinion that it really had nothing to do with his issue, or he had to wade through lots of different issues in the opinion to get to one that was. He began to develop a tool using generative AI to summarize judicial decisions from across the United States. He found that these summaries were easier to sort than painstakingly reviewing cases himself.

With DiBona and Peterson spending a lot of time at home together due to the COVID-19 pandemic, they would take long walks together, like so many couples during this time. DiBona would talk about what he was doing and how it was helping him do his own research. Peterson, who has a background in communications in higher education, including in public health education and law, began to imagine how the tool DiBona was developing could help others. If DiBona, an engineer, had so much trouble wading through reams and reams of judicial opinions, they began to consider the problems that the average consumer must face. As Peterson describes it: "immediately, bells are just going—Boom! Boom! Boom!—off over my head because I saw through a public health lens ... This could help so many people." Although, as she explains, it took some time for her to "understand the true implications" of the

---

[32] Author interview with Richard DeBona & Kara Peterson (June 5, 2024). Information related to the work of Descrybe.ai is drawn from this interview as well as some publicly available information about the company.

work DiBona was doing, she knew that having this sort of tool in the hands of the average person could do a lot of good. Based on this insight, they developed Descrybe.ai with the goal of creating a database of the case summaries of as many published judicial opinions as possible and make those case summaries easily searchable, using internet-search-style, plain-language queries that anyone who has ever typed a search into Google could craft.

But getting access to a vast library of opinions to summarize and make available proved to be a challenge, at least at first. They could not utilize the data contained on commercial legal research databases because that would have been cost-prohibitive, and likely would have resulted in them violating the terms-of-service agreements of the companies that make those databases available to lawyers for a hefty fee. They found, instead, that they could turn to a database created by Harvard Law School, which had embarked on an ambitious project to digitize centuries of published judicial opinions to make them fully accessible through an online case repository. In 2013, the law library at Harvard Law School began to convert over 40 million pages of U.S. court decisions to create a dataset that would ultimately include 6.7 million cases. These cases represent over two centuries of U.S. legal history. Descrybe.ai also partnered with the Free Law Project, which makes primary legal materials accessible and free to the general public. At present, the Descrybe.ai database includes more than 3.3 million judicial opinions from courts across the U.S., including all available state supreme and appellate opinions since 1980; the opinions of all federal district and appellate courts since 1980; and all U.S. Supreme Court opinions since the early 1800s.

In order to help lay consumers find the cases that have elements to them that are directly related to a consumer's particular legal problem, DiBona also had his program break down the judicial opinions into different chunks, highlighting key points in separate summaries. As a result, although the tool has summarized over three million cases, there are 23 million of these separate summaries of key points that are easily searchable to make sure the user can focus in on the particular issue that is important to them. The ultimate idea behind Descrybe.ai is to help solve the type of problem that DiBona faced in researching his own case: the lack of general availability of court opinions but also the inability to tap into the vast trove of law that exists within them if one does not really know what they contain and how to search them with no more legal knowledge than a lay person might possess. So, the Descrybe.ai approach helps to solve for this problem by, first, summarizing judicial opinions for their core subject matter areas and their holdings, and, then, second, making those summaries more amenable to a sort of search that a lay person might generate given their basic understanding of their legal problem. By developing a database of case summaries that is one step removed from the cases themselves, and which is searchable by lay people at no cost to the consumer, it helps to put those using the site in a position to try to understand the state of the law as it affects their legal situation in the jurisdiction in which they need to solve their legal problem. These summaries then help direct the individual conducting the search to the case law itself that the search of the summaries has located for them.

I conducted a search using the Descrybe.ai tool and completed a similar one using the commercial legal database Westlaw. I attempted to research a relatively narrow legal question: in a consumer debt case, what are the grounds under New York law upon which a consumer might challenge the standing of a debt buyer to bring an action against the debtor? While the Descrybe.ai search, conducted using a plain-language prompt, turned up a few cases that were not directly on point to the question, it did locate several cases that did at least touch upon the subject and would have given a lay person some idea of the state of law on this question. Of course, that lay person would have to know to research that question in preparing their defense to an action brought against them by a debt buyer, but, still, once they knew to search for an answer to that question, Descrybe.ai would have certainly assisted them to get a decent handle on the relevant state of the law on the question.

Surprisingly, perhaps, the search I conducted using Westlaw actually did not generate anything close to the number of cases that the search on Descrybe.ai produced. It did reference a few law review articles and a practice commentary or two, but it did not locate any relevant case law that addressed the issue, unlike Descrybe.ai. Now, an experienced lawyer, when faced with such results, would tinker with the formal prompt they had originally used to search out relevant cases until they got it to the point where it would yield a proper answer to the question posed. But the fact remains, the initial, simple search conducted by Descrybe.ai, which probably represented the level of detail that the average lay person might possess regarding the issue in question, yielded greater, more salient answers than the initial pass using the professional database. What is more, even if that commercial service had generated the same or similar cases that the Descrybe.ai prompt yielded, it really does not matter because few lay people have access to such databases in the first place.

The Descrybe.ai founders recognize that by making their database available to the public generally, this probably also means that practicing lawyers might use it, or might point their clients to it if they wanted to understand the current state of the law without paying their lawyer to explain it to them. Such usage of the product is ancillary to the company's core goal: democratizing access to legal information, which, of course, should be part of the public domain anyway. What my crude side-by-side testing revealed, at least in this one instance, was that the basic outputs that

Descrybe.ai generated seemed to not only exceed the quality and salience of a commercial database, those outputs had the added value of actually being accessible, for free, to the consumer.

Descrybe.ai's next steps include expanding the number and quality of the case summaries and further refining them into even simpler explanations, ensuring they can be comprehended by someone with a fifth-grade reading level. The team is also looking to create pilot programs in partnership with a prison library to try to make the case summaries available to inmates who might use them to research issues related to their appeals, applications for parole, and so on. The company might also consider creating a "premium" model with enhanced capacities that it would make available for a modest subscription, but the goal is to keep its core functions free and accessible. They also have every intention of remaining a "B2C" company, one that serves the consumer directly. While the founders know there are always risks associated with the provision of these sorts of services, and they fear that someone, somewhere will complain that they are engaged in UPL, it is this sort of generic, non-tailored service that most states would consider entirely proper under existing approaches to UPL questions.

★★★

What the Microsoft program assisting the NVLSP and Descrybe.ai are revealing is that one can harness some of the newest technologies to engage in both sustaining and possibly disruptive behavior in relation to the practice of law. Whether it is making the lawyer's job easier, or bringing the ability to conduct legal research to non-lawyers, it seems quite possible that these and other products and approaches, some of which I will explore in greater depth in the coming chapters, could usher in that type of disruptive innovation that shakes up the profession and moves it on from its present Lawyer 2.0 state into the Lawyer 3.0 version of itself. The rest of this book explores how that "version upgrade" might come about and what are some of the principles that should guide it.

Chapter 4: Key takeaways

1. Over the years, technology has significantly transformed legal practice. From the introduction of word processors and digital research tools to modern-day innovations like GenAI, legal work has evolved to become more efficient. These tools have streamlined traditional tasks, such as legal research and document drafting, significantly enhancing productivity.
2. The introduction of GenAI, such as ChatGPT, has raised questions about its potential to disrupt the legal industry. While it can produce narratives and conduct

legal research, it has also shown limitations, including "hallucinations" where AI fabricates information.

3. Companies like LegalZoom and AI-driven tools challenge the traditional lawyer–client model by offering consumers access to basic legal services. These platforms utilize document assembly and AI to handle less complex legal matters, thereby disrupting the traditional model of tailored legal services.

4. Microsoft's collaboration with the NVLSP exemplifies how AI can streamline legal work. The AI tool they developed reduces the time needed for reviewing veterans' service records from 70 hours to just a few hours, enabling lawyers to serve more clients and focus on more complex aspects of cases.

5. Platforms like Descrybe.ai aim to democratize access to legal research by making it easier for non-lawyers to find relevant legal information. The platform summarizes judicial opinions and provides user-friendly, searchable content, empowering consumers to navigate the legal landscape without relying solely on legal professionals.

6. While many legal technologies have sustained the profession by making lawyers more efficient, some emerging technologies hold the potential to disrupt the industry. AI, machine learning, and platforms providing direct legal guidance to consumers represent innovations that could reshape the future of legal practice.

Understanding Clients:
Their Job to Be Done

The groundbreaking veterans' service project described in the previous chapter and fueled by generative artificial intelligence (GenAI) may provide a glimpse into how lawyers and maybe other professions will deliver legal services in the future. In fact, with respect to the clients served through that initiative, the future is already here. The central premise of this book is that, on account of advances in technology that are likely to transform the practice of law dramatically in the next decade, the legal profession is about to enter what I call its third iteration: Lawyer 3.0. The profession can either manage this change of state, or have this evolution thrust upon it. In order to best manage this change, the profession and those who would like to see it transform for the better should harness technology to ensure that it fulfills its purpose and serves the community in a more effective and more beneficial way than it does now. This requires an assessment of that purpose and how the legal profession can best meet it. I have borrowed the job-to-be-done framework to help the profession understand its appropriate role, a role that can sometimes shift with the needs of clients in different contexts. In each such context, there are four key clusters of variables: the values at stake; the functions the client wants the profession to carry out; the nature of the client's problem or problems; and the characteristics of the client themselves, both in terms of what they want the lawyer to achieve in a particular context as well as their capacity to utilize a technological solution to address their problem should one exist in a given situation. These different elements of the job-to-be-done framework help us to assess in what contexts and for which clients, a technological solution, to the extent one is available, might enable the client to achieve their goals in a given situation. Technology is an important lever for helping the legal profession meet its broad purposes, but it is not a cure-all and will not offer an appropriate solution in every situation. The purpose of the job-to-be-done framework is to identify those clients, those problems, those interventions, and those instances where a technological solution does as good a job, if not better, than the alternative: in some instances, that may be a lawyer providing full-service representation to the client, but, in many others, it involves no lawyer at all.

In this chapter I will explore several of the job-to-be-done variables in one of the first phases of the legal services continuum described in Chapter 3, that of assessing client needs. This phase includes an exploration, first, of what a prospective client wants out of a given representation in a particular context. This aspect of the analysis touches upon the values and functions the client would like the lawyer to satisfy, but also their own capacity to utilize the delivery of legal services through different service modes that I will describe in subsequent chapters: information-based services, brief assistance, or full-service representation. But the aspect of the investigation I will conduct in this chapter examines a second issue: how to analyze the characteristics of a particular client in a particular situation to ensure any service modes selected satisfy the client's legal job to be done, and whether any such mode might include some type of technological intervention that delivers services in an effective way. I will refer to this phase as the client "triage" element of the legal services continuum. It mostly centers around the characteristics of clients: their needs and capacities, the functions they want the lawyer to carry out in a particular context, and the values they are looking for the lawyer to fulfill. I will leave for the next few chapters questions surrounding the characteristics of the legal problems clients face in any particular context, which will also have an impact on the ultimate job-to-be-done assessment. This analysis will set the stage for the discussion about the legal needs of Americans by exploring some data that address the scope of unmet legal needs in the United States, particularly of Americans of low income. I do this for two reasons. Since disruptive innovation tends to start in the lower end of a particular market, understanding the legal needs of lower-income Americans will help us to understand where such innovation could and should occur, at least at first. At present, what we are seeing in the legal sector is a different phenomenon playing out: that is, much of the energy driving technological innovation in the legal sector is directed at the higher end, targeting the large, private law firms that have the financial muscle to afford the costs associated with incorporating new legal tech into their practice.

What is more, a focus on just those who can afford legal services offered in the traditional, Lawyer 2.0 way does not improve and expand the provision of legal services. As the following discussion shows, for far too many Americans, the Lawyer 2.0 version of the profession is not fulfilling what should be its important values and functions. If that is the case, as it certainly is, a new version of the profession, one that can meet the job-to-be-done needs of more clients, and in a more efficient and effective way, will help the profession assume its rightful role in society. As the following discussion shows, the profession at present is not meeting the needs of far too many Americans. Thus, some change is necessary, and technology may offer a way to help usher in such change. One critical metric we must use to gauge whether new approaches will improve the delivery of legal services is whether such new approaches will meet the needs of more of the community. A profession that promises broad services to a fraction of the population is not just failing to satisfy the functional needs of the community, it is also undermining the core values it is supposed to uphold. It is to that assessment of the extent to which Lawyer 2.0 is meeting the legal needs of the nation that I now turn.

Are lawyers meeting the needs of most Americans?

Many Americans face their legal problems without the assistance of a lawyer, or even legal guidance.[1] There are many reasons why this is the case. The most obvious one is that for far too many Americans, the cost of legal assistance is too high for them to afford. Free legal assistance is offered to low-income individuals in many criminal matters, but, for civil matters—like eviction, bankruptcy, consumer debt—there is some non-profit legal assistance available to those who qualify for such services, but funding for such services, from the federal, state, and local government and philanthropy, has never been sufficient to meet the need. But even the funding that is available to non-profit legal service providers is limited in a significant way: nearly all of the funding sources for such non-profits place income restrictions on who can benefit from such services. Under regulations governing those entities that receive federal funding, they cannot represent anyone whose income exceeds 125 percent of the federal poverty rate, which, for an individual, is about $15,000 a year and for a family of four a little more than twice that number.[2] So, someone can certainly earn a modest income but still make too much to qualify for free legal assistance. And just because someone makes more than is permitted under such guidelines does not mean that they can afford the cost of a lawyer, even one charging a relatively modest amount per hour. If a family facing a home foreclosure is not paying their mortgage because they have probably experienced an economic shock to their household income, it is unlikely that they have extra money lying around to pay a lawyer to help them stave

---

[1]   LEGAL SERVICES CORPORATION, THE JUSTICE GAP: THE UNMET CIVIL LEGAL NEEDS OF LOW-INCOME AMERICANS 72 (2022) (hereinafter JUSTICE GAP REPORT) (estimating that approximately 92 percent of low-income Americans do not receive the level of legal assistance they need to address their legal problems).

[2]   See Federal Poverty Level (FPL), Healthcare.gov, https://www.healthcare.gov/glossary/federal-poverty-level-fpl/ (last visited, Oct. 4, 2024).

off the loss of their home. An understanding of the nature of the justice gap in America is to see, in stark relief, the reality that the Lawyer 2.0 version of the legal profession is not satisfying its obligations to the community. It is to this gap that I now turn.

The legal needs of lower-income Americans

Every year, tens of millions of Americans face their legal problems without a lawyer. Sometimes they do not even know that they have a legal problem or are unaware their problem is the type of problem that a lawyer might assist those individuals in resolving. This justice gap, as it is called—the difference between who has a lawyer and who needs one—has profound implications for our democracy, the rule of law, personal well-being, physical and mental health, economic justice, and fundamental notions of equity and equality.[3] A recent report from the Legal Services Corporation (LSC)[4] documents the current state of this crisis, and the following are just some of their most salient findings:

- [N]early three-quarters (74 percent) of low-income households have experienced at least one civil legal problem in the past year. Additionally, 38 percent of low-income Americans have personally experienced a civil legal problem that substantially impacted their lives in some way. Even for these "substantial" problems, they only sought legal help 25 percent of the time.[5]
- Over the course of a year, low-income individuals will approach LSC-funded legal aid organizations for help with an estimated 1.9 million civil legal problems that are eligible for assistance. They will receive some legal help for 51 percent of these problems, but even then, they will only receive enough legal help to resolve their problem about one-half (56 percent) of the time.[6]
- [In 2022] low-income Americans did not receive any legal help or enough legal help for 92 percent of the problems that substantially impacted their lives in the past year.[7]
- LSC-funded organizations are unable to provide any or enough legal help for 71 percent of the civil legal problems brought to them; this translates to an estimated 1.4 million problems over the course of a year.[8]

---

[3] For a book-length treatment of the contours and impacts of the access-to-justice crisis, see, generally, DEBORAH L. RHODE, ACCESS TO JUSTICE (2005).

[4] JUSTICE GAP REPORT, *supra* note 1.

[5] *Id.*, at 18.

[6] *Id.*, at 19.

[7] *Id.*

[8] *Id.*

Most of the individuals surveyed for the report who sought help from LSC-funded organizations received something other than full representation. According to the LSC's 2022 study, of those fortunate enough to receive some assistance from LSC-funded organizations, only 21 percent of those received what were regarded as "extended services," what I will consider full service. Such services are described in the report as follows: "Preparing complex legal documents (for example, advance directives, appeals for benefits, real estate documents)"; and "Representing a client in court, in administrative proceedings, or in interactions with third parties."[9] A larger percentage of these individuals—28 percent—received "general information and self-help resources," which included: "[g]iving guidance on how to complete legal forms/documents" and "[e]xplaining the requirements on how to file for custody or apply for benefits."[10] A majority, 51 percent, "receive[d] brief services and advice," which included such things as: "[p]roviding advice about how to handle a custody hearing" and "[w]riting a demand letter to a landlord to repair a rented home."[11] This sort of typology—describing the range of legal services as information based, brief services, and extended services—which tracks several components of the legal services continuum I described in Chapter 3, will help animate the discussion in subsequent chapters.

The LSC would ultimately conclude that more than nine-out-of-ten respondents who sought assistance from LSC-funded groups did not receive the assistance they needed to resolve their legal problem: "[l]ow-income Americans did not receive any … or enough legal help for 92 percent of the problems that substantially impacted their lives in the past year."[12] In terms of the types of problems respondents faced, a majority, 51 percent, said they needed assistance with consumer law issues,[13] and other common problems included issues surrounding access to health care (39 percent), public assistance (34 percent), and housing (33 percent).[14] The LSC report also explored why otherwise eligible potential clients of the LSC do not seek out legal assistance. Forty-six percent of respondents who did not seek out legal help cited concerns about the costs of legal services and "more than one half (53 percent) of low-income Americans doubt their ability to find a lawyer they could afford if they needed one."[15]

While these numbers are striking, they are not surprising. They also largely only address the fact that the overwhelming majority of low-income

---

[9] *Id.*, at 72.

[10] *Id.*

[11] *Id.*

[12] *Id.*

[13] *Id.*, at 33. Survey respondents indicated they had multiple legal problems, which resulted in the number of individuals with such problems exceeding 100 percent.

[14] *Id.*

[15] *Id.*, at 18.

Americans face their legal problems without the assistance of or guidance from a lawyer. But it is not just low-income Americans who struggle with securing legal help. Admittedly, we know less about the question of the extent to which middle-income Americans also struggle to secure legal assistance to address their legal problems. But what research does exist indicates that at least half of moderate-income Americans also have a hard time finding a lawyer to help them handle their legal problems.[16] While the justice gap is itself somewhat difficult to measure, we know, at bottom, that the overwhelming majority of Americans are presently going without the guidance of a lawyer when they face a legal problem, even one as serious as the loss of a home, lost wages, or discrimination in the workplace. In many of those instances, a family may experience eviction, an inability to meet their economic needs, and suffer psychological trauma due to the consequences of failing to protect their rights. But the numbers alone tell just a part of the story. And they do not offer guidance to those who might aspire to close the justice gap, other than to say "give everyone a lawyer." Let us put aside the fact that such a response is not particularly realistic: lawyering in a Lawyer 2.0 way is expensive, and there simply are not enough lawyers in the country to meet this need, even if money was no object.

What if we treated civil legal services as something that was every American's right? What if we believed, say, that the federal, state, and local government should provide it to everyone through some kind of "LegalCare" program (so, treating it as more important than health care)? This is something we do, with limited success, in the criminal context for those who cannot afford an attorney. Such a program on the civil side alone would likely cost tens of billions of dollars, if not more. The political will is simply not there at present to accomplish such a feat.

The numbers on the scope and scale of the justice gap in American tell just part of the story, however. If we try to look beyond the numbers, start to view them from the vantage point of those who might need legal assistance, and consider the new technologies now available to the legal profession to expand access to justice, a way forward might emerge that harnesses such technology and recalibrates how Americans address their legal problems. What is more, by using the tools of design thinking introduced in Chapter 2, we can begin to see the justice gap from the perspective of those who need legal assistance and not strictly from the perspective of the legal community. That is, we will take the consumer's view of the extent to which the legal profession is meeting consumer need for legal assistance

---

[16] Deborah L. Rhode, *Until Civil Gideon: Expanding Access to Justice*, 41 FORDHAM URB. L.J. 1227, 1228 (2014) (describing unmet legal needs of middle-income Americans) (citation omitted).

to address their legal problems. What that would require would not just involve developing an understanding of the scale of the justice gap but also an appreciation of how it is that consumers see this gap: their view on their legal needs and their ability (or inability) to find legal representation to address them. To start to develop such an understanding, I turn to some of the important work being done in this area by the sociologist Rebecca Sandefur, who has made a central focus of her research the question of not just to what extent but also why so many Americans appear to face their legal problems without a lawyer. Once we can establish an understanding of these phenomena, we can then begin to build a legal system that is more responsive to the needs of more Americans, and to do so in an accessible and even affordable way.

Beyond the numbers: looking at legal problems from the consumer perspective

In a study published in 2014, Sandefur reported the results of surveys of the residents of a representative, mid-sized, mid-western U.S. city to gauge the civil legal needs of its residents. The city was selected because it was "typical of many U.S. communities in terms of its size and socioeconomic and demographic composition."[17] Given this profile, Sandefur believed one could expect its residents to "represent typical experiences in the U.S. context."[18] What Sandefur would find about the needs of the respondents of a typical American city are illuminating. Sixty-six percent of respondents "reported experiencing one or more" civil legal problems "in the 18 months prior to the survey."[19] The most common of these problems "involved their livelihood and financial stability."[20] Twenty-four percent of respondents "reported at least one situation involving employment (for example, termination, wages, unemployment benefits, disciplinary procedures)"; 21 percent reported "at least one situation involving money (for example, mismanagement of pension funds, disputed bills)"; and the largest group, 25 percent, reported "at least one situation involving debt (for example, being behind and unable to pay credit cards, student loans, taxes, or utility bills)."[21] In addition, and not surprisingly, "poor people were significantly more likely to report civil justice situations than people in high- or middle-income households, and African Americans and Hispanics were more likely to report civil justice

---

17 REBECCA L. SANDEFUR, ACCESSING JUSTICE IN THE CONTEMPORARY USA: FINDINGS FROM THE COMMUNITY NEEDS AND SERVICES STUDY 4 (2014).

18 *Id.*

19 *Id.*, at 7.

20 *Id.*

21 *Id.*

situations than were Whites."[22] Sandefur would extrapolate these findings to consider what they might mean for the nation as a whole: "In a nation of over 316 million people, these rates represent a tremendous amount of civil justice activity—tens of millions of civil justice situations."[23]

But the study did not just seek to estimate the number of legal problems Americans might face. Sandefur's research also explored how Americans deal—or do not deal—with them: while "Americans respond to their civil justice situations in a wide variety of ways," there is also "a powerful consistency: rarely do they turn to lawyers or courts for assistance."[24] In fact, according to Sandefur, "the most common source of assistance for people facing civil justice situations is actually themselves" because the "most common way in which people report handling civil justice situations is by taking some action on their own without any assistance from a third party." Indeed, survey respondents referred to "self-help" to address "46% of civil justice situations."[25] The second most common way in which respondents attempted to face their legal problems was by "turning to their immediate social network," including family and friends, which occurred in "23% of situations." Only 22 percent of situations "were handled with the assistance of a third party who was not a member of respondent's social network."[26]

Another important finding from Sandefur's study is that respondents did not treat all legal problems in the same way. It was more common for people with legal problems to seek out the assistance of a third party outside their social circle when they had a personal injury claim or a matter involving the "breakdown of romantic relationships," like a divorce or when they had a need to apply for support payments.[27] Even in these types of situations, however, a majority of individuals did not seek such third-party assistance. What is more, respondents "were least likely to turn to outside third parties for situations involving housing, whether owned or rented (16% and 17% of the time respectively), and debts (12% of the time)."[28] Similarly, when individuals did nothing to respond to a legal problem, this response was more common in certain situations than in others. For example, this response was most common when facing a problem involving employment, government benefits, or insurance.[29] Still, even when individuals did seek out assistance from a third party to address their legal problems, that did not mean they

---

22   *Id.*, at 8.
23   *Id.*
24   *Id.*, at 11.
25   *Id.*
26   *Id.*
27   *Id.*
28   *Id.*
29   *Id.*

automatically sought help from a lawyer. In fact, in most instances, they did not. Sandefur did more in-depth qualitative research to determine instances where individuals did seek out third-party assistance, and, in such situations, only 42 percent sought out the help of an attorney. If the problem did not involve a court, individuals sought help from an attorney in only 5 percent of cases.[30]

For those who did not go outside their immediate social network for assistance, 46 percent did not seek such assistance because they did not see the need to do so: "either the problem had resolved or they expected it to resolve without getting advice, or they simply felt that they did not need advice."[31] Others (24 percent) thought that seeking help with their problem would not make a difference.[32] Just 9 percent of respondents who did not seek help outside their immediate network explained that they did not know where to turn or how to go about finding such assistance.[33] In only 17 percent of cases where individuals did not seek out third-party assistance, including help from lawyers, respondents cited the cost of such assistance as the main reason they did not seek that assistance.[34] As Sandefur explains: "How Americans handle their civil justice situations is clearly not just about money. Often, they believe there is no need to seek assistance, or that there is nothing to be done about their situation."[35] While not a lot of respondents identified cost as a factor in their choosing not to seek the assistance from a lawyer, "[a] majority of respondents ... believe[d] that lawyers' fees are out of reach for poor people: 58% of those surveyed agreed with the statement that 'lawyers are not affordable for people on low incomes.'"[36]

What is more, Sandefur found that a significant reason many Americans appear to not take "their justice situations to lawyers or courts" is that "they do not understand these situations to be legal." Indeed, 56 percent of the situations individuals faced were described by them as "bad luck/part of life" or "part of God's plan."[37] Twenty-one percent of the problems people faced were considered "private or as matters properly dealt with within the family or community."[38] Not surprisingly, there was a connection between "[h]ow people think about these events matters for what they do about them."[39] Individuals who faced problems they considered to be legal in

---

[30] *Id.*, at 12.
[31] *Id.*
[32] *Id.*, at 12–13.
[33] *Id.*, at 13.
[34] *Id.*
[35] *Id.*
[36] *Id.*, at 15.
[37] *Id.*, at 14.
[38] *Id.*
[39] *Id.*

nature would consider seeking out legal assistance 39 percent of the time; if they did not see their problems in that way, they would only do so in 14 percent of instances.[40]

The consumer's view of the legal profession

Sandefur's findings offer some of the most in-depth and useful insights into how American consumers think not about lawyers so much as their legal problems. Putting ourselves in the shoes of these respondents, and trying to see the issues they may face in their lives that might be, in some way, legal in nature, and which call for a response from someone with legal expertise, presents us with a quite different picture of the justice gap—and it might just help point towards a different way of approaching that gap, and the delivery of legal services in general. A typical assessment of the justice gap often starts with an analysis of the number of individuals who affirmatively seek legal representation from a non-profit organization and then concludes with a calculation of the number of clients those organizations tend to serve (which is often a small fraction of those who seek such help). This number often becomes the so-called justice gap: the difference between the number of people who seek out legal assistance and those who receive representation. But such an analysis fails to take into account those Americans who do not seek out such assistance, nor does it include those who do not even realize they have a problem for which a lawyer might be able to help them.

Other analyses might calculate the number of individuals who appear in a court system pro se, that is, representing themselves. But even that number is deceptive. Take a court system that deals with evictions from rental housing. In most of these systems, unrepresented tenants predominate, even though some jurisdictions have adopted a right to representation in such cases for tenants of low income. But not every situation in which a landlord seeks to evict a tenant makes its way into court. A tenant might move out voluntarily and abandon their home when they receive a notice from their landlord that their lease has ended or they have fallen behind in their rent payments. There is also a rise of "self-help" evictions across the country—instances where a landlord violates the law and simply uses force to get the tenant to leave without going to court.[41] An analysis that takes into account only the appearance of pro se litigants in formal court proceedings misses a large

---

[40] *Id.*

[41] Cecilia Reyes, *Locked Out: Reports of Illegal Evictions Are on the Rise. Yet Police Rarely Enforce the Law*, BUSINESS INSIDER (July 10, 2024), https://www.businessinsider.com/illegal-wrong ful-evictions-law-enforcement-police-court-2024-7 (last visited, Apr. 27, 2025).

number of instances where a tenant has a legal problem regarding their home but that problem does not show up in court records.

There is no question that a simple picture of the justice gap that exists in the present Lawyer 2.0 world reveals a tremendous disconnect between known legal problems and the extent to which many Americans face those legal problems without a lawyer. But a deeper analysis reveals that many of the problems that are, in fact, legal in nature are either ignored, not recognized as such, or consumers do not seek legal representation to try to resolve them. While no one wants to impose legal guidance on anyone who does not want it, the picture that emerges from this deeper analysis is that the scope of the justice gap is far greater than presently acknowledged. What is more, paradoxically perhaps, the Lawyer 2.0 solutions that have largely created this state of affairs are unlikely to help us get out of it.

Understanding the job to be done

While it may be part of business school lore to frame the client's need as not to purchase a quarter-inch drill but a quarter-inch hole, what at least some of Sandefur's research tells us is that potential consumers of legal services are apparently making at least three fundamental misperceptions about their legal problems. It is also possible that they are making a fourth misperception—not understanding the need to access legal guidance to assist with their legal problems—but I will return to that issue in a moment.

First, let us try to view legal problems through the eyes of a typical consumer to get a sense of these three misperceptions. The metaphorical quarter-inch-hole equivalent in the legal services context would entail a client understanding both their legal problem and exactly what they need from a lawyer to address that problem. Sandefur's research suggests that potential consumers of legal services do not appear to have this level of understanding of, and appreciation for, their situation. Instead of viewing the delivery of legal services from the perspective of the legal professional, recalibrating the delivery of legal services to take into account and understand the consumer's perspective on their legal problem helps us to consider new types of interventions that are driven by this understanding of the needs of the consumer rather than the needs of the lawyer. This requires that we engage in the type of analysis of the characteristics of the client described in greater detail in Chapter 2. A critical element of this analysis is to consider whether, and to what extent, the consumer fully grasps the nature of the legal problem in their lives. This type of analysis considers both the capacity of the consumer to understand the situation as well as the characteristics of the problem itself. Putting aside for now the possibility that a consumer might operate under some sort of diminished capacity, either because of age or infirmity, let us view the three consumer misperceptions that seem relatively widespread based on Sandefur's research and assume that a particular consumer has the capacity and wherewithal to grasp the nature of their problem as legal if appropriately described to them as such. But let us take our consumer as we find them—that is, with the information they possess about their problem based on their lay understanding of their situation. With such a consumer in mind, here are three consumer misperceptions about their potential legal problems that appear evident from Sandefur's research.

Misperception one: the consumer does not understand they have a problem

It is sometimes said that anyone who believes they are healthy simply has not undergone enough tests. I do not necessarily believe that is the case with the typical American consumer when it comes to the possibility that, unbeknownst to them, they are being stalked by a legal problem. At the same time, there are certainly instances where individuals may not know they have a legal claim or may not understand that someone else may have a potential legal claim against them. If someone works at a restaurant and they receive a portion of their wages through tips, their employer might be illegally siphoning off a portion of those tips and not sharing them with the employee. The employer might also have a discriminatory pay scale, one that pays women workers less than male workers for the same work. If workers do not share information about their respective salaries, a victim of this discrimination might not understand that there is anything nefarious going on.

Similarly, a consumer might have some outstanding medical debt that accrued some time ago, or they served as a guarantor for a relative in the past on a service contract or lease and the other party to that agreement believes the family member is delinquent in making a payment. The consumer might have changed their residence several times since they last had contact with the business on the other end of either of these transactions. The consumer, if made aware of either of these potential debts, might dispute them. But in either situation, the creditor in the matter could sue the consumer, using the prior address on file to commence the action and the consumer might never know that a case has been filed against them. Perhaps the family member is too embarrassed to admit that there is a case involving the consumer and that family member could fail to defend the action effectively. The plaintiff in either case could end up getting a judgment that renders the consumer liable, with the consumer never even knowing a case was brought against them, at least not until the plaintiff seeks to enforce the judgment and the consumer's bank accounts are frozen!

There are certainly other instances where legal claims might exist about which a consumer has no knowledge, which is common in such cases. The neighbor of a homeowner might have installed a fence that encroaches on the property line between the two properties. A consumer might be the victim of identity theft, with the perpetrator engaging in surreptitious actions to slowly drain small amounts of money from the consumer's accounts. The consumer might not realize that there is a manufacturing defect in a car or other product that is the subject of a class action lawsuit to which the consumer could be a party, which could result in payments to the consumer or replacement of the defective product, should that consumer come to know of the action and their right to compensation or some other intervention.

What these hypothetical examples reveal, and as Sandefur's research seems to confirm, is that the first misperception under which as least some consumers may operate is that they might not even understand that they have a problem, let alone one that is legal in nature. Sometimes, that problem will surface and come to the attention of the consumer in such a manner that they can take steps to protect their rights, but it is also likely the case that some harms may never come to light, like a discriminatory compensation scheme at a worker's place of employment. But this is not the only category of misperception that could plague a consumer when it comes to understanding their legal problems and their potential need for a quarter-inch legal hole, so to speak.

Misperception two: the consumer does not understand the legal nature of a problem

The second potential misperception is that, unlike with the first misperception, a consumer might understand they have a problem but not consider it to be legal in nature. This we might consider a "false negative": that is, the consumer understands something is wrong in their life but they do not appreciate that the problem relates to their legal rights. This should be contrasted with a "false positive": the type of situation where a consumer thinks that the way in which they might have been harmed does give rise to a legal claim when one does not exist. An employee might think they have been discriminated against in their place of employment, but in reality their termination was just the product of a downturn in the economy, their employer falling on hard times, or the employee failing to meet the legitimate expectations of their employer. I will concern myself with the first of this type of misperception: the false negative. The false positive can certainly cause considerable distress to a consumer, and a conversation with a lawyer might put them at some ease when it is explained to them that there might have been nothing illegal about what the employer did, but I am admittedly less concerned with these situations than I am with instances of false negatives.

False negatives—instances where a consumer does not understand they have a legal problem—can mean not only that a consumer's rights are being violated without them knowing that there might be a legal solution to their problem, but also that the consumer is not utilizing legal resources in an attempt to resolve their problem and improve their situation in life. In such instances, it is possible that legal interventions could address an adverse situation, and, when a consumer does not access legal assistance to resolve such legal problems, an injustice occurs in the community and the legal profession does not carry out its functional role—to resolve legal problems. There are also other aspects of the legal role, like the affective and political components of legal representation, that go unfulfilled.

Moreover, as with the first misperception, the existence of false negatives contributes to an underreporting of the justice gap: if a consumer does not realize their problem is legal in nature, they will not present such a problem to a lawyer to try to resolve it. For this reason, at least with respect to efforts that track requests for legal assistance, these consumers' problems will not show up in those records. Similarly, the third misperception will also impact such recordkeeping.

Misperception three: the consumer does not believe a lawyer can help

The third misperception also appears common according to Sandefur's research: that is, that consumers do not believe their problem is one a lawyer can solve. They might understand they have a problem. They might even understand it to be legal in nature. But they might look at this problem as something that is their fate and something they should just accept, or they might think it is intractable and a lawyer will not help them fix it. We can call this misperception the "inefficacy" perspective. They do not understand the nature of their problem or the role a lawyer might play in resolving it in an effective and beneficial way.

Another way this misperception manifests itself is when the consumer turns to some third party other than a lawyer, like an elected official, neighbor, friend, or religious leader in their community, to try to address their problem. This might be because they believe this situation is best resolved within the community and informally rather than by turning to formal legal channels. There are many reasons why a consumer might attempt to resolve their problem short of turning to such channels, including the legal profession and legal channels, with many of them legitimate. The parent of a young adult who is engaged in abusive behavior toward that parent might, because of the family's race, fear involvement with the legal system to address the situation as it could have significant and undue legal ramifications for their child. Because of a person's religious faith, they might feel that a marital dispute is best resolved through their congregation rather than by involving the courts. There are many reasons why a person might not want to subject a problem, even one that is legal in nature, to the legal system. I will call this the "conflict-aversion" perspective. I know that referring to this as conflict aversion can cast concerns under this misperception in a negative light, but I do not intend to do so. There are many very noble and laudable reasons a consumer might not seek to resolve their problems—even those they recognize as legal in nature—through formal legal channels.

For the last several decades, out of a recognition of these types of concerns, there has also been a growing movement towards community mediation and even alternative dispute resolution: modes of resolving conflict that are generally less "legalistic" and formal, where parties might be able to bring an end to a dispute without having to turn to the legal system itself.[42] Some of these modes of dispute resolution are even baked into the judicial system, as a sort of off-ramp that helps individuals avoid some of the costs and consequences of drawn-out legal battles in the courts.[43] In communities that have developed these sorts of channels for alternative dispute resolution, the consumers of such services often leave satisfied that they have been able to resolve their legal issues without having to resort to an expensive, time-consuming, and drawn-out judicial proceeding. But sometimes such less-than-formal options result in less-than-optimal results, where a consumer does not realize the important values that the rules, procedural protections, and mechanisms of the adversarial system are supposed to promote.

Just as I do not intend to cast the conflict-aversion perspective itself in a negative light, I do not intend to demean these forms of dispute resolution. They are likely essential elements of a comprehensive approach to resolving legal problems in a Lawyer 3.0 world, as I will explore in greater detail in Chapters 8 and 10. Indeed, to the extent that such less-cumbersome, less-opaque, and more-accessible systems and outlets satisfy a particular consumer's job to be done in a particular setting, such options will face no opposition from me. In fact, when they satisfy the client's functional, affective, and political needs, and do so in an effective and efficient way, they are entirely consistent with the Lawyer 3.0 way.

At the same time, and to the extent they do not satisfy the consumer's needs, they are not up to the task of providing justice at scale. What is more, the honorable intentions that often drive the conflict-aversion perspective can leave a consumer worse off than if they had pursued more formal avenues of redress, meaning the values that the legal system is supposed to promote, and which the legal profession is supposed to advance, are undermined. Of course, in order for the profession and the legal system to realize its values

---

42 For some of the early history of the community mediation movement, see Amy J. Cohen & Michael Alberstein, *Progressive Constitutionalism and Alternative Movements in Law*, 72 OHIO ST. L.J. 1083, 1093–97 (2011).

43 On litigants' experience in alternative dispute resolution settings, see Donna Shestowsky, *Civil Litigants' Evaluations of Their Legal Experiences*, 19 ANN. REV. L. & SOC. SCI. 19 (2023).

and functions when a consumer has a legal problem that they could resolve by recourse to lawyers and that legal system, the consumer must be able to secure meaningful legal representation. While these misperceptions can make it difficult to fully comprehend the scope of the justice gap, let alone address it, there is another perception—this one all too real—that also widens the access-to-justice crisis.

Legitimate perception: the consumer does not know how to access a lawyer

Of course, another "version" of the misperception that discourages consumers from turning to lawyers to address their problems, even ones they recognize as legal in nature, may not be a misperception at all: that is, the consumer does not know *how* to access a lawyer to solve their problem even if they do understand it to be legal in nature, they understand a lawyer could address it (so they do not suffer from the efficacy fallacy), and they are willing to turn to a lawyer if they can (they do not suffer from the conflict-aversion problem).

Turning to this one consumer "perception" (and not a misperception) of the relationship between legal problems and lawyer-assisted solutions, it is not incorrect for a consumer to appreciate that, even if they understand their problem to be legal in nature and of the type a lawyer might be able to help them resolve, for many consumers, they simply do not know where to turn for legal assistance. We are a far cry from the days when a small-town lawyer maintained their office in their community and residents with legal problems might simply walk down the street and drop in on that lawyer to inquire about the state of that consumer's affairs. Today, lawyers in the U.S. tend to have their physical offices in city centers and in the commercial districts of those urban areas. In addition, there has been a steady exodus of small-town lawyers from rural communities across the nation. In low-income and working poor communities, although one might see billboard advertisements for personal injury or immigration lawyers, such communities are generally woefully underserved in many other areas of the law.

While I will spend more time in subsequent discussions exploring ways to get information to consumers about how they might come to learn about the availability of legal services, such services must be available for consumers to come to such knowledge! We already know that there is a vast *documented* justice gap in the United States. Making matters worse, with a greater understanding of the misperceptions that beset many American consumers about the nature of their problems and the role the legal profession might play in helping to resolve them, it is clear that the present justice gap is far more extensive than currently recognized. If the consumer's legal job to be done should drive the delivery of legal services, one must understand this legal job in each situation in order to enable the legal profession to fulfill its appropriate role in each consumer's situation. It seems clear that at least some work needs to be done by the profession to educate the consumer on what that job to be done is in any particular situation where legal interventions might satisfy a particular consumer's need. In the remaining section of this chapter, and in light of the discussion had so far in it, I will return to several aspects of the legal job-to-be-done framework that are essential elements to this analysis: the characteristics of clients and their legal problems.

Triage in a different light: overcoming consumer misperceptions in discrete situations

In Chapter 2 I identified the characteristics of clients as one of the four critical variables in any given legal situation that can help us tailor the delivery of services to match an array of needs in that situation. Described there, the characteristics include the client's goals for that situation and their ability to pay for legal services. There is also what I called their sophistication, which includes an ability to understand the nature of their situation; their capacity to act on guidance; and their technological capacity. For our purposes here, given the previous discussion that highlighted the critical misperceptions that Americans seem to harbor about the existence of problems, their nature as legal problems, and those Americans' ability to resolve them with legal assistance, I am going to focus here on the characteristic that is most relevant to the apparent disconnect between Americans' appreciation for their problems as legal problems and their willingness to turn to formal legal guidance for assistance. Since at least some consumers appear willing to turn to a third party in their community to address their problems, it is not that they do not want assistance. It is that they either do not want to involve a lawyer or they do not know how to access one should they want to do so. But there are also two additional misperceptions that we need to address to make sure that we can accomplish what should be every consumer's goal: resolution of legal problems. First, a consumer must recognize that they have a problem and, second, they must realize that it is legal in nature. We will get to the third misperception—failing to believe that a lawyer, or at least some legal guidance—will help resolve it, in a moment.

The central driving force in a job-to-be-done framework is the idea that we should strive to understand a consumer's goal in any setting. When a consumer's job to be done becomes a *legal* job to be done is when the problem the consumer wants solved is legal in nature. That is, it requires a solution for which some sort of legal guidance or representation is necessary to achieve the consumer's goal: resolving the problem. Therefore, the first step in a consumer developing a legal job to be done is understanding their problem as legal in nature, as requiring some sort of legal intervention. In some ways, turning back to our characteristic matrix from Chapter 2, this question will not hinge on the characteristics of the consumer. Rather, it will center on the characteristic of the problem. But, in order for a consumer to turn to legal guidance to address their problem, assuming it is legal in nature, they will still need to appreciate that their problem is, in fact, legal in nature. For our purposes, to determine that appropriate legal job to be done in any situation, the "job" must require a lawyer, or at least some legal guidance, to address it.

In some ways, the evolution of the Lawyer 2.0 framework as it currently exists developed mechanisms for addressing some of these misperceptions. At the beginning of the Lawyer 2.0 era, however, that was not the case. When the American Bar Association (ABA) helped to usher in this era through taking such steps as creating the Canons of Professional Ethics in 1908, it prohibited lawyers from engaging in advertising.[44] The approach of the ABA was that such advertising was demeaning to lawyers and gave the impression that lawyers were not professionals but merely seeking profits by trolling for clients. For elites in the bar, that is, the same people who wrote the rules, this prohibition was quite convenient: they had clients already and steady work. Those who did not have clients were the upstart lawyers looking to make their way in the profession and at least some of these were looking for clients who would appear on the opposite side of disputes with the clients of the elites of the profession. The prohibition on advertising probably did little to improve the standing of the profession; it certainly made it more difficult for consumers to find lawyers.

Although it took nearly 70 years from the passage of the Canons for the Supreme Court to hold that prohibitions on many forms of lawyer advertising violated the First Amendment,[45] accessing legal *guidance*, even guidance that helps a consumer understand that they have a problem that is legal in nature, is still not readily available. Yes, if a consumer is injured in a car crash, or has a loved one who has died of mesothelioma due to exposure to asbestos, they might see an advertisement from a lawyer saying that they can help. Sometimes this type of advertising can form the brunt of jokes. There's a viral photograph going around on social media today that has a picture of a sophisticated-looking Golden Retriever in a business suit with the caption that says "Did your human break a treat in half and try to pass it off as a whole treat? You may be entitled to compensation." Lawyers who practice in the field of personal injury play an important role in our society and can satisfy a consumer's legal job to be done in many ways, so I do not want to mock them. But it is instructive that information-based assistance around personal injury law tends to drive consumers to a lawyer who can help address their job to be done. In fact, much of this information

---

[44] AM. BAR ASS'N, CANONS OF PROFESSIONAL ETHICS 27–28 (1908).
[45] Bates v. State Bar of Arizona, 433 U.S. 350 (1977).

has two goals: not only to inform an injured consumer that they can turn to a particular law firm for legal assistance to address their legal problem, but also to inform that consumer that they might have a legal problem in the first place. Remember, though, this form of advertising is still stuck in the Lawyer 2.0 approach: the twin purposes of the information is to let potential clients know they might have a legal problem and to convert that consumer into a customer/client.

Regardless of the area of law, whether it is personal injury or some other legal-needs context, the overarching purpose of the legal system is not to enable lawyers to obtain more clients. It is to resolve consumers' legal problems. So, what would a system that addressed some of the consumer misperceptions around legal problems and legal guidance while also achieving this overarching purpose look like? What do the informational deficits of consumers tell us about what tactics might help the profession achieve that purpose? Are there ways that technology can help to overcome those deficits? And can it also help the profession both frame consumer problems as legal in nature while also placing a priority on the consumer's job to be done—resolution of their legal problems—as opposed to having the goal of the legal profession that it will continue to create jobs for lawyers? In the next chapter, I will explore the next phase of the legal services continuum and examine ways that the provision of information-based assistance can aid consumers with legal problems. Such information-based assistance, infused with technological innovations that are now available, will attempt to accomplish two things. Not only will it assist in taking steps toward overcoming the misperceptions that consumers have about their legal problems, it will also attempt, wherever appropriate, to satisfy the consumer's job to be done. I recognize that it is not possible to resolve all legal problems through information and guidance alone. Still, there is a value to trying to address those problems that are amenable to such limited services. If the technology is there to help accomplish such a goal, if such an approach can satisfy the values the profession is supposed to advance in a particular context, and if the characteristics of the client and the problem are suited to such information-based assistance, the profession should strive to deliver such assistance, at the right time, and in the right place. I explore these questions in depth in Chapter 6.

Chapter 5: Key takeaways

1. The legal profession is on the cusp of significant transformation due to advancements in technology. Lawyer 3.0 represents the future of lawyering, where legal services are delivered more efficiently and effectively through the integration of technology, potentially reshaping the profession over the next decade.

2. The "job-to-be-done" approach is central to understanding a client's need for legal services. Lawyers must assess not only the values and functions clients seek but also the clients' capacity to utilize technological solutions. This framework helps identify where technology may offer better or equivalent solutions to full legal representation.

3. The legal profession needs to adopt a client triage system to assess clients' needs effectively. This involves understanding what clients require in various contexts, whether they need information-based services, brief assistance, or full representation. Tailoring services based on client needs and capacities is key to providing appropriate legal solutions.

4. There is a significant justice gap in the U.S., where tens of millions of low-income Americans face legal problems without proper assistance. Many cannot afford legal services, and current funding for non-profit legal aid is insufficient to meet the demand.

5. Many individuals do not seek legal assistance because they do not recognize their issues as legal problems or believe that legal help would not resolve them. This highlights the need for greater public education and outreach to help people understand when and how legal services can assist them.

Information-Based Assistance

In a Lawyer 3.0 world, there will be more than one way to delivery legal services to those in need of them: those who have a job to be done that requires legal intervention. The simple version of Lawyer 2.0 draws few distinctions between a consumer receiving no legal assistance or guidance whatsoever or receiving bespoke services: services tailored to the full-service needs of each client. What is common in the Lawyer 2.0 version of the legal profession is that the key determinant that controls whether a consumer receives nothing or full service is that consumer's ability to pay for such services. Given the high cost of legal services generally, this means that tens of millions of Americans are effectively priced out of legal assistance to help address their legal problems. Yes, there is free legal assistance available to some who cannot pay for it. Such assistance has been extended to many indigent defendants in criminal contexts by virtue of constitutional requirements regarding effective assistance of counsel, although the adequacy of such assistance is constantly questioned.[1] In the overwhelming majority of situations where legal guidance could help a consumer address their legal job to be done, the assistance is not available to them at a price they can afford, even if they understand their problem to be legal in nature, they believe a lawyer can help, and they would turn to that lawyer if they had the capacity and wherewithal to do so.

As described previously, disruptive innovation in markets for different products and services tends to happen at the lower end of the market, where consumers tend to be priced out of engagement with incumbent providers who might offer services beyond those the consumer might want, as many of these services are outside those consumers' financial reach. In the market for legal services, it is easy to see that this market is ripe for

---

[1] On the history of the American system providing indigent defense in criminal matters, and that system's many inadequacies, see SARA MAYEUX, FREE JUSTICE: A HISTORY OF THE PUBLIC DEFENDER IN TWENTIETH-CENTURY AMERICA (2020).

the sort of disruption that Clayton Christensen believed was common where innovation might lead to the delivery of products and services that might more closely align with the needs—and budgets—of consumers. To date, the legal services market has largely not yet fallen "victim" to the effects of disruptive innovation, probably because the technologies that might disrupt the profession have been, at least up to now, expensive to incorporate into the delivery of legal services. That cost means it has been difficult, at least until now, to really use technology in a manner that translates into more affordable and accessible legal services to consumers at that lower end of the market. What is more, because those service providers operating at the high end of the legal services market are those who have been able, to date, to begin to build expert systems to leverage new practice technologies in their delivery of legal services to the higher end of the market, it is likely that Christensen might consider these sorts of interventions sustaining rather than disruptive innovations: that is, they empower incumbent providers to serve their current customers in more efficient and effective ways, and those innovations tend not to lead to any large-scale change in the market landscape. What is more, the legal sector is unique from many other markets where new entrants can freely enter the market and challenge the dominance of incumbents: there are strict controls on the delivery of legal services through rules against the unauthorized practice of law (UPL). In other words, while anyone can, say, create a new system for watching movies at home, as Netflix did to unseat companies like Blockbuster, in the market for legal services, incumbents control access to that market through regulatory restrictions, and new entrants have a much harder time challenging the dominance of those incumbents as a result.

With the introduction of the newest technologies that appear to assist in the delivery of legal services in some form, are we on the cusp of an actual disruption that would transform the market for legal services in significant ways? This chapter begins to explore this question and starts with the first stage of the legal services continuum described in previous chapters: the provision of information-based services. This phase of the continuum is generally not considered an important one in the delivery of bespoke services to clients who can afford full-service legal representation. But it is at the lower end of the market where such services are currently being offered by non-profit providers. In addition, new technologies are making this type of service more readily available. This chapter will focus on this stage of the legal services continuum and show when and how the services offered to consumers to address their legal job to be done will satisfy all of the needs and values the legal system is supposed to advance. It will do so by not only describing some of the interventions that are doing this well, but also by incorporating the characteristics matrix from Chapter 2 to identify those instances where such services are all a consumer needs to achieve their job to be done.

When is a particular problem, with a particular consumer, appropriate for guidance alone?

Information-based assistance will not resolve every legal problem. In fact, it might merely help the average consumer address only a small fraction of such problems. But, when we look at the characteristics of clients—their goals, their perceptions and misperceptions, and the values they need to satisfy—in relation to the problem they might face, we can see that information-based systems that deliver the right amount of guidance, at the right time, can actually accomplish at least some of what we want the legal profession to accomplish when it comes to fulfilling its critical role. As we saw in the last chapter, there are many reasons why consumers fail to access legal services even when they have a legal problem. Sometimes, of course, it is because they cannot afford a lawyer. Sometimes, it is because they want to try to resolve their problem without the assistance of a lawyer. But there are also instances when they do not even realize they have a legal problem in the first place. While information alone will not address the issue of consumers not being able to afford lawyers when they need them, a lot of the mismatch between consumers and the availability of legal services has at least something to do with the fact that consumers do not have an adequate understanding of their situation: that is, they may not even realize the situation they face may be legal in nature.

One of the first things that information-based assistance can do is to give consumers a clear sense of the problem they may be facing. It can even help them identify the very fact that they have a problem to begin with. It can then help people understand that their problem is legal in nature and that a lawyer might help them solve it. At the same time, it could help the consumer understand that the problem is not legal in nature at all, or that it will be solved with fairly minimal guidance even if that problem is, in fact, legal in nature. The first step in an analysis of a problem requires us to utilize several components of the job-to-be-done framework described in Chapter 2. We must understand the nature of the problem and then determine what information might serve to resolve the problem to address the consumer's functional, affective, and political needs. It must also assess the consumer themselves: can they utilize the guidance given in an effective way? These are all questions baked into the diagnostic function. But once it is determined that (1) there is a legal problem, (2) information might go a long way toward solving it, and (3) the consumer can act effectively based on that information, the next step in the provision of information-based assistance is to determine just what guidance the consumer should receive. What information-based assistance can do is provide consumers with actionable intelligence: information that can guide conduct in the future, whether that conduct is directed at solving a problem, avoiding a problem, or ensuring that a problem does not get more serious and consequential. Sometimes the actionable intelligence will simply include guidance to seek out a lawyer. The diagnosis of the problem might identify the problem as being complex in nature, requiring a response that is beyond the scope of assistance the consumer can obtain through information-based guidance alone.

Benefits of information-based assistance

Consumers should have as full an understanding of their rights and obligations as is possible. In a liberal democracy that is supposed to operate in a manner that is consistent with the rule of law, a knowledgeable citizenry aware of the ways in which the law should govern behavior and which turns to our legal system to resolve our disputes is essential to that functioning democracy. Knowledge of how one should operate in the world helps the individual to both protect themselves and also act in accordance with legitimate community expectations. It allows members of the community to order their affairs, preserve their rights, plan for the future, and avoid violating the rules by which that community functions. With an understanding of one's rights and obligations, one can avoid problems in the first place, either because they appreciate what is expected of them in a particular setting, or they know what they can legitimately expect of others and can speak up when they believe those expectations are not being met. This sort of knowledge represents perhaps one of the most important uses of information: it helps consumers avoid problems in the first place or prevents those problems from getting unmanageable to the point that they can only be addressed by serious legal interventions.

If we return to the job-to-be-done variables introduced in Chapter 2, we can see that information-based assistance can serve to address many of them in appropriate circumstances. Of course, this begs the question: what are "appropriate circumstances," but I will return to this critical question shortly. According to these variables, the legal profession is supposed to serve certain values like the rule of law and access to justice. In some situations, information-based assistance can certainly serve these ends, at least at the outset, meaning that when consumers are aware of their own obligations under the law, many will adhere to those obligations. Adherence to law is where the rule of law starts. Making sure others adhere to their obligations starts with the consumer being armed with information to understand what they owe others and what those others owe them. While such information, internalized or shared with others, will not prevent all acts of illegal conduct that violate the rights of others, it is possible that it can reduce at least some instances in which legal interventions are necessary to vindicate rights. In this way, and turning to another of the values that the legal profession is supposed to advance, that of access to justice, a system that prevents legal problems from occurring in the first place is certainly one that will make strides towards reducing the justice gap. If there are fewer problems that require legal interventions, there will be fewer consumers who will not have their legal needs met.

When we turn to the functions the legal profession is supposed to fulfill, we can see that information-based assistance alone might be enough to address many of these functions in the right situations. Depending on the nature of the problem (another variable in the framework), there are situations in which a bit of information will serve the instrumental needs the consumer has with respect to a particular problem or issue. This is particularly true where the consumer's goal is to obtain information so that they might understand whether they have a legal problem in the first place. This might be why they contact a lawyer, if they know one who might be able to provide such assistance. If they can receive the information necessary to understand that their problem is not legal in nature, or at least it is one for which there may be no legal solution, the instrumental goal they have for the communication has been satisfied. The consumer will also satisfy that threshold goal if they learn that they do, in fact, have a legal problem. That can then activate further appropriate and timely action to address the legal problem as such.

When it comes to the emotional element of the search for legal guidance, it goes without saying that the consumer may have some degree of anxiety about their situation and information-based assistance may help assuage those concerns. Learning that what is happening to them is, in fact, illegal might give them some comfort that, with the right interventions, they may be able to achieve a successful resolution to the situation. Learning that their concern that someone is violating their rights is incorrect, or that even though they might have a problem, there might be no legal solution to it, might, in some circumstances, also give them some comfort. In Sandefur's research referenced earlier, at least some consumers seem to believe their problems are insoluble, and perhaps even their fate. Learning that there might actually be a way to solve their problems and that they do not have to simply accept them could give some consumers a sense of hope. At the same time, realizing one has a problem where one was unaware of it beforehand might not make one's mental or emotional state better. It might actually make it worse. Still, at a minimum, consumers should have an accurate sense of the fact that they might have a problem and whether it is legal in nature. There are certainly situations where one might argue, using the old saw, that "ignorance is bliss" or "what you don't know can't hurt you." It is a rare legal problem where that is the case. For these reasons, information-based assistance, even at the cusp or threshold of a problem, can address at least some aspects of the affective element of the job-to-be-done framework.

Such assistance can also serve the political aspects of that framework. Information can help consumers understand the political nature of their conduct and the conduct of others, when we view this element as dealing with the relation between individuals and others within the community. Assistance centered around providing information to the consumer can help them understand not just their rights and the way others must treat them, it also helps the consumer appreciate the way they must behave toward others. As a result, information-based assistance certainly can help address the political aspects of the job-to-be-done framework.

While we can see that information-based assistance might, as I have said, help consumers address their job to be done in appropriate circumstances, what are such circumstances? Perhaps a little bit of information, combined with brief guidance from a lawyer, can help to address the consumer's problem adequately. There are also significant risks in either scenario, whether simple information or slightly more involved action by a legal services provider is offered. There are many risks associated with either of these forms of assistance, risks I will explore in greater depth in the next chapter. There is also another problem with information-based or even brief service when it is delivered by non-lawyers: it might result in UPL violations. The remainder of this chapter is devoted to this question, and recent developments suggest that we are, perhaps, entering a moment where the relaxation of such rules may serve to help usher in a Lawyer 3.0 world.

The unauthorized practice of law

Another significant risk when it comes to providing even information-based assistance is that at least some might consider that a portion of such action constitutes the practice of law. Now, if a lawyer or law office provides such services by making them available to the public generally, there is no UPL concern. In such situations, the lawyer is creating the information and is accountable to the public for the accuracy of the information. Should a consumer act on such information and it turns out the advice was flawed, the lawyer could face charges of malpractice: that providing the information created a duty of care which included the provision of competent assistance. When that duty of care is violated because the information is incorrect, the lawyer may find themselves the subject of a malpractice action. This can even happen in instances where no formal lawyer–client relationship is formed by the execution of a retainer agreement. When a lawyer gives legal advice, and such legal advice constitutes the practice of law (and the provision of legal advice generally does constitute the practice of law because only lawyers can provide it), the lawyer is at least held accountable under the standard of care to give advice that is accurate and aligned with the needs of the consumer. When a non-lawyer gives the same advice, they are not held to the duty of care that lawyers must uphold; instead, we say they are engaged in UPL, which, in every state, is illegal.[2]

We saw in Chapter 4 that when a service provider offers tailored assistance to a specific consumer in a specific situation, such an act may constitute the practice of law, and, when that service provider is not a licensed attorney, such actions constitute the *unauthorized* practice of law. Some providers of services that look a lot like legal services have tried to avoid crossing the line into UPL by insisting that they do not provide such tailored services, but, rather, merely offer generalized guidance to consumers that helps them make decisions for themselves about how to address their legal problems. Such generalized guidance is considered appropriate in many jurisdictions and does not constitute a violation of UPL rules. For example, the company LegalZoom provides a range of information and services to its customers in discrete areas. It uses disclaimers that try to make it clear to its customers that the services that organization provides are not legal in nature, are not tailored to any particular consumer's needs, and are no substitute for the guidance of a lawyer.[3] Courts reviewing claims against groups like LegalZoom have found that these types of disclaimers are generally sufficient to shield them from claims of UPL.[4]

This line between generalized services and tailored assistance is sometimes blurry, and some states, like Washington State, have experimented with models where non-lawyers can engage in what would otherwise amount to the practice of law, there, in the area of family law. That program, which authorized the training and practice of "limited license legal technicians" (LLLT), was shuttered less than a decade after it was first instituted for a range of issues, including a lack of support from the state's Supreme Court which had originally initiated it, a failure to expand it to other areas of law, inadequate funding to support the training of the technicians, some opposition from the established bar, and a lack of interest among

---

[2]   For her landmark work assessing UPL rules across the U.S., see Deborah L. Rhode, *Policing the Professional Monopoly: A Constitutional and Empirical Analysis of Unauthorized Practice Prohibitions*, 34 STAN. L. REV. 1 (1981).

[3]   LegalZoom, Terms of Use, https://www.legalzoom.com/legal/general-terms/terms-of-use (last visited, Oct. 5, 2024).

[4]   See, for example, Janson v. LegalZoom.com, Inc., No. 2:10-cv-04018-NKL, 2012 U.S. Dist. LEXIS 60019 (W.D. Mo. Apr. 30, 2012). As part of the Settlement Agreement, LegalZoom agreed to change its business practices in Missouri. See Nathan Koppel, *Seller of Online Legal Forms Settles Unauthorized Practice of Law Suit*, WALL ST. J. L. BLOG (Aug. 23, 2011, 11:47 AM), http://blogs.wsj.com/law/2011/08/23/seller-of-online-legal-forms-settles-unauthorized-practiced-of-law-suit (last visited, Apr. 27, 2025).

paraprofessionals to pursue the license.[5] Still, the more one strives to improve information-based systems to make sure they are appropriate to a particular consumer's situation and avoid some of the other risks described here—of mismatch and other types of errors—the more those systems will come close to, if not cross, the line constituting the practice of law.

At the same time, recent developments in the law might suggest that we might be close to the point where rules against UPL might fall in the face of legal challenges brought by those looking to expand access to justice. As this book goes to print, a case pending in the federal court in New York State might just show the way forward when it comes to creating opportunities for non-lawyers to provide quality, information-based assistance to consumers in need, even when that assistance might otherwise constitute UPL.

In *Upsolve v. James*, a non-profit organization based in New York City brought an action against the New York State Attorney General's office which enforces that state's UPL rules in order to get out ahead of any action that office might take to shut down the organization's operation. Upsolve is a community-based organization that trains non-lawyers to offer advice and guidance to consumers facing debt-collection actions. A lawyer tends to participate in the training and the preparation of materials on which that training is based, but the individuals who provide the services, who are called "justice advocates" by the group, are not licensed attorneys themselves and are not directly supervised by the lawyer who trained them when those advocates are in the community providing advice and guidance to community members. If Upsolve operated as a law office, and had non-lawyers who were trained and supervised by a licensed attorney such that any advice they supply had been vetted by the lawyer and those advocates know the types of questions they can answer and which they cannot, such an approach would not run afoul of UPL rules. But the fact that the justice advocates did not receive ongoing supervision of their work by a licensed attorney meant that these practices could not constitute the *authorized* practice of law. Upsolve did not really attempt to argue that the justice advocates were not engaged in the practice of law, however. They challenged New York's UPL rules themselves as content-based restrictions on speech that violated the First Amendment to the U.S. Constitution. And, at least for now, the trial judge agreed with the group's characterization of the rules against UPL as they relate to the activities of the justice advocates.

Here's how the court described the activities of Upsolve and its justice advocates:

> Plaintiffs have crafted a program that would train non-lawyers to give
> legal advice to low-income New Yorkers who face debt collection

---

[5]   Lyle Moran, *How the Washington Supreme Court's LLLT Program Met Its Demise*, ABA JOURNAL (July 9, 2020).

the information provided by the justice advocates to consumers seemed to address and allay any concerns about the consumer-protective aspect of the UPL rule at issue in this case. The group requires that advocates "must attend a training—designed by lawyers" and "abide by State ethical guidelines for assisting clients, including for conflicts of interest and confidentiality."[15] In addition, the advocates "must refer clients to licensed lawyers if those clients' needs exceed the scope of the Training Guide."[16] Those advocates are also not permitted to "appear in court or file documents."[17] According to the court, this "eliminat[es] any risk of providing bad advice in more complex or adversarial settings."[18] Citing prior precedent of the U.S. Supreme Court, the judge in the *Upsolve* case would note that lawyers make up a "noble profession" and "play a unique role in our society."[19] At the same time, he would also point out that Upsolve and the other defendants had "designed a unique program of their own." Because of this, "they have demonstrated a narrow exception, under the First Amendment, to New York's UPL rules, and they will be allowed to implement that program without the threat of prosecution."[20]

As this book goes to print, the New York Attorney General is appealing the lower court's decision. While it is possible that the appellate court might scale back some of the court's holding and undermine the justifications for its decision, it seems clear that the sorts of arguments raised by the plaintiffs are not going away any time soon and we might see other, similar efforts across the country to rein in the reach of UPL rules in other jurisdictions. This can certainly occur by litigants providing services like those supplied by Upsolve bringing challenges to the application of UPL laws to their practices, but it might also come in the form of legislative changes to those prohibitions that advocates and consumers, working together, might achieve. If the most important and beneficial purpose of UPL laws is to provide a modicum of consumer protection, to ensure that providers of services are properly trained to dispense appropriate advice in particular settings, to the extent that intermediaries like Upsolve are able to ensure that the services they offer are otherwise consistent with the standard of care in a particular setting, that will vindicate and achieve the consumer-protective purpose of UPL prohibitions.

---

[15] *Id.*, at 118.

[16] *Id.*

[17] *Id.*

[18] *Id.*

[19] *Id.*, at 120, citing Mallard v. United States Dist. Ct. for the Southern Dist. of Iowa, 490 U.S. 296, 311 (1989) (Kennedy, J., concurring).

[20] *Id.*, at 120.

What is more, when such intermediaries provide accurate services to consumers in appropriate situations, it also vindicates other important values, interests, and principles from within the job-to-be-done framework: not just protecting the consumer's legal interests in a particular setting, but also expanding access to justice and upholding the rule of law. UPL rules should serve the job-to-be-done framework in a Lawyer 3.0 world and should not merely serve to protect and preserve the legal profession's monopoly on the provision of legal guidance. When appropriate guardrails are in place, like quality-control measures that ensure the correct assistance is provided, to the right client, and at the right time, the consumer-protection concerns melt away, and all that is left are those related to the naked preservation of the lawyer cartel. When those UPL restrictions do not advance the values the profession is supposed to uphold, they do not serve an appropriate purpose, and we should jettison them when it is necessary to do so to promote and protect those values.

This discussion about UPL underscores a core piece of the analysis that can help usher in the transition from the Lawyer 2.0 version of the legal profession to its Lawyer 3.0 state. An essential component of this shift is to align the values the profession is supposed to uphold with the goals a consumer might seek to achieve when they seek out legal assistance in some form. As we saw in the previous chapter, there are times when a consumer is unable or unwilling to try to secure legal assistance with a legal problem they face, or fear they face. It is also the case that many consumers do not even realize they have a legal problem, or a problem that calls for a solution that is legal in nature. Another goal of the legal profession should be to ensure that everyone who has a legal problem has enough guidance and assistance to resolve it in a meaningful way. That requires that there is a sufficient and adequate *quantity* of service to go around; that it is of appropriate *quality*; and that consumers have adequate awareness that they have a problem, it is legal in nature, it is the type of problem that legal assistance can help them address, and they have the wherewithal and capacity to access such assistance in a meaningful and accessible way. As a threshold matter, I have explained here that information-based assistance can, in appropriate circumstances, help consumers appreciate their problem as legal in nature and then might provide a level of assistance, appropriate to the circumstances and delivered at the right time, that might resolve that problem before it increases in complexity and severity that it will require more than just information-based assistance to resolve, and where the stakes are so high that full-service legal intervention is necessary. An effort to ensure that all Americans are aware of their legal problems in a way and at a time when we might provide guidance to them to resolve them in an efficient way, before they get worse, would not just allow us to develop an appreciation for the true scope of legal need in this country, but also help address an array of problems before they get worse, when more intensive and expensive legal interventions are necessary to resolve them. In the final part of this chapter, I will explore one potential technological approach, one I will call a "legal symptoms checker," that might address some of the threshold issues essential to developing an appropriate sense of the scope of the justice gap in the U.S. while also providing a level of initial guidance to a consumer to help them begin to address their legal problems in an appropriate way.

A legal symptoms checker

I am not a doctor, but I assume the conversations that start with "Doc, I was checking WebMD last night and ..." are ones that most physicians dread because their patients might have convinced themselves that they have come down with something like Legionnaire's disease and fear they have just days to live. Still, there are times when such online diagnostic tools can serve an essential function. During the worst parts of the COVID-19 pandemic, searches for symptoms of the illness likely helped those suffering from it realize that they probably needed prompt medical attention, to the extent that treatments were available in those first months, but also probably put some people at ease, rightly, that they might merely have a cold, allergies, or some other more benign affliction. The availability of such online diagnostic tools may give some doctors fits as their patients contact their medical professionals in a panic that they might have some obscure and/or serious disease, but these resources likely have saved some doctors' offices time because their patients conclude that they do not need to consult that office based on their symptom profile. Hopefully, such instances provide examples where the information made available resulted in an accurate diagnosis of the consumer's medical situation that empowered them to take appropriate action.

In the legal field, there no functional equivalent, no "WebLaw," but perhaps there should be. What is most prevalent in the field today is that lawyers engage in some degree of advertising that targets specific potential clientele based on the type of services the lawyer provides. This is most common in the area of personal injury law. In their advertising, lawyers might ask consumers general questions like whether they have been "injured in a car crash." They might also utilize advertising in a way that is much more targeted and specific, like explaining that they offer services to individuals who have suffered side effects of a specific drug. They might even advertise to a group of people that might be relatively small, like first responders who might have fallen ill after working to sort through the wreckage of the attacks of September 11, 2001, at the site of the former World Trade Center. These forms of advertising certainly are designed to attract potential clients and to help solve the justice gap for such consumers by making it clear that legal services are available to certain classes of people. They also do something else: they let people know, who might already appreciate they have a problem, that this is a problem that legal interventions might help them address. Until a lawyer sits down with the consumer to assess whether that consumer has a claim, it is one the lawyer is willing to take on, and it is one for which the consumer wants to retain the lawyer, it is hard to know whether the claim is viable or the lawyer and prospective client will decide to work together. At least the consumer will have developed an understanding, based on the information provided through the means of the lawyer's advertising, that they might have a legal problem and it might be one for which legal services are available. These are both essential, threshold elements of any plan designed to ensure full access to justice.

How might the benefits achieved by this form of legal advertising expand to other areas? Well, that is where a "WebLegal" approach might come in, modeled on the WebMD diagnostic tool. A legal symptoms checker would broaden the areas in which these types of communications could give consumers a sense of whether they have a problem that is legal in nature and conduct an initial assessment of the best way to resolve that problem. To be clear, I am not advocating for a dramatic increase in lawyer advertising. No one wants to see that. But one could envision a portal, not unlike WedMD, where consumers could log on and identify some of the issues they are facing in an effort to understand whether they have a legal problem in the first place. With generative artificial intelligence (GenAI), they might even simply describe their problem in lay-person's terms and the AI-powered interface might be able to analyze the information provided to determine, at least in broad strokes, the nature of the problem and then ask follow-up questions that might result in a narrower assessment of the problem the consumer faces. Some organizations that I will describe in the next chapter have accomplished something akin to this sort of symptoms-checking interface in discrete areas of law. To the extent that advocates could begin to build these out more, or connect those that do exist, we could start to see the emergence of a more comprehensive system that can overcome one of the threshold questions many consumers face, if they even know to ask it: do I have a legal problem in the first place?

Over a decade ago, with a team of law students I supervised who worked in conjunction with computer science students and faculty from the University at Albany of the State University of New York, and in partnership with a local non-profit organization, we created an interactive website that provided a range of information and strategic advice to homeowners facing mortgage foreclosure. This was at the height of the foreclosure crisis in the early 2010s, and the non-profit was overwhelmed with consumers seeking their assistance. The organization had created an analog guide to the foreclosure process that ran well over 100 pages in length, and the organization mailed out copies of this guide to every homeowner it could not represent. Our team took that guide and created a digital version of it, which provided a range of information to homeowners who were either facing foreclosure or felt they might be at risk of having a foreclosure action filed against them. The site helped the homeowner not just understand their rights in the process and provided guidance on what steps they could take to defend themselves if necessary, it also broke the complex process down into easy-to-understand steps. Moreover, instead of overwhelming homeowners by imparting, at one time, all of the information surrounding foreclosure actions in a comprehensive book, the site helped the consumer understand where they were in the process (if they were in the process at all). They could conduct a "symptoms check" to understand the law and procedures surrounding mortgage foreclosures and whether they might be in some kind of legal jeopardy. Once the consumer understood that they might have a legal problem related to their mortgage arrears, and where they might be in the foreclosure process if one had commenced, it offered specific countermeasures they could take at the appropriate time. But it also helped them to understand that they might not have a legal issue at all, at least not yet. If they had received a phone call from someone purporting to be a representative of their bank (or more likely, just someone from what is known as a loan servicer) saying that the homeowner was behind in their mortgage and, because of that, the bank was preparing to take legal action, the homeowner would know that they had legal rights, even if such an action was commenced, and that they had steps they could take to protect themselves. They would also know that just because they received such a call, that did not mean they would be out on the street the next day. In other words, they got a read on their legal "health" from information they could glean from the website—get a legal checkup—and have a sense of what actions they might need to take, and when, in order to protect their rights. This intuitive and easy-to-navigate site provided unrepresented homeowners with specific guidance not just on how to defend themselves in a foreclosure action, it also helped them diagnose their situation and offered them tailored information based on the nature of their specific case in real time.[21]

More and more, as I will explore in subsequent chapters, we are seeing these sorts of web-based portals serving this sort of diagnostic—if not also a "treatment"—function, not unlike what a more comprehensive "WebLegal"

---

[21] For a description of the development of this site, see Raymond H. Brescia, Walter McCarthy, Ashley McDonald, Kellan Potts & Cassandra Rivais, *Embracing Disruption: How Technological Change in the Delivery of Legal Services Can Improve Access to Justice*, 78 ALB. L. REV. 553, 601–5 (2015).

interface might provide. Designing tools that might help to serve these sorts of functions could help address some of perceptions and misperceptions consumers have about the legal issues they face, their rights, and the role that lawyers might play in solving their legal problems.

★★★

Critical to unlocking the benefits of the job-to-be-done framework is determining whether a consumer even has a legal problem. One can then turn to assessing what form of assistance might help them solve it. There are times when information-based assistance alone will satisfy the functional, affective, and political needs of the client. But there are also many situations, for a variety of reasons, where such information would not be enough to meet the client's job to be done. In the next chapter, I will explore the next stage in the legal services continuum—brief assistance—which lawyers often deploy when legal information is not sufficient to address a consumer's needs. There are certainly significant risks involving both the provision of information-based assistance and brief services only to consumers facing a legal job to be done. I will do my best to identify and address those risks in the next chapter as well.

Chapter 6: Key takeaways

1. The legal services market, traditionally dominated by high-cost bespoke services, is ripe for disruption. Innovations aimed at the lower end of the market, such as information-based assistance, have the potential to provide more affordable and accessible legal services, especially to those priced out of full-service representation.

2. Information-based legal services can help consumers recognize their legal problems, understand their rights, and take action to resolve issues. This type of assistance may be sufficient for less complex legal problems, empowering individuals with actionable information without the need for full legal representation.

3. By providing consumers with a better understanding of their legal rights and obligations, information-based assistance can help prevent legal problems from escalating. This type of assistance supports the rule of law by promoting adherence to legal standards and reducing the likelihood of disputes requiring costly legal interventions.

4. While information-based assistance can be beneficial, it carries risks, such as the potential for consumers to misunderstand the information or apply it incorrectly. Ensuring that guidance is accurate, clear, and appropriately tailored to each situation is crucial to the effectiveness of these services.

5. Non-lawyers providing legal information or brief assistance face the risk of violating UPL rules, which restrict who can provide legal advice. However, a recent court case,

Upsolve v. James, challenges these restrictions as content-based limits on free speech, suggesting potential reforms that could allow non-lawyers to offer certain types of legal assistance.

6. Similar to medical diagnostic tools like WebMD, a "legal symptoms checker" powered by artificial intelligence could help consumers assess whether they have a legal problem and guide them toward appropriate solutions. This technology could provide early-stage legal guidance and improve access to justice by helping people recognize and address legal issues before they get worse.

The Benefits, and Risks,
of Limited Services

What are the situations in which a consumer can advance and protect their interests with only limited assistance, whether it is information-based guidance or brief service? In other words, what are the appropriate circumstances in which such information is sufficient to address the consumer's job to be done? This will largely depend on a full assessment of the variables and characteristics described in Chapter 2. Although we have already looked at the values and functions legal interventions might serve in certain circumstances, we cannot ignore the other elements of the job-to-be-done framework. Indeed, in order to ensure that information-based or brief assistance is appropriate to satisfy a consumer's needs in a particular setting, we cannot disregard the other aspects of the framework. To have some assurance that these forms of limited assistance are enough to accomplish a consumer's needs and goals in a particular setting, we must place a heavy emphasis on addressing the nature of the presenting problem and the characteristics of the consumer in any given situation. When a consumer has the capacity to retain a full-service lawyer whenever that consumer has any sense that they have a legal problem, these sorts of questions are less important. But when we are trying to devise a system that will meet everyone's needs and match their needs to the appropriate mode of service delivery, these questions are central to such an effort. To do this, we must return to our job-to-be-done framework from Chapter 2 and use the variables described there to determine when something less than full service is adequate to satisfy a consumer's needs in any given situation.

The characteristics of the problem

We have already seen that there might be situations where information-based and brief assistance will satisfy at least some of the values legal intervention might advance in a particular setting as well as the functions the consumer needs fulfilled to accomplish their job to be done. But not all problems are amenable to these forms of assistance, and not all consumers can take action consistent with the guidance they receive in a way that protects their rights and interests. While an individual with experience in business might achieve just what they need legal intervention to achieve with a modicum of information or brief assistance, another individual, with the exact same information, and in the exact same situation, might not have the same success. We always need to assess all four elements of the job-to-be-done framework when it comes to considering whether a particular intervention will satisfy the consumer's need in a particular setting. When it comes to assessing whether information or brief assistance will satisfy the range of needs that might arise within a particular setting, much of the analysis will hinge on the nature of the problem when viewed in light of the characteristics of the consumer and their ability and willingness to move forward on the basis of the assistance they might receive.

Turning to the nature of the problem, one would need to ask whether the problem is itself of such relative complexity and the stakes so high that the provision of information alone is not sufficient to protect the consumer's interests. I am the first to admit that many—and probably most—true legal problems are of such complexity that information-based and/or brief assistance will not assist the consumer in resolving them. That is what makes them legal problems in the first place. Whether a consumer is looking to create a financing deal for a startup business, secure patent protection for an invention, organize their property and assets so that they have some peace of mind that their estate will pass on to loved ones upon the consumer's death, or avoid jail time in the event they are charged with a crime, in many such instances, looking just at the nature of the problem, it will be of such complexity that even someone with some degree of understanding of the law and their legal rights and obligations will still need full-service representation to address that problem. Putting aside what is at stake (which I will talk about next), many, and, once again, probably most, true legal problems are not ones that a consumer can address through information-based or brief assistance alone given the complexity of the problem. Information and limited guidance can only get you so far, and sometimes learning that a problem is of such complexity that the consumer should probably consult a lawyer to try to address it is a critical piece of information that the consumer should learn. While knowing one has a legal problem is sometimes a significant step toward trying to resolve it, so is knowing that one should not try to go it alone and should seek some form of assistance that is more than just information or brief service. By taking into account the true nature of a problem, and understanding its relative complexity, this will help to determine the type of response that is needed and whether something other than full service will enable the consumer to solve that problem, to meet their job to be done in a particular setting.

Another factor in determining whether full-service legal representation is needed in a particular situation is what is at stake. This question might also drive other functions that the consumer wants fulfilled in that situation. For example, as discussed previously, a straightforward and simple transaction involving the transfer of property, even one that includes entering into a mortgage to secure that property, is often one in which both the purchaser and seller will want legal representation. The legal work involved might involve changing some identifying information in the form documents used in the transfer, and lawyers who engaged in this line of work often have paralegals carry out a lot of the steps necessary to complete the transaction. The complexity of the matter is not high, but the stakes are. The affective and political elements of this situation will likely encourage most parties to the transaction to seek out a lawyer to represent them in it, regardless of their own sophistication or their prior experience with such transactions. Therefore, even where a problem's complexity might not necessarily determine whether counsel is necessary or desired in any particular situation, what is at stake (with those stakes determined from the client's perspective of course), might also have an impact on whether information-based or brief assistance alone will suffice to satisfy the consumer's job to be done in a particular situation.

The characteristics of the consumer

Another critical element of the job-to-be-done framework is the characteristics of the consumer. Each consumer is different, and different things will matter to them in different situations. Once again, when we see the world through a Lawyer 2.0 world, the official line, and there is nothing necessarily wrong with this, is that every consumer should have a full-service lawyer to help them with every legal problem they might have. The only problem with this view is that it is utterly unrealistic. Without an influx of tens of billions of dollars that will supply a full-service lawyer to every American who needs one, we will never achieve the Lawyer 2.0 ideal. Still, it is one that persists for several reasons, not the least of which is that any encroachment on the legal services monopoly by interventions other than a full-service lawyer at every turn puts lawyers' jobs at risk. And the profession seems comfortable resisting efforts to deliver some other form of legal assistance, even when it is adequate to meet the consumer's needs in a given situation, and that means millions of Americans receive no legal help at all. This is not a situation that anyone should accept; and lawyers, with a duty to ensure access to justice, the rule of law, and community well-being, should actually serve at the vanguard of efforts seeking to rectify this situation rather than having too many lawyers defending the status quo at every turn.

For those consumers able to afford a full-service lawyer whenever they need one, they might not agree that the system is broken. In fact, there are some that utilize legal services that might prefer the status quo: like landlords whose tenants are unable to defend themselves in eviction cases, or entities holding relatively small personal debts whose lawyers almost never face a defendant who is represented by counsel. I am confident they appreciate the current state of affairs and prefer that their lawyers face unrepresented litigants who are unable to present the same sorts of defenses as a defendant who is represented by counsel. But I am not interested in satisfying the interests of those consumers who prefer the status quo because in a world of unequal access to justice they just happen to be in the camp that has representation.

That is not to say that even those who have access to a lawyer would prefer that they did not need one, wish that lawyer did not cost as much as they do, or might prefer settling their differences with others without having a one-size-fits-all approach to dispute resolution: that is, with so many disagreements ending up in the courts, with their resolution taking time, money, and often a great deal of aggravation. While there are many consumers with no access to justice at present who would like some assistance in addressing their legal problems, there are also many current consumers of legal services who likely wish there was a better way, one that was more cost-effective and less complicated and burdensome.

But this is the Lawyer 2.0 world in which Americans live at present. We largely have a one-size-fits-all approach to the provision of legal services, but not everyone has the same interests, needs, financial wherewithal, or desire to resolve every legal dispute in only one way: that is, to have a full-service lawyer step in to address their problem in a bespoke fashion. If given the choice, many consumers, even those who presently retain lawyers and have the financial ability to do so, would likely opt for something different, a more accessible and easier way to resolve those disputes that might lend themselves to interventions that do not involve a full-service lawyer operating at full speed (and expense).

What this discussion helps to bring into focus is that the Lawyer 2.0 system might not actually satisfy the job to be done of even those consumers it does serve. We know that it certainly does not help those who are not able to obtain representation when they might need it. Yes, there are those who the current system benefits (other than lawyers). That the status quo might benefit those who have representation and whose lawyers face unrepresented litigants can hardly be a reason to maintain this status quo. Thus, putting aside the interests of incumbent providers of legal services and those consumers of legal services who might prefer the present system because of the asymmetry of power both groups enjoy because some have representation while many do not, developing a different framework for the delivery of enough legal services, at the right time, and in the right place, will depend on what we can ascertain to be the true and valid interests of consumers of legal services. Again, maintaining the status quo because a particular class of consumer benefits from the justice gap is not one of these valid reasons.

Then what are the true and valid interests of a prospective consumer of legal services, which is another way of asking, what is that consumer's job to be done and what are the unique characteristics of different consumers in different settings? To answer this question, let us return to our job-to-be-done framework with a particular emphasis on the characteristics of clients. One of those characteristics is the consumer's ability to pay for legal services. This will, of course, vary by consumer. But it might also vary depending on the particular problem that the consumer needs solved. Some problems will cost more to address than others. And a consumer might be willing to expend the resources necessary to solve certain problems rather than others. Having different service options that would better enable a client to calibrate the services for which they will pay to address their problem, rather than a one-size-fits-all, bespoke approach, is one way to address the consumer's job to be done and matches the characteristics of the client.

Another characteristic of a particular consumer in a particular setting that we must take into account is whether that consumer has the capacity to utilize the services available to address their needs. This is particularly important where we are providing information-based and/or brief services alone. In order for those services to address the consumer's problem in an effective way, it is critical that such guidance is sufficient to advance their interests and solve their problem, to address their job to be done. In addition, the consumer must be able to receive such guidance or direction, understand it, and take appropriate steps in light of it. It goes without saying that, in many instances, information-based and brief services alone will not be sufficient to meet consumer need. But, given the growing sophistication of technologies that can help diagnose consumer problems and provide information to them to act to protect and preserve their interests (more on this in a moment), there will be instances where the right information, at the right time, with the right consumer, will suffice to address their needs. But every situation is different, as is every consumer. And even where a consumer receives fairly complex and sophisticated information and direction in one setting that offers them all they need to address their problem, in another setting, that consumer might need more guidance than information-based or brief services alone might deliver. For these reasons, any system for delivering strictly information-based services alone will also need to have baked into it a mechanism for determining not just the nature of the consumer problem, but also the characteristics of the consumer in that setting. It will have to assess the extent to which a particular consumer can comprehend the guidance received and act in accordance with that guidance.

The Lawyer 3.0 model will have as a core element of the services offered through it the fact that some consumers will receive information-based services only to address their legal problems. Such assistance can address at least some of the jobs to be done in an effective way and can even simply inform consumers that they actually have a problem, can put them at ease in the event no legal problem exists, offer them some potential solutions, and also provide guidance that can keep what might be a small problem today from turning into a much larger problem tomorrow. Thus, at this stage in the legal services continuum, we might ensure consumers perceive their problems accurately; are armed with information and guidance to try to address them; and, at least in some situations, help them address their job to be done in a way that satisfies their need to address the instrumental, affective, and political dimensions of their problem. The right information or brief assistance, delivered at the right time, to the right consumer, can, in at least some instances, serve to satisfy the appropriate functions and values that we want the profession to address. Since this book is, in no small part, about emerging technologies that might improve the quality and reach of legal services, does the technology exist already to deliver meaningful and actionable information in an effective way, to satisfy at least some consumer's jobs to be done? It is to that question that I now turn.

A lab for new immigrant advocacy

Rodrigo Camarena is the co-executive director of Pro Bono Net, an organization that has been at the forefront of the digital transformation of the practice of law over the last 30 years. Camarena has been behind the development of Justicia Law, a web-based portal for the provision of legal advice, guidance, and referrals for new immigrants in the U.S. facing a range of different legal issues. Whether it is helping them apply for citizenship if they qualify, or to determine whether they have been the victim of wage theft and offer them assistance in reclaiming those wages, most of Justicia Lab's services constitute both information-based assistance or brief advice and guidance, all through a digital interface. According to Camarena, Justicia Lab has emerged from work done among the immigrant advocacy community to share common tools and a common infrastructure for providing legal assistance to new immigrants. That network had grown to include about 12,000 advocates who would collaborate and share resources, policies, information about changes in the law affecting their clients, and so on. Justicia Lab is that and much more.

The web-based interface now offers a range of services along the legal services continuum, including the type of diagnostic work described in Chapter 6, as well as referrals when a consumer might require the full-service assistance of a lawyer. It starts with a program called Immi, which offers a range of basic information to new immigrants who might want to learn more about their rights and whether they might have the ability to adjust their immigration status. It also has a program, which I will explore in greater depth in the next chapter, called Citizenshipworks, which helps immigrants who qualify to apply for citizenship using a fully online tool that walks someone through the process of completing this application. By answering a series of questions and providing the information relevant to the application, the system both screens users for their eligibility to apply for citizenship and prepares the application itself if it is determined the user is eligible to do so.

Justicia Lab also offers services to immigrant workers—a group that is often taken advantage of in the workplace—an opportunity to determine whether they are the victims of wage theft or their employer is not paying them in accordance with law for things like overtime pay. As Camarena describes it, "it is like TurboTax for getting money."[1] The ¡Reclamo! program as it is called, has only been piloted in New York City for now. It offers a range of services within the brief-services category: it helps the consumer understand their rights and assists them in calculating their proper wages under the law. It then helps them complete a form to file a complaint with the New York State Department of Labor, can draft a letter to the immigrant's employer, or even place a call to the employer to demand it comply with the law. Justicia Lab is also exploring ways to use generative artificial intelligence (GenAI) and other new technologies to provide services to immigrants. In partnership with community partners like Google, it is working on ways to provide new immigrants with tools to translate documents they might receive in English, or to help them navigate the system for applying for asylum under U.S. law.

Started as a suite of tools that advocates could use, Justicia Lab continues to experiment with ways to provide services directly to consumers of legal services, with the caveat that there are many instances where one might need a lawyer or other advocate to help guide them through a more complicated case. To this end, Justicia Lab also hosts Immigration Law Help, a portal for finding legal assistance from a network of non-profit providers of legal services.

Justicia Lab serves as an example of a web-based portal, one that serves both advocates and consumers directly, that can address a range of the legal needs of new immigrants, with an opportunity for such consumers to seek direct and full-service representation if it does not appear that the web-based portal is sufficient to meet their needs. The services provided through the

---

[1]   Author interview of Rodrigo Camerena (June 10, 2024). Information related to Justicia Law is drawn from this interview as well as publicly available information about the site, which can be found at https://www.justicialab.org/ (last visited, Apr. 27, 2025).

portal match the information-based assistance described in the last chapter, helping, first, new immigrants to understand their rights. Second, it provides what some might call brief advice and assistance because there is minimal effort on the part of the organization in providing services to any individual consumer, other than creating the systems (which is no small feat for sure). At the same time, this assistance is real and important to the consumer. If there is an appropriate match between the consumer need and what the brief services offered through the portal can provide, this sort of technology-based assistance not only serves more consumers than the network of advocates can assist without this type of intervention, it also frees them up to handle the more complex cases where such brief services are not suitable to satisfy the consumer needs in any given situation.

Such limited assistance is not without its risks however, no matter the context. It is to some of these risks that I now turn.

The risks associated with information-based and brief assistance

No lawyer guarantees outcomes in complex client matters. Even in what might present as a relatively straightforward case, most lawyers will refrain from saying they are certain of the outcome in any course of action. They might say that they have seen many clients with similar problems and outline the successful strategies the lawyers have deployed in the past and what they intend to do in the client's case. This requires an appropriate diagnosis of the problem and for the lawyer to set a course that can achieve the client's desired outcome. Even with living, breathing lawyers, the tactics and strategies they choose may not bring about the type of outcomes the client wants. And the lawyer may have done nothing wrong. This happens to even the best, most successful lawyers. Indeed, no lawyer gets every case exactly right. Sometimes a lawyer makes an error in judgment and pursues a tactic or strategy that does not work. This can happen even if everything the lawyer did was to the best of their ability and carried out in accordance with the lawyer's duty to provide competent, even zealous, assistance. If this happens when skilled, competent, zealous lawyers are assisting clients in a full-service way, we can assume that when information-based or brief assistance is let loose in the world, consumers who rely on that assistance are not always going to get exactly what they want out of the intervention either. Any limited form of assistance is going to have to protect against a number of different ways in which such interventions can go bad. It will also have to engage in an assessment of the consumer to determine the extent to which they can utilize a limited form of assistance in an effective way. No system will be perfect. The present system certainly is not, and many Americans do not have the luxury of having their lawyer make mistakes on their behalf simply because they do not have a lawyer. But we should not measure a new system merely by whether it is better than nothing. I would certainly hope that it would be. The true measure is whether some consumers might be worse off for their use of any system that is an alternative to the present one. What follows is a description of the types of arguments against the adoption of a service-delivery model that is largely based on limited forms of assistance, at least in terms of those consumers for whom such a system is appropriate and would not make their lives worse if they relied on it. It is to these risks that I now turn.

Errors in assistance

The first concern with delivering information-based or brief assistance alone is whether the information or guidance is itself accurate. To the extent that competent and skilled experts are preparing the assistance that is made available to consumers, this should address this concern. Given that other professionals might assist a legal expert in the delivery of information-based or brief services, there needs to be some oversight to ensure that appropriate legal experts have vetted the information that is provided to consumers. In the project on which my students and I worked during the foreclosure crisis in the 2010s, described in the last chapter, we had prepared materials that would explain the rights of homeowners facing mortgage foreclosures in New York State. We carefully reviewed the material that we wanted to post on an interactive and consumer-friendly web-based interface that would provide this guidance to such litigants. We provided this carefully curated information to the web designers constructing the site only to find, when they presented their work product in its Alpha version, that at least some of the information contained on the site was inaccurate. We asked the designers where they had gotten that information and they told us that they had simply edited what we had given them to make it easier to understand. That was nice of them to have edited our work, and their content was probably easier for a lay person to understand, but it was also wrong! I am not saying anything terribly radical when I insist that any effort to provide information-based and/or brief assistance must always ensure that the guidance made available to consumers is itself accurate.

Failure to understand/follow guidance

If we rely on information-based and brief assistance alone in the delivery of assistance, even when that assistance is perfectly accurate and attuned to the specific needs of a consumer, there is always the risk that a consumer will misinterpret the guidance and take action—or fail to take action—based on their misunderstanding of the guidance. I remember one time sitting in court and a litigant who was there without counsel looked at my jacket and tie and assumed, correctly, that I was a lawyer. She asked me what she should do to fight her landlord's aggressive effort to engage in wide-ranging and intrusive discovery, the type of process that is not common in most landlord–tenant disputes such as the one she faced. I scanned over the motion made by the landlord's lawyer and muttered something like "this is just a fishing expedition": a common refrain from lawyers when they feel the process of discovery is going far afield from the matters at issue in the case. The litigant heard me say that and her case was called shortly thereafter. I could see her arguing with the landlord's lawyer before the judge but could not hear what was being said. I did note that at one point the judge laughed at something the tenant said. When she returned, she was also laughing a little and I asked her how the argument went and what it was that she had said that made the judge chuckle: "I told the him that the landlord's lawyer was bottom feeding with his demand for discovery just like you said!" In turn, I told her what I had actually said and we also had a laugh. Fortunately, she prevailed on the motion, but in countless experiences in court I have witnessed what one might call "pro se telephone tag": litigants trying to argue their cases in front of judges when it seems they talked to someone who gave them some guidance, which could have possibly come from a family member, a community activist, a self-proclaimed "citizen detective," a neighborhood busybody, someone they know who had the same thing happen to a friend of theirs or a friend of a friend, a religious leader in their lives, or even a lawyer. Too often, that guidance seemed to degrade quickly in the time between receiving that guidance and their appearance in court.

If information-based or brief assistance serves as the vehicle of choice to provide guidance to consumers, such consumers must be able to act on it and deploy it effectively. With today's mobile technologies, when guidance is available over the web and accessible on a smartphone, we can shrink that gap between the time the consumer reviews the information and utilizes it in their lives. In fact, they could consult such information in real time in certain situations, like when in court or negotiating over the phone with a credit-card company to reduce a debt that was the product of identity theft. Still, those who might create systems that provide information-based or brief guidance will have to ensure, to the greatest extent possible, that the assistance is accessible, understandable, and actionable, while still being accurate for use in a specific situation.

"Misfits": false positives and some false negatives

Making sure the limited service offered is accurate and matches the needs of consumers is obviously the first and most important goal to strive to achieve when developing such systems. But even when the guidance supplied is accurate in a specific situation, two potential issues may emerge when developing such systems and they are put to use in the world. The first of these centers around the appropriate "fit" between the service supplied and the consumer's need in a particular situation. What this first issue raises is whether the information might generate what I will call false positives and false negatives: that is, a consumer might interpret the information to apply to them when it does not, or, when it does, the consumer might not realize that the information might help them. In any automated information-based or brief service-delivery system, it is critical that there is an appropriate fit or match between the consumer's situation and the service they receive to help them address it. A human advocate who is trained in the law generally runs through a mental decision tree as they start learning information about a consumer's case and categorizes that information according to the nature and nuances of that case. They then come up with the right approach to address the presenting problem. It is certainly possible that a digital interface could engage in the same sort of triage function: through a series of questions, it could begin to engage in a sorting function to make sure the right information reaches the right consumer at the right time. One of the main triaging functions a lawyer carries out when determining the right approach to take in a particular client's case is often assessing at what stage they are in any particular matter. In litigation, has the client already been sued or do they have a claim they should bring (and, if so, how much time does the lawyer have to bring it based on the applicable statute of limitations)? In a transactional setting, has a deal already been consummated and is the question now whether it has been breached? If a client comes to a lawyer seeking help because their company is under investigation over compliance with environmental obligations under which that company operates, the lawyer will want to know how far that investigation has progressed.

When a lawyer assesses a client's situation incorrectly it can have significant consequences. Thinking that the lawyer has plenty of time to file a case or respond to a complaint when they do not can mean the client's case is time-barred or the lawyer will have subjected the client to a potential default judgment. When even human lawyers fail to appreciate the correct actions to take, given the posture in which the consumer's problem presents itself, limited-service systems will have to take great pains to ensure that the guidance supplied aligns with the present needs of a consumer in light of the nature of the problem, especially with respect to the timing of any interventions the consumer will have to take. The question of the timing of limited services is just one aspect of "fit" as it relates to the connection between the consumer and the assistance they must receive in order for it help the consumer satisfy their needs in a particular setting.

There are also other types of errors—like category or case-type errors—that flow from a mischaracterization of the problem, either because the consumer misunderstands the nature of the issue they are facing or provides incorrect information to a digital interface that is attempting to carry out the appropriate triage function to assign the consumer a service that is appropriate to their needs. Human designers of these interfaces will have to create appropriate mechanisms to ensure that the information supplied is appropriate for a particular consumer in a specific situation. Once again, though, the more tailored to the needs of specific consumers that information gets, the greater the risk that the provision of services to that consumer in an information-based system will look like the practice of law. And if such information is supplied by non-lawyers, there is the significant risk that it will face a charge that such a system involves the unauthorized practice of law (UPL). Since I have discussed this issue at some length already, I will not belabor it again here. Still, because they can serve important consumer-protection functions, appropriate unauthorized practice concerns should certainly serve to inform any discussion concerning the adequacy of information-based and brief services in discrete settings.

★★★

In a Lawyer 2.0 world, a large gap exists between the static, know-your-rights guidance, like Dacey's book *How to Avoid Probate* discussed previously, and full-service representation, with very little in between. But as such initiatives like Justicia Lab, the tool for assisting veterans outlined in Chapter 4, and Descrybe.ai show, new technologies are helping to fill that gap, creating more opportunities for consumers to receive the right assistance, at the right time, to help them address their legal problems where, in the past, they had few viable options to do so. To this point, I have described the ways that technology can improve the delivery of legal services in the first few stages of the legal services continuum: that of finding and triaging clients, providing information to them, and offering them brief services. These technology-based interventions will become essential in the transition to the Lawyer 3.0 version of the legal profession. Are there ways that new technologies will impact full-service representation as well? It is to this question that I turn in Chapter 8.

Chapter 7: Key takeaways

1. Not all legal problems require full-service legal representation. In some cases, consumers can resolve issues using limited information-based guidance or brief assistance. The complexity of the problem and the consumer's capacity to act

on the information are critical factors in determining whether limited services are appropriate.

2. Many legal issues are too complex for information-based or brief assistance alone, requiring full-service legal representation. However, for less complex issues or lower-stakes situations, limited services may be sufficient. Understanding the problem's complexity and the stakes involved is key to matching the service to the need.

3. The ability of consumers to effectively use limited services depends on those consumers' characteristics, such as their capacity to understand legal process and the complexity of the legal matter at hand. Each consumer's needs and ability to navigate the legal system vary widely, and the current "one-size-fits-all" approach may not be suitable for everyone.

4. While limited legal assistance can be helpful, it carries risks, including the potential for consumers to misunderstand or misapply the information they receive. Ensuring that consumers can effectively follow the guidance provided is essential to avoiding negative outcomes.

5. Digital platforms like Justicia Lab demonstrate how technology can deliver legal assistance, especially for underserved populations like immigrants. These platforms provide diagnostic tools, brief services, and referrals, helping address consumer needs without full-service legal intervention.

6. There are concerns about the accuracy of the information provided through limited services and the potential for consumers to misinterpret or misuse it. Ensuring that guidance is both accurate and actionable is crucial to the success of limited-service models.

8

Full Service, the Lawyer 3.0 Way

The delivery of legal services in a Lawyer 3.0 way will include a heavier reliance on the provision of assistance in different ways, and through different media. For at least some legal problems, information-based or brief assistance will suffice to address a particular consumer's job to be done. At the same time, while a consumer might prefer not to go to court, or not to be charged with a crime, there are many instances where a consumer's preferences will not control what is happening to them. And when those situations rise to the level of complexity or the stakes are so high that it is not a legal problem one would want to leave to anyone but a trained and seasoned legal expert, there is simply no substitute for a full-service, living, breathing lawyer who can assist the client in addressing their job to be done. But the Lawyer 3.0 version of the legal profession will also change full-service lawyering in significant ways. It will make such lawyering both more efficient and effective. In turn, it will also make it more affordable and accessible. When the provision of legal services is less costly to provide, as it will be when lawyers adopt and incorporate the capacities of the Lawyer 3.0 world, such services can reach more people. They will be less expensive to provide in the private sector and organizations in the non-profit sector will be able to serve more clients. When even the supercharged version of information-based assistance and brief service are insufficient to satisfy the consumer's job to be done, that does not mean that new technologies will not also improve the delivery of full-service legal assistance. In this chapter I will examine some of the ways in which even the work of the full-service lawyer will change in a Lawyer 3.0 world. It will start with bringing the process first described in Chapter 3—business process analysis (BPA)—to help us break down the components of what lawyers do in different situations to determine whether there are efficiencies that could be gained by the incorporation of technology into the service-delivery model. It will also explore whether in certain cases lawyers might inject some of the less-intensive modes of service along the continuum of legal care to help meet client needs without resort to a full-service mode of assistance.

131

The value of business process analysis

Meghan Cook got involved in what was then referred to as the "digital transformation" of business processes as a graduate student and then in her work at the Center for Technology in Government, which is part of the University at Albany, one of the flagship research universities of the State University of New York. For several years, I had the great fortune of co-teaching an interdisciplinary course with Cook that was centered around urban innovation and included law students and public policy students. One of the problems our partners—the governments of the cities of Albany and Schenectady in Upstate New York among others—faced was urban blight, particularly vacant and abandoned homes. When properties are abandoned by the owners, they become magnets for crime and arson, and they tend to bring down the property values of neighboring homes.

Generally speaking, local governments throughout the country have the power of eminent domain—they can seize properties for a public purpose if necessary, when, for example, they might need to create a new off-ramp for a highway or engage in some large-scale economic development initiative. While this power might seem somewhat capacious, there is a catch: the government "condemning" the property, as the process is known, must pay the owner fair market value for that property. The process of setting the fair market value of a property and condemning a property can be time consuming and, of course, costly: the government has to actually pay the owner.

In the students' research for tools that our community partners could use to address the problem of vacant properties, they discovered that local governments have a powerful tool to address abandoned properties, what is known as Article 19-A of the state's Real Property Actions and Proceedings Law, or "19-A" for short. This statute provides that a local government can seize the title to property without such compensation when it is clearly abandoned, when it has, in effect, become a nuisance. Since our community partners had many properties within city limits that met the standard for 19-A, this seemed like an effective tool these cities could use to address the problem of vacant and abandoned properties.

Many of the attorneys had never heard of the statute as it is not used with any great frequency in the state. When those attorneys learned about it, though, they seemed intrigued. Then they read the statute; they were daunted by its complicated, seemingly contradictory procedures. Indeed, although 19-A did not require a local government to compensate the owners of properties that qualified for seizure under the statute, the 19-A process itself was quite elaborate and Byzantine. The statute itself seemed to stop and start, doubling back on itself at times. Reading it, you sometimes felt like you were reading poorly drafted instructions for defusing a bomb: "now, cut the red wire, but first, cut the green wire!"

The various stages and processes required to claim property under 19-A did seem daunting at first. The students, using BPA under the guidance of Cook, helped to break down the steps of 19-A into its component parts, which aided the lawyers who might use the statute to understand what actions they needed to take, and in what order: when to conduct background research on parties interested in a particular property, file pre-complaint notices on them, serve the complaint in the action on those same individuals and entities, and bring the case through to judgment. By using BPA, the students were able to break the process down, step-by-step, uncover mistaken assumptions about the process, streamline its complex nature, and make it "digestible," bit-by-bit. Figure 8.1 presents a graphic description of the process that the students developed.

Through the methodical use of BPA to understand and describe how one might enforce this statute, the students empowered the over-worked lawyers interested in using it by providing them with an easy way to understand the statute's processes and put them into practice. The students also developed template forms and pleadings the lawyers could use when initiating 19-A proceedings, something that they would ultimately do with student assistance.

What BPA did in this context was to help break down a relatively complex process into its component parts, which then enabled the lawyers and the students helping them to create streamlined systems for making the work easier to carry out. Cook, who now works at the New York State Division of Homeland Security and Emergency Services, explains the BPA method is of particular use to her in working with lawyers because it can "make the implicit explicit."[1] It helps to uncover both decisions that a group makes when carrying out a process and asks whether such decisions are necessary. It starts by taking a step back and grounds the group in what it is they are trying to achieve in the first place. It then starts to talk through with participants not just *what* it is they do, but also *why* it is they do it. It also asks whether certain steps or actions are necessary: are they driven by the imperatives of the goal they are trying to achieve or might they be a legacy of prior practices, of "that's just how we do things"?

In one example of Cook's work, she partnered with the lawyers who dealt with the financial management of about ten different state agencies. None thought they could ever streamline their unique practices and get everyone to follow the same or similar processes so as to create a centralized accounting system that would be easier to manage and oversee. Each of the agencies said "Oh no, we're different. There's no way we could move to a centralized accounting system." But after getting everyone in the room

---

[1]   Author interview with Meghan E. Cook (Sept. 19, 2024). Information related to Cook's experiences with business process analysis are drawn from this interview.

Figure 8.1: The 19–A process

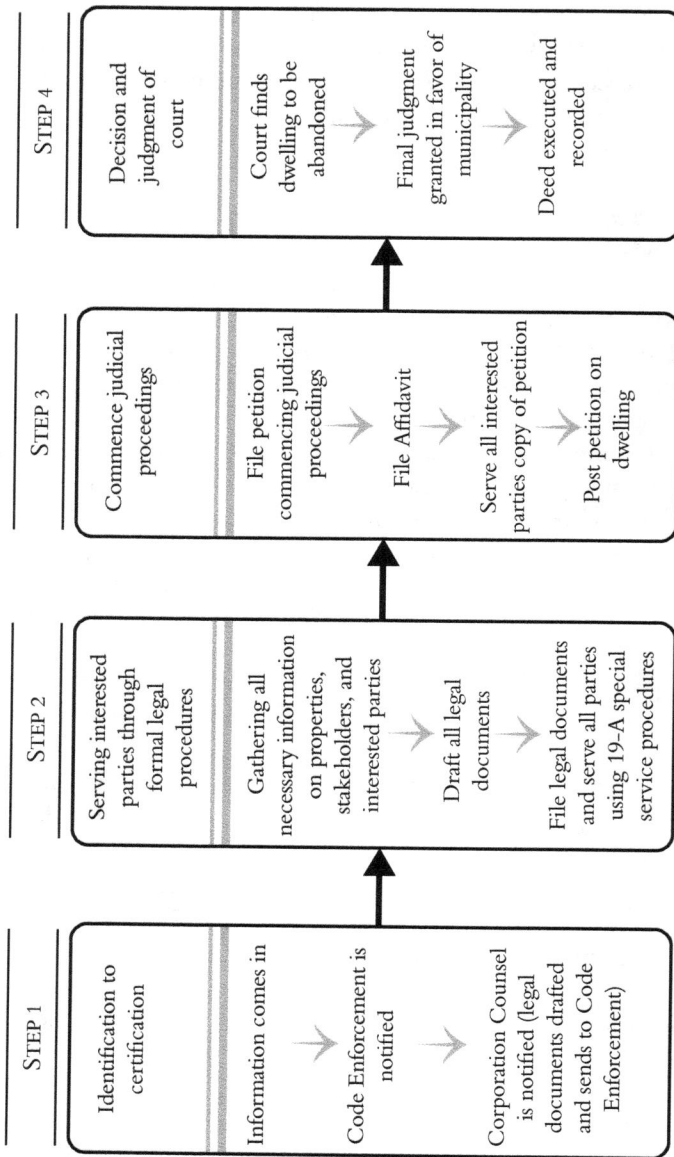

SOURCE: See ROBERT CONNORS, KIMBERLY JONES, MATTHEW LEGER, MICHAEL MUSIALOWSKI, KARA NELSON, ERICA TWOMEY & KARAN VERMA, AN ANALYSIS OF THE PROCESS AND LEGAL CHALLENGES ASSOCIATED WITH ARTICLE 19–A PROCEEDINGS IN THE CITY OF ALBANY AND THE CITY OF SCHENECTADY, Appendix A (2017) (on file with author).

and talking through what it was they all did and why they did it, she was able to show these agencies that simplifying, synthesizing, and harmonizing their actions was less difficult to accomplish than anyone thought possible.

As Cook and I had our students conduct the 19-A analysis, lawyers can utilize BPA to analyze what it is they do, how they do it, and where are they "pain points," as Cook calls them, where a different approach or tactic might improve the process, but that process has to be broken down into its component parts to understand what it is lawyers are actually doing and how what they are doing can be improved. And when we start to introduce the capacities that new and emerging technologies may offer lawyers to streamline their work, it can make what was once the exclusive province of a lawyer working in a full-service capacity into something that the lawyer can offer a client that looks more like brief service, as the following discussion shows.

Deliver services in new ways and through new formats

Adam Stofsky's legal career started as a legal intern with a human rights group in Nigeria.[2] The grandchild of Holocaust survivors, he was drawn to this work. But that internship did not involve work common in such a position, which generally would entail talking to victims of human rights abuses, writing up their stories, preparing legal briefs, and speaking to leaders and elected officials. Adam did a lot of those things throughout his summer between his first and second year of law school, but he also did something else. With the introduction of digital photography and videography, he could afford to purchase a video camera. This offered him a creative outlet in law school and he enjoyed making short film clips as a hobby and a distraction from the grind of his academic pursuits.

Armed with this technology, Adam began taking video testimonials of some of the people with whom his organization was working, including those who had been forcibly removed from their homes to clear the way for transnational companies seeking to tap into Nigeria's natural resources. Many of these interviews were harrowing, and the fact that the experiences Stofsky captured on video allowed the victims to tell their own story, in their own words, proved quite powerful as Stofsky's organization passed them along to decision makers that might take some action to benefit the group's clients. Yes, these stories could have been repeated in a dry brief or report documenting the abuses the victims had experienced, but the video medium proved incredibly effective in getting the victims' stories out into the world, where they had a clear effect and helped Stofsky's organization

---

2   Author interview of Adam Stofsky (Sept. 6, 2024). Information related to Stofsky's work is drawn from this interview unless otherwise noted.

secure some compensation and other relief for the abuses the groups' clients had suffered. Stofsky saw first-hand the power of this medium to communicate information with impact and he wanted to find a way to utilize video and other means of storytelling once he entered the working world as a practicing attorney.

Upon graduation, he would get that opportunity when he secured a fellowship paid for by the Skadden Fellowship Foundation to work for the Lawyers Committee for Civil Rights under Law. There, he was able to provide support to individuals and businesses from Mississippi displaced by Hurricane Katrina. With his emerging videography skills, he would document the human side of this displacement, and although he certainly, once again, did all the things that lawyers tend to do in these situations, like write briefs and advocate for his clients through more traditional channels, he also utilized the medium of video storytelling to help humanize his clients and make the impacts of Katrina seem more real to policy makers and government officials in charge of dispensing relief to the storm's victims.

After a relatively brief stint in a private law firm after his work for Katrina victims, Stofsky began to devote more of his time to developing video-oriented content that helped to tell effective stories. To that end, he created the New Media Advocacy Project (NMAP), which has as its current mission "to partner with change makers to tell stories that promote a more equitable world." In this new organization, Stofsky began to utilize the power of innovative forms of storytelling and new media to assist groups internationally working on critical human rights issues, often those, like the ones he came across while working in Nigeria, that involved victimization of local communities in the march of transnational entities to extract natural resources from those communities, with devastating local effects. Stofsky honed his skills as an advocate with NMAP for several years and then began to look for ways to transition to more work within the U.S., and, admittedly, the type that involved less trauma. He was starting to feel the impact of working for years with victims of human rights abuses and felt it was time to turn his attention to other uses of his communication skills.

With this idea in mind, he began to engage in one-off projects, mostly with non-profit legal groups, largely to help them develop more engaging know-your-rights guides and to put them in digital and video formats. He also began to work with private clients, looking to pull together training videos and other tools that could help the employees and customers of such companies understand their legal obligations in different situations. In December 2019, before the COVID-19 pandemic made us all familiar with video technologies, Stofsky organized a free webinar for non-profit organizations that would teach them some basic principles of effective communication in the digital space, whether that was using videos of speakers presenting on information, animated graphics, or other techniques.

He thought this webinar might get a few dozen participants. Within about 30 minutes of the release of information about the event, Stofsky got over 400 people to sign up. Clearly there was a hunger for knowledge of the effective use of these tools to convey critical information to consumers that would improve the work already being done by these organizations. But even they knew a fundamental truth of the reach of their services: through direct services to individual clients alone, they would never serve all those who qualify for such services let alone all those who need them but cannot afford them. What Stofsky has learned about the power of different media to convey legal information in engaging and even delightful ways cannot only extend the reach of legal services, in both the non-profit and even for-profit world, but it can also make that delivery more efficient and effective. What is more, as innovation in the ways in which advocates can build legal interventions on different types of media platforms proceeds apace, and such tools become easier and less expensive to use, there is a tremendous opportunity to harness new ways of conveying information and delivery meaningful legal assistance at scale. And this innovation in the storytelling and other information-sharing tools will only serve as an accelerant that could help transform the way in which legal services are delivered in the U.S.

Saying the same thing over and over again

A lot of what lawyers do, even lawyers providing full-service assistance, is provide basic information to their clients. As many lawyers who counsel clients will tell you, especially if they handle a particular type of case, whether that is representing a landlord in eviction proceedings or technology startups, they spend a lot of time having the same conversation with many different clients. They might start by explaining the types of services they will provide a client in a particular case should the client want to retain the lawyer. If representation follows, the lawyer will ask the client to bring certain documents or other materials to the initial meeting with the lawyer. The lawyer and client will then sit down at that meeting and provide an overview of what the representation in the matter will entail and what the client can expect to happen as the work unfolds. The lawyer will have these conversations over and over again; they might even have a bit of a rehearsed speech. Perhaps they will modify this information based on the needs of a particular client, the client's demeanor, the time the lawyer has before their next meeting, or the level of sophistication the lawyer believes the client possesses. But the basic information is often quite similar. In fact, the only difference in the presentation of information might be when a lawyer neglects to mention something they usually discuss.

But what if the lawyer could "bottle" these conversations and share them with the client ahead of time? What if, instead of the lawyer spending time giving the same speech again and again (and perhaps messing it up), the lawyer could prepare explainer videos that captured this information, made sure it was accurate, and made it available to clients prior to sitting down with the lawyer? Not only would this ensure the information delivered was accurate, it would save the lawyer a lot of time and the client at least some of the expense associated with paying the lawyer to give the same speech they give to clients time and time again.

Through his new company, Briefly, Stofsky and his team have created just this sort of system for the non-profit Lakeshore Legal Services in Detroit, Michigan, and that group uses it even for those clients they know they are going to represent. Those clients have a wide range of information available to them before they even meet with their lawyers after a decision is made to represent them. The clients can watch explainer videos on the process they are facing, like an eviction, and are instructed on how to prepare for the initial meeting with their lawyer: for example, what are the types of questions the lawyer is going to ask and what sorts of documentation should the client bring to the meeting. This makes that initial meeting between the lawyer and client so much more efficient, and saves a lot of time for both the lawyer and the client. It also probably saves the client from having to come back on a separate day because they did not realize they had to bring some evidentiary proof or other document to the lawyer for that meeting. The tool can also work to triage those seeking assistance from the group, identifying those the organization is not going to serve, but even those consumers receive a range of informational assistance, delivered through the video content Briefly and the organization have created.

Stofsky finds that these sorts of tools are also helpful not just in litigation, but also compliance and corporate work, and can go a long way toward not just saving lawyers time and effort but also keeping clients out of legal hot water. Briefly helps lawyers create short explainer videos on topics relevant to their practice that they can share with employees of the companies they serve. A lawyer might field multiple calls from different members of a company's salesforce on issues related to the products and services the company offers. Stofsky says that there is a high demand for these legal explainers, which lawyers can use to address issues like cybersecurity, non-disclosure agreements, and intellectual property. These tools provide guidance to employees of a company as to their legal engagements with customers. Where a lawyer might have the same conversation about one or more of these topics multiple times throughout the week, that time can be spent on other matters if the lawyer can prepare a relatively short video that captures the appropriate guidance about that topic and the lawyer and company can push it out to its staff in the field as part of a regular training, or when they need such information in real time.

In the non-profit sector, since non-profit organizations are themselves corporations, and have corporate obligations they must meet, lawyers serving such organizations also practice corporate law, with a smattering of tax law included for good measure. One element of non-profit corporate practice is making sure the lawyer's clients are complying with their obligations under federal tax provisions so that they can maintain their tax-exempt status. Since at least some non-profit organizations might engage in social change work, and such work might involve legislative lobbying, there are limits on the types of political work that non-profit organizations can do. For example, they cannot endorse candidates for political office. But when does lobbying for some type of legal change by, say, protesting at an elected official's office or calling them out on social media, constitute legitimate forms of advocacy under the tax code, or illegitimate forms of "electioneering" that could jeopardize a non-profit's tax-exempt status? Similarly, even "legitimate" forms of lobbying cannot constitute the bulk of what a non-profit organization does, so making sure the staff of a non-profit organization "colors within the lines," so to speak, and does not risk the organization's non-profit status is an important role that many lawyers for such organizations must fulfill.

In order to make the work of non-profit organizations a little easier, several years ago, my law students and I again worked with computer science students from the University at Albany to create a website that provides guidance to non-profit leaders and their staff to help them understand their obligations under the law. This website includes multimedia elements to it, including podcasts, explainer videos, and even slide decks in PowerPoint to provide basic information to lawyers who might want to make presentations to their clients about those organizations' legal obligations when it comes to lobbying. A non-profit leader could share these podcasts with their staff who might engage in social change work to make sure they avoid any type of improper conduct. In addition, since many lawyers who work for non-profits do so on a pro bono basis and this area of law might not be the main focus of their work, we make these decks available in editable form to such lawyers so that they can use them as starting points should they want to make their own presentations to their clients.

Similarly, when my students and I helped to create the web-based tool described earlier that was designed to provide guidance to homeowners facing a mortgage foreclosure without the assistance of a lawyer, we soon learned that even consumers who had the benefit of legal services, even though it was difficult for them to afford them, were using this tool as well. Because the site offered detailed accounts of the stages of the foreclosure process and what one would have to do at each stage of that process to protect one's interests, lawyers representing homeowners advised their clients to use our website to develop a basic understanding of the mortgage foreclosure process. These lawyers knew that their clients did not have a lot of disposable income lying around to pay for legal assistance (this is why the homeowners were in a mortgage foreclosure in the first place). In order to save their clients the expense of paying their lawyer for the time it would take to explain the mortgage foreclosure process to those clients, many lawyers directed their clients to our publicly available website, which offered those clients information so that they could understand that process without having to pay the lawyer to provide that overview.

No matter the context, many lawyers offer some modicum of routinized services even to their full-service clients. To the extent the lawyer can capture some of the information-based services and present them in a way that saves the lawyer time and the client money, it can mean the lawyer can do other, higher-order work, and perhaps to do it for more clients. What the work of Briefly and some of these other examples show, is that when we break down the work that lawyers do on a day-to-day basis, there are elements of that work that might lend themselves to other forms of service delivery, forms that save time and money, and might even prove more accurate.

Full-service lawyering in a Lawyer 3.0 world

Returning the core principle that animates this work, which is one that should serve as the centerpiece of the legal profession's service to the community, the purpose of the legal profession is to help members of the community resolve their legal problems. Since the profession has a monopoly on the provision of legal services, at least for the time being, it has a responsibility to ensure, to the greatest extent possible, that every American has access to some form of legal assistance that can help them satisfy their legal needs. Given that the technology exists today to extend the reach of legal services to many who, at present, do not otherwise have access to such services, there is an imperative to harness that technology to delivery assistance to the community that can help more consumers address their legal needs in a meaningful way. As I have tried to show in previous chapters, an array of technologies can facilitate the provision of information-based assistance and brief service to reach more consumers, and when these forms of assistance are sufficient to address such consumers' jobs to be done, then the profession has fulfilled its appropriate role in those settings. But are there ways that some of those same technologies, when applied to full-service representation, can also help improve even the delivery of more traditional legal services?

One of the main benefits of new law-practice technologies is that they can make the lawyer's work more efficient. As someone who began his legal career right before the introduction of email (and experienced the adoption of something as simple as voicemail into my office's phone system), I would estimate what might eat up close to 10 percent of my work week was trying to track down clients and adversaries. What is more, one might be working on something that required one's complete attention only to get interrupted by a phone call from someone with whom you had been trying to speak for days, meaning you had to drop what you were doing to speak to them, disrupting any momentum, rhythm, or flow you had entered into in that task. It is still difficult to fathom how much time was spent back then just setting up meetings and calendaring court appearances. Even finding mutually convenient times to speak with someone by phone, or simply to set up a meeting, itself took way too much time. Today, a lot of this is done instantaneously and, in some instances, through automation.

New technologies will improve on even these basic efficiencies. We have already seen that tools that make information-based assistance possible and aid things like document assembly might make the delivery of something less than full service an effective means of meeting consumer needs. But those same means of delivering services will also help the full-service lawyer provide assistance to clients in more efficient and effective ways. Let us focus on two things that lawyers, even full-service lawyers, do day in and day out: providing basic information to clients and preparing court filings and other legal artifacts. Lawyer 3.0 lawyering will make these tasks far easier, less expensive, and more efficient. In turn, this will mean lawyers' services are less expensive to deliver, meaning they will reach more consumers. The innovations available today, and those that will soon become more available and more reliable, can extend services to more clients through something less than full service and can also improve more intensive services.

The tools that make the delivery of information-based and brief services available to clients can also improve that more intensive mode of service delivery. Just as I was able to help my office develop a rudimentary document-assembly tool for the creation of a "kitchen sink" housing court answer, lawyers already use document-assembly technologies to make their work more streamlined. While the introduction of new technologies like generative artificial intelligence might have some lawyers and lay people thinking that it will just write legal briefs for them, there is a catch with such technologies, one that should give lawyers pause when they think about how they tend to engage in document assembly, which most do, whether that is using some form of automation or through something more crude like "cut-and-paste" in common word processing applications.

Here's a dirty little secret of full-service lawyering. Lawyers tend to harvest a lot of content from prior work product whenever they engage in preparing materials for a new client. Whether it is putting together a will or preparing a complaint in an anti-trust action, they sit down with the client, consider a path forward, and then go to work. Let us call that client Cleo. After the lawyer sits down with Cleo to consider what course of action the lawyer will take on the client's behalf, the lawyer typically thinks about the extent to which Cleo is like other clients the lawyer has represented in the past. If you ever wondered how Netflix comes up with those recommendations selected just for you, well, to the extent we know how these sorts of algorithms work, Netflix takes note of your viewing habits, finds other viewers that have similar habits, and lumps you in with those other viewers. The technical term for this is "user-based collaborative filtering." In other words, Netflix takes what those other viewers have chosen to watch next and recommends it to you as well.[3] Lawyers do something similar. They think about which of their past clients is most like Cleo and tend to start with whatever legal documents they used for those clients and update them to account for Cleo's unique facts and circumstances. Sometimes that might require extensive revisions of the prior work; sometimes it will mean just changing the names of the parties involved and other identifying information.

One advantage of beginning from this prior work and updating it as necessary is that the lawyer has already proofread it, vetted the case citations or references to the law for accuracy, and curated it as necessary to make sure it accommodates any relevant changes to the law. The rehashed documents are unlikely to contain spelling or grammatical errors, and the lawyer feels the framing of the issues and the presentation of arguments—essential elements of advocacy—are both done well. They might have tweaked the rhetoric or style of the arguments over time as different approaches seemed to work better than others. The work product, honed in the fire of advocacy, has likely become better over time. The lawyer can take this work and build on it further for Cleo, knowing that much of the lawyer's craft has been baked into the work through, potentially, years of advocacy.

No lawyer wants to recreate the wheel, to use an expression I have used previously. And what the current version of generative artificial intelligence (GenAI) does do is precisely that. When prompted, it creates a new version of any document every time in response to the query. In fact, you might pose the same query and it might generate two different responses. And even something simple like asking it to write a letter to a creditor to inform them that they are improperly pursuing the lawyer's client for a debt that came about by virtue of identity theft will still have to be read carefully for accuracy, tone, and to ensure it has not generated some fictitious legal source. What a lawyer would prefer to do is turn to their computer and call up the letter they wrote for a different client where the lawyer made the same argument—presumably successfully—in a different matter. They would just change the relevant names and any other information that is unique to the new client. If the lawyer changes only, say, 10 percent of the

---

[3]   See Yiran (Amanda) Wang, *Netflix's Recommendation Systems: Entertainment Made for You*, ILLUMIN MAGAZINE (Feb. 14, 2022) (describing what is known as Netflix's user-based collaborative filtering model).

document, they are confident that they do not have to carefully proofread the remaining 90 percent of it because that has already been done before. This is not true for the product of GenAI. For decades, lawyers have used word processing tools including macros and other rudimentary and off-the-shelf document-assembly applications to complete these sorts of routinized practices with relative ease. GenAI, on its own, is not necessarily a time-saver in such situations.

Still, new document-assembly tools and interfaces will make even these sorts of actions easier. Several years ago, Jonathan Pyle, who now works for a non-profit legal services provider, Philadelphia Legal Assistance, created the product Docassemble, an open-source tool for creating templates of legal filings that works through an interrogatory interface to generate the types of work product that lawyers create all the time. The products that this site can generate can be customized for jurisdiction, type of case, and so on, and lawyers have been tapping into it since 2017, when Pyle, a lawyer with a background in coding, started to explore ways to cut down on the repetitive tasks that he saw lawyers engaged in all the time. For Pyle, this was a "nights-and-weekend" project that he undertook in his spare time, which he worked to make, with a nod to a popular insurance advertisement, "so easy a lawyer could use."[4] Pyle believes that these sorts of tools can reduce the expense associated with providing legal assistance to consumers from $4,000 to something more like $50 per service. At that price, even lower-income consumers could afford them, if someone has the wherewithal to build them. For Pyle, though, lawyers are not exactly working to build such systems and make them available at such a low cost. He explains that he can go to a video on YouTube to "change the motor in my washing machine," but if someone has a "question about some high-volume legal case in Philadelphia courts, nothing is going to come up that's any good" because "lawyers don't put their brain power onto the internet."

In addition to making more information available to consumers, products like Docassemble and Microsoft's Power Automate can enable lawyers to pull pre-prepared information and portions of documents that have been fully vetted, and can be easily updated, into new documents with a few keystrokes or clicks on a few check boxes. Whether someone is preparing a contract, putting together a trust document, or preparing a complaint or answer, newly improved document-assembly tools can make even full-service lawyers more efficient in their work. They might also blur the lines between full service and brief service. In addition to information-based assistance and

---

[4] Author interview with Jonathan Pyle (June 5, 2024). Information related to Pyle's work is drawn from this interview.

document assembly, there are other ways that new technologies improve the delivery of full-service lawyering.

Other Lawyer 3.0 capacities

I have spent a fair amount of time so far in talking about GenAI, and that is where most of the buzz around lawyer capacities has hovered since early 2023, but there are other types of AI that are likely to focus the work of lawyers in important ways in the coming years. The first of these is predictive analytics. A form of AI, it differs from GenAI in that, instead of producing answers in narrative form (although it can be asked to do so), it analyzes large amounts of data to make predictions about future outcomes. This is particularly useful to lawyers when trying to assess the likely results of different types of cases, with different factual profiles, that are filed in different courts and before different judges. Based on experience in bringing different cases, on research about different judges, and assessments about the types of arguments that might work in different settings, lawyers will exercise their judgment in determining how, when, where, and whether to assert certain claims. But those judgments are limited by their own experience and their ability to assess and synthesize available data for a range of clues and insights.

What predictive analytics can do for lawyers, as it is already started to do, is synthesize vast quantities of data about case outcomes in different types of cases to help lawyers make more educated judgments about the types of arguments they might make, before different judges, and in different courts, to maximize their chances of success. It might even discourage lawyers from taking on some cases that they might otherwise accept if the data and information they have, or their "gut instincts," are off. Legal technologist Nicole Black says that lawyers can certainly do this sort of assessment with information outside their own records and case files, but they can also do this with information they already possess.[5] They can analyze the types of cases they have filed in the past, the factual elements of those cases, the lawyer teams the firm assembled in different contexts, and the outcomes achieved in those contexts, to think about which cases might be worth taking on in the future and which they might want to pass up, given their analysis of whether those cases ended up bringing value to the firm or were not really worth the effort in hindsight.

Predictive analytics and other forms of AI can also help lawyers and in-house counsel involved in compliance work. David Rosen, a technologist and lawyer, started the company Catylex using machine learning and other

---

5   Author interview of Nicole Black (June 6, 2024).

forms of AI, what he calls an "ensemble" of such technologies. Catylex uses this ensemble to help lawyers that work both inside and outside of companies understand those companies' legal obligations embedded in the hundreds, if not thousands, of contracts that govern those entities' relationships and actions. Rosen's company helps to summarize and extract critical information drawn from those contracts to enable legal compliance staff to ensure employees understand and comply with their contractual obligations.[6]

The technologies harnessed by companies like Catylex may someday do more for lawyers than just monitor current company obligations. Lawyers in compliance settings might use AI and predictive analytics to spot anomalies that might indicate the entity is at risk of engaging in some form of illegal conduct. A transnational organization that has to interact with foreign governments might notice unusual expense reporting from a unit in a particular country known for having government officials who are "open for business," so to speak; that is, who welcome graft and bribes. The company's activity, which might otherwise fly under the radar, might indicate that employees are engaged in improper conduct in violation of the Foreign Corrupt Practices Act. As more companies enter the business-to-business space and utilize new technologies to help scale the delivery of real-time legal services in a wide range of contexts, at a fraction of the time, energy, trouble, and expense that such services might demand today, this will likely lower the cost of such services and enable companies to spend less on legal services and more on delivering value to their customers.

★★★

Regardless of the context, and regardless of whether one is engaged in providing brief advice and counsel to clients, or engaging in more traditional, full-service representation in a manner consistent with the incumbent form of practice so common in Lawyer 2.0 settings, new technologies can make even these traditional, bespoke forms of practice more streamlined and cost-effective. And when they do both of those things, they make it possible to expand the reach of legal assistance to more people who might otherwise not have access to it. The technologies that are presently available, and which will be available in the coming years, might make it possible to usher in a new version of the American legal profession. What would it take to make that happen? I explore this question in the final chapter. In the next chapter, I examine how legal

---

[6]   Author interview with David Rosen (June 3, 2024).

education will need to change in order to train the legal professionals who will operate in a Lawyer 3.0 mode.

Chapter 8: Key takeaways

1. Through technological innovation, lawyering in a Lawyer 3.0 world will involve changes that do not just impact information-based and brief services. It will also affect the delivery of what we might normally think of as full-service representation in profound ways.
2. The use of video and digital media can tell advocacy stories in powerful ways, and can also save lawyer and advocate time by enabling the communication of routinized information that lawyers provide to clients with great frequency, like explainer videos that help prepare clients for meetings, making the initial attorney–client interaction smoother and more productive.
3. Digital tools like explainer videos, websites, and podcasts can extend the reach of legal services, enabling legal professionals to provide basic guidance at scale and allowing them to serve more people while reserving more intensive assistance for complex cases.
4. Document-assembly tools can help lawyers automate routine legal tasks such as filling out forms for clients, saving time and reducing costs. By using these tools, lawyers can reduce the cost of legal services significantly, making them accessible to a broader population.

Teaching to the Tech

As I have argued elsewhere, the turn of the 19th to the 20th century represented a critical inflection point in the profession, one where it took a decidedly pro-lawyer turn.[1] Elites in the profession partnered with representatives of some of the more established law schools to halt the growth in the ranks of the profession. Throughout the 19th century the main pathway to the profession was through the apprentice system, where one worked for very low pay for a period of years at the law office of a practicing lawyer.[2] This served as a means by which practicing lawyers could control access to the profession: only those lawyers accepted as apprentices could find their way into the profession, and only those who could afford to work under such conditions could even consider it as an option. By century's end, the profession was, for all intents and purposes, exclusively white and male.[3] But a rise in immigration, with more jurisdictions permitting access to the profession through some form of legal education, including schools that offered flexible schedules for working people, meant that the profession was starting to let in immigrants "by the hundreds," in the words of prominent lawyer and diplomat Elihu Root.[4] Indeed, according to one American Bar Association (ABA) report, given the relatively low barriers to entry to the profession, even the "illiterate foreigner who can hardly read or write English, who wishes to become a lawyer almost as soon as he becomes a citizen, with the lowest ambitions and ideals, who earns his living while

---

[1]   I discuss the transformation of the American legal profession that occurred around the turn of the 19th to the 20th century at length in RAY BRESCIA, LAWYER NATION: THE PAST, PRESENT, AND FUTURE OF THE AMERICAN LEGAL PROFESSION 61–93 (2024).

[2]   For a description of the apprenticeship system, see LAWRENCE M. FRIEDMAN, A HISTORY OF AMERICAN LAW 302–3 (4th ed. 2019).

[3]   On demographic trends in the profession, from the late 19th century to the late 1980s, see RICHARD ABEL, AMERICAN LAWYERS 78–111 (1989)

[4]   AM. BAR ASS'N, SPECIAL SESSION ON LEGAL EDUCATION OF THE CONFERENCE OF THE BAR ASSOCIATIONS DELEGATES 19–23 (1922).

studying law as a runner or pettifogger," could join the profession.[5] These immigrants, according to Henry Drinker, who we met in the first chapter, worked on the factory floor by day, learning their ethics in the "slums" from their fathers who "sold strings and other merchandise."[6] For Drinker, these unethical charlatans were largely "Russian Jew boys," who besmirched the good name of the profession.[7]

In order to control access to the profession, elites in the bar turned to the example of the American Medical Association, which had successfully lobbied for changes to medical education, to make such education more rigorous, more time-consuming, and more expensive.[8] The legal profession could do the same.[9] It could elect to impose pre-law educational requirements, create more obligations on law schools to have full-time faculty members, expand the course of study of law schools, and even do things like require that such schools have extensive law libraries. Choosing any of these requirements would make it more difficult and more expensive to operate a law school, and thus more expensive to attend law school. Elites in the profession, focusing on the interests of the profession in controlling access, and not really concerning themselves with the potential impact this would have on consumers and the fact that this would limit not just the supply of lawyers but also who could enter the profession, imposed all of these requirements. It is bad enough that these restrictions helped suppress the forces of supply and demand that might have increased access to justice by increasing the number of lawyers and thus lowering the cost of representation. It is reprehensible that such restrictions were also motivated, at least in part, by bias. It is no surprise that, in the 1980s, over 100 years after the profession started to explore ways to limit more widespread access to it, and 50 years after these educational requirements began to take effect, lawyers were still mostly white and male,[10] and the demographics of the profession today still do not reflect the diversity of the American population as a whole.[11]

---

[5] AM. BAR ASS'N, *Report of the Committee on Legal Education and Admission to the Bar*, 26 ANN. REP. A.B.A. 395, 419 (1903).

[6] AM. BAR ASS'N, *Proceedings of the Section of Legal Education and Admission to the Bar*, 52 ANN. REP. A.B.A. 605, 622 (1929).

[7] *Id.*, at 623.

[8] PAUL STARR, THE SOCIAL TRANSFORMATION OF AMERICAN MEDICINE: THE RISE OF A SOVEREIGN PROFESSION & THE MAKING OF A VAST INDUSTRY 112–18 (2nd ed. 2017).

[9] See, for example, AM. BAR ASS'N, *Proceedings of the Section of Legal Education and Admissions to the Bar*, 44 Annu. Rep. A.B.A. 656, 662–67 (1921) (recording comments by several attendees that the legal profession should impose the same sorts of educational barriers to entry adopted by the medical profession).

[10] ABEL, *supra* note 3, at 90–108.

[11] For an overview of current demographics of the profession, see BRESCIA, *supra* note 1, at 129–40.

At a critical inflection point in the evolution of the American legal profession, elites in the profession took a decidedly pro-lawyer turn, and we are still very much living with the profession they created at the time. But changes in technology today mean that we are at such an inflection point again, one that presents an opportunity to refocus the profession to make it more client-centric than lawyer-centric. Legal education has a significant role to play in this inflection point, to help usher in a new version of the profession: Lawyer 3.0. We have already explored some elements of this version. It will certainly involve the deployment of new technologies to deliver services to at least some Americans and will generally make the practice of law more efficient, and, hopefully, more affordable. But it will also make the needs of the consumer the focus of members of the profession and as well as others who would provide legal assistance in some form. This will require a significant change not just in the way the profession functions, but how it sees its role in society and in relation to the consumers who would benefit from legal assistance that would help them address their legal problems. This will not just require a recalibration of how lawyers operate, but also how they are trained, which will necessitate an overhaul of legal education itself in a way that is no less significant than the one that occurred a century ago.

What would legal education in a Lawyer 3.0 world look like? As we have seen, one of the most significant drivers of the coming phase-shift in the profession is technological change. There are certainly other ways that legal education itself needs to change to make the profession more accessible and open to individuals of diverse backgrounds generally, to overcome some of those traditional barriers that the profession imposed in the 20th century that created a profession that did not reflect the diversity of the broader population, particularly in relation to gender, race, LQBTQIA+ status, and disability. And I applaud such efforts, have supported them elsewhere, and will continue to do so, even as the legal profession faces aggressive attempts to scale such measures back despite the profession's need to rectify its long history of exclusion.

I will direct my attention here to the role that law schools must play in responding to not just the technologies that are likely to transform the practice of law over the coming decade, but also to instill in aspiring professionals the skills and capacities necessary to function within a Lawyer 3.0 framework. In addition to instructing their students to demonstrate a degree of technology competence, law schools will also have to help their students develop the competencies that practicing in a Lawyer 3.0 world will require and to understand how to apply the variables set forth in Chapter 2 to deliver effective legal services at scale. These include the ability to understand and apply what should be the values and purposes of the profession and match them to the needs of consumers. It also means they should learn to use the tools of design thinking to reframe their role in light of client needs, to master business process analysis and what I will describe in this chapter as systems thinking to improve the delivery of legal services in light of consumer needs, and to adopt a consumer-focused mindset created in light of the variables matrix described earlier in everything they do. These competencies will ensure that the services the law graduate offers are designed to satisfy the consumer's job to be done in each setting. It will also require that they learn to engage in interdisciplinary collaboration to make sure they can accomplish all of these other components of Lawyer 3.0.

What is more, the Lawyer 3.0 version of the legal profession will require a significant reframing of legal education itself. Since this new approach to the profession designs the delivery of legal services from the consumer's perspective rather than the needs and interests of the lawyer and the legal profession, it will also require a reframing of legal education to prepare lawyers and other professionals to use training in the law to serve consumer need, and not simply to create a pathway to a degree that provides a golden ticket to a well-paying career. It is highly likely that a practitioner operating in a Lawyer 3.0 way will still earn a decent wage. Once again, this should not serve as the central focus of the profession, however, nor should lawyer earning capacity serve to justify an otherwise unjust monopoly on the provision of legal services.

A profession that has for too long believed, sometimes implicitly perhaps, that the purpose of the legal system is to ensure employment opportunities for lawyers will have to reframe its core mission and core purpose to one that puts the consumer at the center of delivery of legal services and not the lawyer. Since legal education in some form will prepare a new generation of professionals who will deliver legal services in a new way, legal education itself will have to change to satisfy the need to do so.

The remainder of this chapter is devoted to what legal education for a Lawyer 3.0 world might look like. I hesitate to call it "Legal Education 3.0" because, in reality, legal education played almost no role at all in Lawyer 1.0: the profession that existed throughout the 19th century. Putting semantics aside, Lawyer 3.0 will certainly require a change to legal education in ways I describe next.

The formal duty of technology competence

Because of developments in law practice technology and increasing globalization in the profession at the time, in 2009 the ABA embarked on an effort to review its rules of professional conduct in light of such changes. It created the ABA Commission on Ethics 20/20 to consider potential changes to the Model Rules to account for these developments and their potential impact on the practice of law.[12] The Commission explained how technological change in particular required lawyers to assess what it is they do and how they do it, in light of consumer needs (a very Lawyer 3.0 approach, I must say), as follows:

> [T]echnology has irrevocably changed and continues to alter the practice of law in fundamental ways. Legal work can be, and is, more easily disaggregated; business development can be done with new tools; and new processes facilitate legal work and communication with clients. Lawyers must understand technology in order to provide clients with the competent and cost effective services that they expect and deserve.[13]

Since the ABA tends to be gradualist in nature, despite the recognition that technological change could transform the practice of law in "fundamental ways," in 2012 the Commission recommended, and, in 2013 the ABA House of Delegates would ultimately approve, the addition of language to Comment 8 to Rule 1.1, which covers the lawyer's duty of competence to their client.[14] The Rule itself provides simply that "A lawyer shall provide competent representation to a client." Such competent assistance "requires the legal knowledge, skill, thoroughness and preparation reasonably necessary for the representation."[15] Similar to the way in which I describe the notion of problem complexity in Chapter 2, Comment 1 to this Rule provides as follows:

> In determining whether a lawyer employs the requisite knowledge and skill in a particular matter, relevant factors include the relative complexity and specialized nature of the matter, the lawyer's general experience, the lawyer's training and experience in the field in question, the preparation and study the lawyer is able to give the matter and whether it is feasible to refer the matter to, or associate or consult with, a lawyer of established competence in the field in question. In many instances, the required proficiency is that of a general practitioner. Expertise in a particular field of law may be required in some circumstances.[16]

---

12 See AM. BAR ASS'N, ABA COMMISSION ON ETHICS 20/20: INTRODUCTION AND OVERVIEW 1, https://www.legalethicsforum.com/files/20120508_ethics_20_20_final_hod_intr odution_and_overview_report.pdf [https://perma.cc/GPY5-VD4B] (last visited, May 15, 2023).

13 *Id.*, at 3 (footnote omitted).

14 AM. BAR ASS'N, MODEL RULES OF PROFESSIONAL CONDUCT R. 1.1 (hereinafter MODEL RULES).

15 *Id.*

16 Model Rules, *supra* note 14, at R. 1.1, Com. 1.

While this and other comments related to Rule 1.1 that provide greater detail about how to gauge the level of care required of a lawyer in any particular situation, the ABA amended Comment 8 in an effort to address the growing impact of technology on the practice of law. In order to do so, it added language to existing Comment 8 to Rule 1.1 as follows (the new language noted in italics):

> To maintain the requisite knowledge and skill, a lawyer should keep abreast of changes in the law and its practice, *including the benefits and risks associated with relevant technology*, engage in continuing study and education and comply with all continuing legal education requirements to which the lawyer is subject.[17]

The Commission took the position that it was necessary to supplement the general duty of competence by making "explicit" that there is a corresponding duty of *technology competence* because "technology is such an integral—and yet at times invisible—aspect of contemporary law practice."[18] The added language, according to the Commission, "would offer greater clarity regarding this duty and emphasize the growing importance of technology to modern law practice."[19] Asserting that "this obligation is not new," the Commission went on to explain that "the proposed amendment emphasizes that a lawyer should remain aware of technology, including the benefits and risks associated with it, as part of a lawyer's general ethical duty to remain competent in a digital age."[20]

While the Commission's report acknowledged that "[t]echnology affects nearly every aspect of legal work,"[21] it also pointed out that, in contemporary law practice, there are specific areas where new technologies have an outsized role, including how lawyers "store confidential information, communicate with clients, conduct discovery, engage in research, and market legal services."[22] Even in the early 2010s, the ABA's Commission recognized that "technology has transformed the delivery of legal services by changing where and how those services are delivered (for example, in an office, over the internet or through virtual law offices)."[23] It also noted that "[i]n the past, lawyers communicated with clients by telephone, in person,

---

[17] *Id.*, at Com. 8 (emphasis added).
[18] AM. BAR ASS'N, *supra* note 12, at 8.
[19] *Id.*
[20] *Id.*
[21] *Id.*, at 4.
[22] *Id.*
[23] *Id.*

by facsimile or by letter,"[24] and lawyers "typically stored client confidences in paper form, often inside locked file cabinets, behind locked office doors or in offsite storage facilities."[25] At the time of the report, and in light of technologies available then, lawyers "communicate with clients electronically, and confidential information is stored on mobile devices, such as laptops, tablets, smartphones, and flash drives, as well as on law-firm and third-party servers (that is, in the 'cloud') that are accessible from anywhere."[26] And all of this prior to the onset of the COVID-19 pandemic, which only increased the role of technology on the day-to-day functions of practice, and before the notion of generative artificial intelligence (GenAI) was even a glimmer in most lawyers' eyes. What is more, the Commission also noted that technology impacts "how lawyers conduct investigations, engage in legal research, advise their clients, and conduct discovery[,] ... requir[ing] lawyers to have a firm grasp on how electronic information is created, stored, and retrieved."[27] Technology also affected how clients and prospective clients find and communicate with their lawyers, particularly because of the internet, which "provides immediate access to information about lawyers through search engines, websites, blogs, and ratings and rankings services."[28]

In some ways, though, despite the Commission's sense that technology was already transforming the practice of law in "fundamental ways" in 2012, the adoption of a single sentence fragment embedded in a comment to a Model Rule, as opposed to the body of a rule itself, suggests that, despite the fact that technology has advanced in leaps and bounds over the last two decades, the Commission's—and the ABA's—sense of the duty of technology competence is what I might describe as a "thin" view of that competence, rather than a more robust, or "thick" view. The express terms of the addition to Comment 8—that such competence should take into account the "benefits and risks" of technology—and the Commission's discussions at length in its report about practice technology alone, suggest that the duty of technology competence, as described in that Comment, represents a view of technology competence that requires merely that a lawyer should be aware of the ways in which practice technology and its uses might put at risk other types of professional duties: like the duty to preserve client confidences, when, for example, information is shared in electronic form outside the confines of a law office's internal system. Talking about the duty

---

[24] *Id.*

[25] *Id.*

[26] *Id.* (citing AM. BAR ASS'N, LEGAL TECHNOLOGY SURVEY REPORT: EXECUTIVE SUMMARY 18–22 (2011)).

[27] *Id.* (footnote omitted).

[28] *Id.* (citing AM. BAR ASS'N STANDING COMM. ON THE DELIVERY OF LEGAL SERVICES, PERSPECTIVES ON FINDING PERSONAL LEGAL SERVICES (Feb. 2011)).

of technology competence in this way, as many lawyers do, tends to focus on the "risks" side of the way in which that duty is framed. And when we embrace the "benefits" side of the phrase, a more robust and "thick" view of technology competence emerges.

A thick view of technology competence, and the law schools' role in teaching it

At the turn of the 19th to the 20th century, the legal profession entered its Lawyer 2.0 phase, due, in part, to the advent of technological change, which changed how lawyers practiced, the types of services they provided, and the very substance of their work. Because of the introduction of new technologies into the practice of law, lawyers went about their daily business in new and different ways. They advised clients on new business forms and how to navigate newly created regulatory systems. They also learned new areas of law, like anti-trust, railroad, and privacy law. Few aspects of what lawyers did evaded the impact of technology on their work.

Today, a thick version of technology competence is likely to require similar and broad changes as to how lawyers practice, what they do on a daily basis, and the areas of law where clients require assistance. Moreover, a focus on the *benefits* of technology as part of the duty of technology competence will require more of lawyers than their simply being aware of the way such technology can make law practice more efficient. It will also require a comprehensive understanding of how technology can supercharge a whole new approach to how they do business, one that places the interests of the consumer at the forefront of the delivery of legal services. And the "benefits" of technology are such that the new capacities made possible by emerging technologies permit the lawyer to re-orient their work to be more consumer-centric than ever before. This, too, is not just part of the duty of technology competence, it is also a core component of practice in a Lawyer 3.0 world.

So, what is the role for legal education in imparting to students an ability to maintain this thick version of technology competence? Since law schools have an obligation to prepare law students for the practice of law, they also have an obligation to ensure students can fulfill all of their ethical obligations as lawyers, including meeting the duty of technology competence. A robust view of this duty certainly encompasses ensuring students are aware of the risks associated with new technologies, but imparting to law students an appreciation for and mastery of this more expansive view of technology competence is central to ushering in the Lawyer 3.0 era. In the next section, I attempt to chart out what a version of legal education that embraces the Lawyer 3.0 mindset might look like.

Legal education for a Lawyer 3.0 world: new competencies and capacities

Lawyering effectively in a Lawyer 3.0 world will require that legal professionals place the needs of consumers—their jobs to be done—at the center of everything that they do. This will require the following.

Teaching the values and purpose of the profession

All law schools must instill in their students a set of skills to prepare them for practice, but also the values of the profession. What those values are and should be has certainly been a subject of debate since the end of the 19th century. Imparting to students, generally, that there are formal rules that they must follow so that they might practice in an ethical way advances a set of distinct values but does not provide those students with the array of competencies they will need to succeed in an environment where technological innovation is likely to transform the practice of law significantly in the coming years. Even the "thin" duty of technology competence is not enough to prepare those students to use these new capacities in a way that will help the profession fulfill its broader purposes: to secure access to justice for all Americans so that they can address their legal problems in an effective, efficient, affordable, and accessible way. Promoting access to justice, one of a range of current goals of the profession, should be seen as *the* central value that animates most of what lawyers do. This will require a recalibration of professional values and goals, with a corresponding adjustment in the range of competencies that legal professionals acquire in law school and beyond. In order to realize this essential component of the delivery of legal services, legal education will, in turn, need to teach those who operate within a Lawyer 3.0 ecosystem—whether they are lawyers or not—a range of skills and competencies that will enable them to catalyze broader changes in the ways in which legal services are delivered. But this re-orientation and recalibration is inspired by, and starts with, an effort to place consumers in the center of the legal profession's work, as opposed to the lawyer.

Mastering the tools of design thinking, business process analysis and systems thinking

As described previously in Chapter 3, design thinking always starts from an attempt to understand the perspective of the consumer of a product or service. This requires the nurturing of empathy—an attempt to see the problem the consumer is trying to solve through their eyes, to understand what it is they are experiencing, how the environment treats them (or ignores them), and what sorts of changes could be made in an effort to solve the problem from the perspective of that consumer. This also means defining success as solving the problem the client has identified, and on that client's terms to the greatest extent possible. Design thinking is a multi-stage process that starts from seeing the problem from the consumer's perspective before entering into an ideation and experimentation phase when one can engage in rapid prototyping of ideas that make strides toward addressing the consumer's problem. Once that prototype is ready, one can test it against the problem to see whether it satisfies consumer needs in that context. When addressing the legal job to be done, the solutions designer must appreciate the multi-dimensional needs of the consumer based on not just the characteristics of that consumer in any given situation but also the functional, affective, and political needs they want the lawyer to address. The deployment of the prototype of the good or service, or the legal intervention the consumer and their lawyer will want to utilize in a given situation, will always generate feedback. In the legal context, the lawyer and consumer can evaluate the intervention in real time and iterate new versions of the prototype until an appropriate solution emerges from the process. But that process is always iterative. It might be the case that, in the legal context, a lawyer and their client might settle on a winning strategy from the outset, and it requires little adjustment along the way. That rarely happens in the real world. The teaching of design thinking fits squarely within the broader effort that attempts to get lawyers to better understand consumer needs—as those consumers see them—and strive to satisfy them.

An additional competency that could go along with design thinking is that other approach toward service delivery introduced in Chapter 3: business process analysis (BPA). BPA actually interacts quite comfortably with design thinking and complements it. This is particularly true when one is not only striving to understand and redesign one's business processes from the perspective of the consumer (how they see those processes from the outside looking in) to make them more accommodating and accessible, but also when the reason for doing so is to improve the efficiency and rationality of one's service-delivery system so that one might increase the number of clients one can serve.

Finally, in order to devise holistic, effective, and efficient solutions to consumer problems, lawyers should also be able to grasp both the forest and the trees, to understand where in the legal ecosystem their talents and services are most needed, and where and how they can craft effective solutions to address consumer needs. "System thinking," as it is sometimes called, is also an essential skill that lawyers seeking to devise meaningful and effective solutions to consumer problems will need to develop in order to determine the best and most appropriate intervention, at the right time and in the right place, to address a range of consumer problems a lawyer is typically asked to resolve.[29] If a modest intervention at a particular place and time, even one carried out by the consumer with minimal assistance from a lawyer, would help to reduce the likelihood that the problem will grow to the point where it might require the engagement of a lawyer, the lawyer should take every effort to identify those instances where limited assistance is sufficient to resolve a consumer's problem. This is the appropriate approach, even when it might mean that, because the consumer's problem is resolved in an effective manner and with minimal legal effort on the part of the lawyer, the consumer will not need the more extensive (and expensive) services from the lawyer. Systems thinking looks for those places and spaces within the legal ecosystem where a certain fix or modest intervention can resolve an issue without it becoming a more significant problem down the road. It also looks for points within a specific practice "vertical" where effective and timely interventions can reduce the need for more significant efforts at other points. And it also helps to identify instances where a process "improvement" in one area might create a larger problem somewhere else. Meghan Cook, our BPA expert from Chapter 8, uses the example that a logistics company might start to have its drivers use technology that would help move trucks through residential areas to avoid congestion on highways and larger roadways. But by rerouting trucks to where there are more people, that is likely to cause an increase in accidents involving pedestrians.[30] By making an improvement in one area, one might create a problem somewhere else. Without a systemic view, "court vision," as it is sometimes called in basketball, one might see an opportunity for a positive outcome in one place, but fail to see that it forecloses success in achieving one's overall goal.

These three skill sets—design thinking, BPA, and systems thinking—are all critical competencies that law students must develop in order to function in a Lawyer 3.0 world. They are by no means the only competencies that those operating within this new version of the profession will need to master. But by teaching these skills, it is likely that legal education will see other ways to change not just the things it teaches students, but also who it teaches and how. (More on this in a moment.)

So, how would law schools teach these threshold competencies? At present, some law schools incorporate the teaching of some of these skills, consciously and unconsciously, into their work. The NuLawLab at Northeastern University School of Law and the Legal Design Lab at Stanford Law School both explicitly

---

29   For an overview of systems thinking, see Derek Cabrera & Laura Cabrera, *What Is Systems Thinking?*, in *Learning, Design, and Technology: An International Compendium of Theory, Research, Practice, and Policy* (J. Michael Spector et al. eds., 2019).

30   Author Interview with Meghan E. Cook (Sept. 19, 2024).

incorporate design thinking to explore innovative solutions to the access-to-justice problem. But any experiential course that strives to incorporate the perspectives of their clients into their case selection and service delivery is utilizing elements of design thinking. Client-centered lawyering is also a methodology popular in many clinic/experiential settings, where the student providing services through a program at their school learns to develop empathy and to understand the problem the client faces from their perspective, and also encourages them to see the client's situation through the eyes of that client.

Whether it is the express incorporation of design thinking and all of its stages, or the teaching of basic client-centered and empathetic methodologies, at least at the outset of the representation (and, hopefully, throughout), developing a sense of the consumer needs, their perspective on those needs, and what they want to achieve out of the representation are all critical to the delivery of consumer-centered services. One would hope that all law students, and, ultimately, lawyers, adopt such an approach that puts the interests of the clients ahead of those of the lawyer, and allows the client to identify and shape those interests as they see fit, but the current state of the legal profession, and the failure of the profession to meet the legal needs of every consumer who has them, suggests we are not going far enough in imparting this critical skill to law students, and, ultimately, lawyers.

But law schools should also teach the critical skills of BPA and systems thinking as well. These capacities will enable law students, once they become professionals, to think through the manner through which the offices in which they work deliver services and assess the ways in which technology may improve the delivery of such services so that they fit into the system at the appropriate place and the appropriate time. I am constantly amazed when I speak to my students, digital natives who have grown up with technology, at the simple fixes they are often able to introduce into the law offices in which they work as interns, sometimes even as volunteers. Students with a facility with even such off-the-shelf products as Excel are often able to bring much needed process innovations to their offices workflows simply because they have a better feel for the capacities of many of the technologies presently available that can make the work of law offices more efficient. Empowering these students with BPA and systems-thinking skills, when coupled with their greater understanding for and facility with different technologies, will only increase their ability to help improve the processes through which the law offices of the future will deliver more services more efficiently and at scale.

Developing a consumer-focused mindset in pursuit of the consumer's job to be done

In addition to this array of functional skills, once again, law schools should impart to their students an understanding of something akin to the job-to-be-done framework described in depth in Chapter 3. This requires that sort of client-centered focus introduced earlier, which many law schools do try to instill in their students, particularly through their clinical programs, but it goes beyond just having a client-centered approach to the delivery of services. It also requires the incorporation of a fulsome analysis of all of the elements of the job-to-be-done framework, including an appreciation for the range of important values the lawyer is supposed to represent in serving the consumer and their community, the functions the lawyer fulfills in any given situation, an in-depth and complete understanding of the nature of the problem the consumer presents, and a sense of the particular characteristics of the client that will help shape the type and level of intervention that lawyer might deploy to assist the client in solving their legal problem.

Understanding interdisciplinary collaboration

Finally, in order to do some of this work effectively, and to bring technology into the equation in a meaningful way, law students and lawyers are going to have to learn to work better with other professionals, especially technologists, although there are certainly some individuals who are both lawyers and technologists who know enough law and enough about computers or other technologies to create technological systems that can solve different client problems. David Rosen, who we met in Chapter 8, is one of these lawyer-engineers. But most lawyers will not be in a position to become an expert computer programmer and an expert lawyer at the same time. Instead, lawyers who wish to incorporate technology effectively into the practice of law will not just need to hire engineers and other professionals to develop systems of the lawyer's design, they will also need to learn to work more closely with other professionals in creating those systems from the ground up, to understand the capacities of such systems, but also to contribute their own understanding of the critical services such systems are supposed to deliver. Such "centaur" teams described earlier are going to be the ones that are able to meld the practical, ethical, theoretical, and technical in the most effective way possible. Historically, the bar writ large has mostly limited the extent to which lawyers can work with non-lawyers in formal partnerships. This has likely led to a degree of professional chauvinism and undue exceptionalism. Law schools should begin to try to disabuse law students of this mindset in order to foster environments in which lawyers and other professionals can work more comfortably together to deliver effective services at scale.

Legal education beyond just lawyers

To this point, I have talked about legal education in a very Lawyer 2.0 way. That is, I have looked at legal education only from the perspective of an institution that educates lawyers. At present. This preference for educating legal professionals in a very narrow way has both been a hallmark of legal education for the last century, but, at the same time, does not tell the whole story about who provides legal assistance to clients on a day-to-day basis. Lawyers are aided by what are formally referred to as "non-lawyers" in virtually everything they do. As described earlier, in the traditional real-estate transaction involving the transfer of a residential home, in many communities a paralegal will prepare much of the paperwork that is necessary for the consummation of the transaction. The lawyer generally has put together a compendium of forms in collaboration with lawyers from other entities, like mortgage banks. They have probably pulled a "power-of-attorney" form off the internet or out of a form book. They have received mortgage documents from the bank's attorney and things like title reports from a title search company, an entity that might include lawyers but often does not. At the closing, the lawyer presents a stack of documents that is hundreds of pages thick. These forms contain reams and reams of content, often in very small type print. Although this might look like it has entailed a lot of work to prepare, in reality the lawyers handling the transaction have used versions of these forms over and over and over again. What is more, paralegals have done most of the work to pull them together and adjust them to reflect the specifics of any particular transaction, like the names of the parties, the address of the home, and the purchase price. In other words, some of the most essential updates to the forms, the core elements of the transaction, are usually carried out by non-lawyers.

In other areas of law, non-lawyers also do a lot of the work. And some of this is officially sanctioned. In the immigration context, federal authorities certify practitioners who are not lawyers to handle many different types of immigration applications and disputes. These professionals typically work within law offices where their practice is supervised by an attorney. In many of the legal services offices in which I worked, paralegals and community organizers handled matters involving the termination of welfare assistance and denials of applications for Social Security Administration benefits, all with the support and under the supervision of practicing lawyers. So those colleagues handled much of the work, even assisting clients in fair hearings: modest approximations of adversarial trials, where they had to do a lot of what a lawyer would otherwise do, like examine witnesses, move the admission of evidence, and make legal arguments.

What these simple examples show is that there are many formal and informal ways in which the delivery of legal services is carried out by individuals other than lawyers every day. Some states have created what have come to be known as regulatory "sandboxes" that allow a degree of service-delivery innovation. But in most of those jurisdictions, there has not been much experimentation with respect to non-lawyers providing legal services.

At the turn of the 19th to the 20th century, the legal profession turned to the medical profession to learn how, in just a decade, the American Medical Association had successfully reduced the number of individuals who were graduating from American medical schools by half. That effort was certainly motivated, in part, by the desire to engage in some degree of quality control. But it was also carried out to preserve the monopoly of practicing medical professionals to deliver medical services. A lot has changed in the medical field over the last century. While one of the main things that the medical profession was trying to accomplish in those days was to limit the number of people who were not qualified to deliver medical services, over the last 100 years the medical profession has actually proven itself much more willing to certify a wide range of professionals other than physicians to deliver some types of medical services. In fact, medical practice looks more like a continuum than a monolith, with registered nurses, nurse practitioners, and other types of medical professionals providing a wide range of services to meet the needs of the patient base, which is, simply put, the community. Would it be prudent for the legal profession to embark on a similar endeavor, to explore ways to certify other professionals along the continuum of care to deliver services in an efficient, competent, accessible, and affordable way? The changes that the medical profession instituted at the turn of the last century seemed good enough for the legal profession. I would also think that the issues medical professionals face are likely more complex, and the stakes higher, than the matters that most lawyers handle on a day-to-day basis. Where life-and-death matters are *not* at stake, the legal profession could explore similar types of initiatives to expand the work of other professionals within the legal profession so as to deliver services in a more accessible way.

Legal education for a Lawyer 3.0 world

Legal education for the next version of the legal profession will likely not only prepare future lawyers for a technology-infused practice of law, it will also infuse those lawyers with a profound sense of empathy and an ability to consider ways to reach more consumers with legal services that are accessible and affordable. It will also educate more types of legal professionals, not just lawyers, and instill in those different professionals an ability to work with non-legal professionals as well, especially technologists, to consider ways to deliver those services at scale. Lawyer 3.0 will require a new way of educating not just lawyers, but also legal professionals who are not fully licensed attorneys. If a range of different professionals can deliver medical services to the community, it is hardly inappropriate to explore ways to do the same with legal services.

Chapter 9: Key takeaways

1. The legal profession in the U.S. evolved from an apprenticeship model to a formal education system by the early 20th century. Elite institutions played a significant role in creating barriers to entry, partly influenced by a range of biases. These measures limited access to the profession, helping maintain its monopoly and reducing competition.

2. Technological advancements have drastically altered the way law is practiced, from how lawyers communicate with clients to how legal work is disaggregated and managed. Law schools must adapt to teach technological competence as an essential skill for future lawyers.

3. The ABA introduced a formal duty of technology competence in 2012, emphasizing that lawyers must stay updated on the benefits and risks of relevant technologies to provide competent representation. This duty reflects the growing importance of technology in legal practice, but the profession did not go far enough in embracing the benefits of new technologies.

4. The future of legal education and practice (Lawyer 3.0) focuses on making legal services more consumer-centric rather than lawyer-centric. This involves using design thinking, BPA, and systems thinking to reframe legal services from the consumer's perspective and better address their needs.

5. Legal education in the future must teach law students to collaborate with other professionals, particularly technologists. This interdisciplinary collaboration will be crucial in developing and implementing innovative legal solutions that are both efficient and scalable.

6. Similar to the medical profession, where a variety of professionals provide services, the legal profession could explore ways to certify non-lawyers to perform certain legal tasks. This approach would make legal services more accessible and affordable to the broader population.

10

Ushering in the Lawyer 3.0 World

Despite my somewhat cheeky reference to the staffing patterns of the factory of the future, I do not believe law office personnel will be hounded by dogs guarding the offices' computers as they whir and buzz and deliver legal services to thousands of clients without a human having to do much more than make sure those computers are connected to a functioning power source. While some technologists and "disruptors" might dream of such a world, even if one was possible, even if it provided access to some modicum of justice to every American, it is certain that something important will be lost if the legal profession is displaced in a way that undermines, and does not advance, some of the *value* the profession provides and *values* the profession serves when offering legal assistance. What is more, lawyers also play important instrumental, affective, and political roles for their clients. Even with a profession centered on expanding access to justice, which I advocate should serve as the touchstone of the profession in the Lawyer 3.0 version of itself, the justice that is provided must be meaningful, and satisfy the consumer's full job to be done in order for this new version to represent an improvement over the last. While some consumers will certainly benefit from a world where they can get their legal problems solved accurately, swiftly, and inexpensively with a few keystrokes, I do not think we are anywhere near such a world. While the technology evangelists might want to usher in such a world, I think something significant is lost—for our democracy, the rule of law, client dignity, community—when there is no role for a lawyer to assist individuals in making some of the hardest and most consequential decisions of their lives and to help them navigate through the challenges they may face over the course of those lives.

Similarly, I do not want to live in a world where, in order to receive human assistance with a legal problem, one has to do the equivalent of shouting "agent" while dealing with an automated system in an attempt to get through to a human on the other end of the line. Still, we are swiftly coming to a point where lawyers can automate a great deal of legal tasks, whether those tasks are internal, and empower lawyers to make considerable efficiency gains that are passed along to clients, or whether such automations serve consumers directly. In either case, such interventions could make legal assistance much more accessible to the average consumer. One significant aspect of that accessibility is that legal services will likely be far more affordable.

Taking the adage of Bill Gates that I referenced earlier to heart: we often overestimate the impact of innovation on the next two years but underestimate the changes that will take place over the next ten. As this book goes to print, we are right at the tail of that first two-year window from the introduction of generative artificial intelligence (GenAI) for widespread use. Rumors of the demise of the legal profession with that introduction have been greatly exaggerated. But will they be over the next ten years? Are there ways that the profession can get ahead of those changes, adapt to and incorporate new technologies to better serve the community, and recalibrate the delivery of legal services and other services that look a lot like legal services? Advances in technology are likely to have dramatic impacts on the legal profession over the next decade. It is better for the profession to plan for and bring that future into existence than have that future happen to it, with potentially harmful consequences, not just for lawyers but also for consumers, the community, and society as a whole.

At least two phenomena will lead to significant changes in the capacity of technology to transform the delivery of legal services to the community over the next few years. The first of these is that advances in technology are such that we will soon be at a point where new tools will assume many of the routine tasks conducted by lawyers on a day-to-day basis today. The second is that the market for legal services is broken, and far too many Americans face their legal problems without a lawyer for various reasons, with just one important one being that the costs of such services are out of the reach of many families. The combination of these two forces means that the profession is ripe for the type of disruption identified by the late Clayton Christensen as the "Innovator's Dilemma": the notion that incumbent actors within a market will cede market share to new entrants as they strive to deliver less expensive and accessible products and services to the lower end of a given market. Eventually, those new entrants seize a larger and larger portion of the customer base as their products and services improve in quality and attractiveness to a growing segment of that base. Those new entrants then dominate a given market, ultimately displacing the incumbents entirely.

To date, this phenomenon has not yet played out in the legal profession for a number of reasons. The cost of introducing new technologies effectively into the practice of law is expensive, and few new entrants or market disruptors have been able to bring such new technologies to bear on the lower end of the market at a cost that works. Instead, many of the legal tech innovators have targeted the high end of the market by serving private law firms using a business-to-business model. Such an approach is unlikely to bring about the type of disruptive innovation that is often seen in other contexts. What is more, even when we have seen things like online legal research enter law office practice, the commercial providers of such services have found ways to offer somewhat scaled-down versions of their products for non-profit providers, but these products are rarely used by consumers directly.

Another reason it is harder to introduce technological innovations that might extend the reach of legal services to consumers at a fraction of the cost of traditional providers of such services is the regulatory regime that seeks to curtail the unauthorized practice of law (UPL). Not only do most jurisdictions prevent the provision of legal services by non-lawyers, they also make it unethical for a lawyer to assist a non-lawyer in the delivery of otherwise unauthorized legal services. So, even if a lawyer advised a technology company seeking to deliver services directly to the community that looked a lot like legal services, that lawyer would likely find themselves facing ethics charges that they are assisting others in UPL. Since non-lawyers are not subject to lawyer codes of conduct, those codes incorporate rules against UPL into their provisions by making it unethical for lawyers themselves to assist third parties in delivering legal services. This means that even those from outside the profession who might want to use technology to help close the justice gap cannot turn to lawyers to help them to do so if what those non-lawyer entrants are doing is engaging in what might be considered the practice of law. Since the criminal codes of most jurisdictions include prohibitions on UPL rules, and those apply to non-lawyers and lawyers alike, it is not possible for non-lawyers to evade punishment, even if lawyers' codes of ethics do not extend to them.[1]

Such UPL rules have their place, for sure, and serve important consumer-protective purposes. We cannot have those not trained in the law holding themselves out as capable of solving legal problems for consumers when their services might actually end up harming those consumers. This could happen where such advocates might fail to register a copyright; make a business filing in a timely fashion; or submit an error-ridden application for an adjustment of immigration status that ends up resulting in a finding that the applicant, unbeknownst to them, engaged in some form of immigration fraud based on the contents of the filing.

UPL rules certainly can also have their dark side. They chill activities that could improve the lives of millions of Americans in meaningful ways with little downside risk, particularly in settings where the matters about which a consumer might receive guidance are of low complexity; the consequences

---

[1] On the range of punishments often associated with UPL, including criminal sanctions, see Quintin Johnstone, *Unauthorized Practice of Law and the Power of State Courts: Difficult Problems and Their Resolution*, 39 WILLAMETTE L. REV. 795, 800–807 (2003).

of not having assistance are significant; and a little bit of information, at the right time, and in the right place, might go a long way in bringing a successful resolution to the consumer's problem. Too often, the UPL rules do little more than preserve the lawyer monopoly rather than provide an appropriate level of consumer protection. They also stand in the way of innovation, especially disruptive innovation, if such disruption tends to occur from new entrants into a market at the expense of incumbents. What the market for legal services has unlike many other markets, other than, say, medicine, are significant barriers to entry, including UPL rules. Such barriers make true disruption—that is, disruption that occurs at the lower end of the market—more difficult to achieve when it comes to providing services directly to consumers in a meaningful and accessible way. In the end, UPL rules and other barriers to both entry to the profession and the provision of legal services by non-lawyers tend to place the interests of lawyers in maintaining their monopoly and suppressing competition for their services ahead of the interests of consumers who might prefer more affordable, accessible, "just-in-time and just-enough" services, services that might resolve their legal problem without the expense often associated with retaining a lawyer.

But the notion that there is no substitute for full-service representation provided by a licensed attorney in every situation in which a consumer faces a legal problem has been a prominent force driving the legal profession's (self-serving) pursuit of a monopoly on the delivery of legal services since even the early days of its existence in the colonial era, which was a time when many jurisdictions, facing a lack of lawyers in the community, tended to have fewer restrictions on both entry to the profession and even the delivery of legal guidance by non-lawyers. Still, beginning in the early part of the 19th century, the model of providing bespoke legal assistance tailored to the needs of each client has largely served as the mode of service delivery, and it certainly is the dominant mode of the provision of such services in the Lawyer 2.0 era. What is more, this vision of the lawyer as the "craftsperson," providing unique and specialized services in a way that is customized to each client, certainly serves the interests of lawyers who wish to maintain their monopoly on the provision of such services. In a world where such services are affordable and accessible to everyone who needs a lawyer, that monopoly power causes few problems. But we are not in that world.

Rather, at present, far too many Americans face their legal problems without the benefit of legal guidance. Given this state of affairs, the persistence of the justice gap, when combined with the emergence of new technologies that might help to close that gap, means that the old ways of doing business could soon face serious threats. Once again, the purpose of the legal profession is not to ensure full employment for all lawyers, even if the trouble and costs associated with joining the profession might require some incentives to get individuals to do so. The fact that the market for legal services is clearly broken because so many face their legal problems without a lawyer, and that new and emerging technologies could help address this market failure, means that the time is right to consider ways in which consumers can have their legal needs met in an effective, accessible, and affordable way without losing the benefits, in appropriate circumstances, that full-service, customized, and bespoke services might bring to particular consumers. The challenge is to determine when technology might aid in the delivery of legal services in appropriate settings; might completely displace human lawyers in some situations; or simply will not substitute for a full-service, human lawyer in others. When the purpose of the American legal profession should be to ensure that all Americans have access to legal assistance to satisfy their legal needs, as opposed to merely protecting the profession's monopoly, devising a methodology for assessing the best and most appropriate mode of delivery in different settings represents the central challenge facing the profession in the immediate future. That methodology, I submit, is what could usher in the next phase of the American legal profession: what I have called Lawyer 3.0. Such a methodology will center around a few core organizing principles.

Putting the consumer at the center of the legal profession's universe

The first and most critical shift in mindset that the legal profession will have to take is for it to place the consumer at the center of everything the profession does. This means not just looking at the access-to-justice crisis from the perspective of consumers. It also demands that the profession must recognize that its purpose is to ensure that every American who has a legal problem has some means of addressing it. What is more, the profession must also take the steps necessary to realize that purpose. New technologies are likely to create the conditions necessary to provide some of legal services through other means: that is, consumers will access services in ways that do not involve a lawyer delivering them in every instance. I will repeat this one last time: the purpose of the profession is not to ensure the legal system operates as a full-employment plan for lawyers; it should ensure that it serves the needs of the community and its citizens and not the profession.

Such a shift in focus and mindset will require a fairly significant change in the way in which the trade guild that is the legal profession sees its role within society. The profession is supposed to place the interests of its clients above those of the lawyers within it. This is true even if that means that there will be times when full-service, bespoke services, delivered by lawyers, especially when such services are out of the economic reach of many Americans, are not the solution to the problems consumers face. When we see this state of affairs from the consumer's perspective, we recognize that there is an abject need to develop alternative, more affordable, more accessible methods of service delivery. At the same time, newly emerging technological capacities will make alternative forms of delivery that satisfy the needs of clients in effective ways a reality. When that capacity exists, the profession should embrace it in order to ensure that as many consumers who need legal guidance can receive it, which leads to the second organizing principle for Lawyer 3.0.

The access-to-justice imperative in light of new technological capacities

A core tenet of the profession, one to which its members already commit, is the need to ensure access to justice for all Americans. The Preamble to the American Bar Association's (ABA's) Model Rules of Professional Conduct already provides that, "[a]s a public citizen, a lawyer should seek improvement of the law, access to the legal system, the administration of justice and the quality of service rendered by the legal profession."[2] It also implores lawyers to "further the public's understanding of and confidence in the rule of law and the justice system because legal institutions in a constitutional democracy depend on popular participation and support to maintain their authority" and to "be mindful of deficiencies in the administration of justice and of the fact that the poor, and sometimes persons who are not poor, cannot afford adequate legal assistance."[3] Because of this, "all lawyers should devote professional time and resources and use civic influence to ensure equal access to our system of justice for all those who because of economic or social barriers cannot afford or secure adequate legal counsel."[4] At a minimum, then, the profession does at least pay lip-service to the notion that lawyers should support access to justice and the legal system. At least in word, if not in deed, we see that the profession explicitly links meaningful participation in the justice system with the rule of law. A legal system that does not ensure full access to it for those who need recourse through it is not upholding the rule of law itself. But mere lip-service to such notions is not the same as delivering on the promise of the rule of law and access to justice.

We are in a position today that new technologies may place the capacity to bring us closer to that promise of access to justice if the profession harnesses them in ways that advance these broader interests, but only if we know when they are adequate to the task. A failure to satisfy one's legal needs, either

---

[2] AM. BAR ASS'N, MODEL RULES OF PROFESSIONAL CONDUCT, Preamble ¶ 6.
[3] *Id.*
[4] *Id.*

by inaction, or inappropriate action, is still a failure. If we do not know when and under what circumstances different approaches and modes of service delivery, at different times, can fulfill the values the legal profession is supposed to fulfill and meet the needs of the consumers in meaningful and accessible ways, disruption for the sake of disruption—that is, using technology to displace lawyers in circumstances when it is not fully up to the task of doing so—may actually make the consumer's situation worse, or it may widen the justice gap by making technological innovation only available to those who already have representation and are able to engage those lawyers whose work is supercharged by new technological capacities. Developing the ability to discern when and under what circumstances alternate forms of service delivery can provide meaningful and effective services that satisfy consumers' functional, affective, and political needs, and uphold the values the legal system and legal problem solving is supposed to advance, will be an essential skill that is necessary to usher in the next phase of the American legal profession.

Analyze legal problems along critical dimensions to devise appropriate solutions

As first introduced in Chapter 3, there are four critical fields that help us analyze a given situation to determine the appropriate intervention that can help address a consumer's job to be done. First, what are the values that the delivery of legal services might advance in a given situation? Second, what are the specific functions legal interventions might serve in that setting, including the extent to which there are instrumental, affective, and political dimensions to the legal problem? Any solution to the problem must take into account these functions. Third, what are the characteristics of the problem and the types of interventions that are necessary to solve it? This will include an appropriate accounting of its relative complexity as well as what is at stake for the client. A matter that might threaten the consumer's liberty is quite different from one in which a relatively small sum of money is involved. Still, what is at stake in every situation is not necessarily simply a question of some objective measure. Indeed, it is entirely relative, and just as the stakes for each client will vary, how we gauge those stakes, and the importance of legal services to address them, will also vary.

An institutional landlord might see a $2,000 civil penalty for a housing code violation as the cost of doing business for that entity. Or a giant technology company might see a $5 billion fine as little more than a parking ticket. At the same time, a consumer who lost a case involving an outstanding credit card debt valued at the same amount, say, as the landlord's civil penalty could find themselves having their wages garnished and a bank account frozen to satisfy the debt, which could lead to more significant adverse consequences down the road, like a dramatic reduction in their personal credit rating, or even homelessness and familial disruption. The characteristics of each problem must always be viewed in light of the client's relationship to that problem. This leads to the fourth and last metric for assessing each legal setting: what are the characteristics of the consumer themselves? That is, how does the legal problem impact that consumer? What are the stakes as they see them? With respect to potential technological solutions in a particular situation, what is their personal capacity to benefit from and activate different tech-based solutions if they are asked to take a more—or less—active part in their response to their legal problem? These four fields all help us assess the consumer's job to be done in each setting and help us craft a unique solution for each situation. And sometimes, what is appropriate in a particular setting will include a technology-based solution, as I explore next.

Can a computer do it better, and what does better even mean?

Given our four-fields analysis, it is likely that situations will arise in which a technology-based solution will do just as good a job as a human lawyer providing full-service representation in the same situation. And whether the technology-based service is superior to the one delivered by a human will be measured by its accuracy, affordability, accessibility, and suitability for use by the specific client in need of specific services in a specific situation. Assessing these elements of the technology-based services will require an analysis of the values at stake, the functions the consumer wants the lawyer to fulfill, the nature of the problem, and the characteristics of the consumer in that situation. In addition, we might not always analyze the relative superiority of technology-based solutions against a lawyer operating to provide the full range of services that the consumer might desire when that lawyer is not really available to a particular consumer for whatever reason, including the following: there is no lawyer who handles that type of matter in the community, the consumer cannot afford such a service, or the consumer is unaware of how to access that lawyer. Still, even when a lawyer might serve a particular consumer, that consumer must be able to afford that lawyer or must be able to gain access to that lawyer's services in some other way, either because the lawyer is willing to provide those services on a pro bono basis or the lawyer works for a non-profit organization and the consumer is both eligible for services from that organization and there is a lawyer with the capacity to assist that consumer. Unless the technology-based service will leave the consumer worse off than if they had no representation whatsoever, which is not completely out of the question, in most instances, where the technology-based service provides accurate, accessible, and affordable services that are suitable for a specific client, and the alternative is no assistance at all, it is hard to argue that the delivery of such services are in any way inappropriate or inferior to the alternative: that is, no assistance whatsoever.

Still, assuming a lawyer is available to a consumer in a particular setting, let us measure a technology-based solution against that type of lawyer ideal: the provision of bespoke, traditional services from a human practitioner. Even there, it is possible that there are instances where the consumer might prefer a technology-based solution to a human one. There is a reason millions of Americans file their taxes every year with an online company like TurboTax. It is a relatively accessible interface that provides services at a fraction of what a tax preparer might charge. These services tend to be fairly accurate, but the service provider typically offers a measure of accountability and will agree to defend a consumer in the event there is an audit of the taxpayer or there is some error in the filing. Because of the ease of use and its affordability, consumers are largely satisfied with these sorts of services. Millions of consumers choose these services every year: they decide they are "good enough" and serve the consumers' job to be done in a discrete and particular setting: filing their taxes.

Could a provider of legal services offer a similar sort of interface in other contexts? With the Citizenshipworks initiative introduced previously, immigrants who might qualify to adjust their immigration status and apply for citizenship are able to answer a series of interrogatories about their situation, including: providing information about their current status, whether they have had any run-ins with law enforcement, and whether they have resided in the U.S. lawfully for the requisite period of years to apply for U.S. citizenship. The interface develops the case on behalf of the applicant and moves them through the system as they answer the questions posed to them and supply the requisite information. If at any point it appears that the immigrant has a case that is not relatively straightforward, and for which the tool is not the right mechanism to file the application for citizenship, the system will inform the consumer of that fact, let them know the tool is not appropriate for them, and direct them to other resources that might be able to help in their specific situation.

Let us analyze the scenario to which the tool applies. First, the person is eligible to apply for citizenship and there are no legal barriers to that application, other than the requirement that the consumer completes the application. Second, there are no apparent red flags that the Citizenshipworks interface identifies. Third, the system can accurately fill out the required paperwork and provide directions to the consumer as to how to file it to complete the application. In the end, what the consumer wants from legal services—their quarter-inch hole—is to file an accurate and successful application for adjustment of immigration status. If the Citizenshipworks tool helps them to do that, it is likely that this tool will satisfy the functions the consumer wants fulfilled, even an affective one: the peace of mind that comes with knowing that the application is accurate and complete as filed. It certainly satisfies the instrumental purposes for which the consumer is seeking assistance as well as their political goal: assisting the consumer to secure their role within the body politic. What is more, if a specific consumer presents a straightforward case that the interface can process accurately, and the consumer is capable of completing the tasks required to utilize the online portal, a consumer might feel quite comfortable completing this sort of application process using an online interface from the comfort and convenience of their home.

Of course, this rosy scenario assumes a lot. It assumes that the client can successfully and accurately navigate the interface and supply appropriate answers. The interface is available in several common languages spoken among immigrant communities in the U.S., including Spanish and Mandarin. For this reason, at least that potential barrier to access is addressed for those for whom the system operates in their native language. It also assumes that the system itself can identify red flags in the consumer's application such that they cannot rely on this straightforward application process to pursue their citizenship. A user might also input incorrect information about their status, which they might do intentionally, fearing that they do not want to give the system the "wrong" answer when a wrong answer is actually just an answer that is not factually accurate. The consumer might also make an honest mistake as well, one that a human conducting an interview of the person sitting across from them might catch. Seeing doubt in the consumer's eyes as they answer a question, or some other aspect of their story might contradict the new fact the client is presenting, might prompt the advocate to ask a follow-up question if they fear the consumer is not supplying a correct answer. If it is safe to assume that Citizenshipworks can accurately identify those cases where the service is not suitable for a particular individual, then the consumer will be no worse off than if they had not sought assistance from the service, except for the fact that perhaps they spent some time trying to figure out the system, or they got their hopes inappropriately raised, thinking that they had found a service that could help them achieve their goal.

There is no question that creating such expert systems as Citizenshipworks takes time and expense, especially because of the energy and expertise needed to ensure that the system produces neither false negatives (that the system "ejects" consumers from the service inappropriately, based on the mistaken assessment that the consumer is not appropriate for the service), or false positives (that the system moves forward with an application for a consumer when they cannot really rely on the simple and straightforward services that Citizenshipworks provides). But what a tool like Citizenshipworks does, and does well, is reverse the relationship between consumer and the services they receive: the job that is done on their behalf. It determines whether the consumer is appropriate for the service, rather than creating a bespoke strategy from scratch for each consumer who seeks services. While this critical shift in approach is an essential element of any expert system that might displace the full services offered by lawyers in particular circumstances, or steps in where no or few lawyers currently tread, what is also particularly important about a service like Citizenshipworks is that it reverses the traditional relationship between consumer and service. It is this reversal that is also an essential pillar of the Lawyer 3.0 approach.

Product first

What I mean when I say a program like Citizenshipworks reverses the traditional relationship between consumer and service is the following. In the traditional and dominant approach that is prevalent in Lawyer version 2.0, the lawyer sits down with each client, assesses their needs, and develops a unique plan for that client that addresses those needs. Each legal intervention is tailored to the unique needs of each client. Even with such a tailored approach for each client, the lawyer will likely pull ideas, pleadings, old contracts, legal memoranda, and legal research from their work on other cases to start to create a game plan that is tailored to the particular client they are serving in a particular setting. The lawyer will also exercise their judgment about what they think the client needs to hear at a particular moment in the lawyer–client relationship, will express their assessment of the client's situation, and will explain to the client what it is they intend to do on behalf of the client, at least at first. They will discuss the benefits and risks associated with different tactics and strategies and come to a conclusion about the right path to take for that particular client. All this is well and good, and it represents the lawyer operating at the height of their craft. It also represents a highly inefficient and expensive way to do business, especially in an industry that largely charges by the hour, where time is literally money.

But what a Lawyer 3.0 approach does is look for opportunities to reverse this process. To lead with product rather than consumer. That is, the lawyer should spend time devising *pre-packaged* legal strategies or products and then assess specific consumers for the suitability of those interventions to satisfy the consumer's needs. Such products might serve a significant percentage of consumers, at a fraction of the cost, and satisfy their legal needs along a number of dimensions, not the least of which is accessibility and affordability. The lawyer can spend time developing these products, tailoring them to the extent necessary to accommodate a range of specific and common exceptions and make those products available to consumers. The lawyer evaluates the *consumer's* suitability for a particular product instead of devising a new legal strategy for each prospective client who walks in the lawyer's door.

In a way, by taking this approach legal services will be commoditized. Taking a "one-size-fits-many" approach, even if it does not fit every consumer in every situation, will still deliver high quality services, at scale, that satisfy certain consumers' jobs to be done. When the out-of-the-box solution fails to meet a consumer's needs in specific situations, such consumers could turn to the more traditional model of services, which should still be available, even in a Lawyer 3.0 world. They will just be far more expensive than those services delivered in a commoditized way, but likely no more costly than they are at present. Putting aside whether a particular consumer can afford the more expensive, bespoke services, at least some consumers who could not afford those bespoke services, and even some who could, might opt for the more affordable, accessible, commoditized version of services, if they are adequate to meet each consumer's needs. Just because a consumer can pay for more services than they really need or might desire does not mean they should or will. And this delta between what a consumer needs and will pay for simply because there are no affordable options that are more aligned with their needs is what makes the situation ripe for the type of disruptive innovation at the center of the Innovator's Dilemma. When alternative options are available to consumers, both those who can afford more services and those who cannot, and those alternative options satisfy those consumers' jobs to be done in an effective way regardless of their ability to afford more services than they need, disruption is not just possible, it is inevitable. What is more, in the case of the legal profession and its responsibility to serve consumer needs and place those consumers' interests ahead of their own, disruption is not merely possible or likely, it is an imperative.

Simplification

Another important component of a technology-infused legal practice is going to include making sure that there are what are known in the field of artificial intelligence (AI) as humans in the loop. The humans in question in this equation are on both sides of the transaction in which legal services are provided. When we talk about AI and the importance of having a human in the loop, usually what that means is that there is a human who is monitoring the work of the AI entity to make sure the output is consistent with the anticipated work product and is carried out in a manner consistent with human values. The human in the loop operates on the legal services side of the transaction to analyze the work product of a technology service to ensure it is accurate and free of "hallucinations" and other errors. They will monitor the inputs from which the machine is drawing information, like its legal sources, and also watch its outputs. The human's main function is to ensure that any advice, information, and documents that are produced or disseminated by the technology are consistent with the legal services providers' standard of care. This will be the most important quality-control element of the delivery of legal services through technological means. So, there will be a human watching what goes into the machine, the information it processes, as well as the outputs, that is, the legal service (for lack of a better term) that it produces.

There is also another human involved in this so-called loop though. That is the consumer. One of the things that lawyers do not do particularly well is assess the ways in which the services they deliver are received by the consumer. And this starts with how information is shared with a prospective client who might be interested in retaining the lawyer. A lawyer might deliver information in a cold and unemotional manner even though they are discussing highly charged legal issues. They might also pass along negative information in a way that is insensitive to the state in which the client is receiving it. When we start delivering services to consumers in a consumer-centered way, we will have to do a better job of taking into account how consumers process information that is delivered to them. For too long, law firms have focused on things like having elegant waiting rooms and some non-profits have tried to do the same. User experience (UX) in a Lawyer 3.0 world will focus on much more than having accommodating and comfortable waiting rooms.

If we go back to our design-thinking approach, we will strive to take into account UX at all points of the legal services continuum. What is more, when we engage in rapid prototyping of service-delivery models, we will test them against users' interactions with those models. Those interactions will generate feedback about whether or not those models are confusing or clear, inviting or discouraging, accessible or difficult to deploy. Lawyers do very little of this UX testing in their work. When we begin to utilize more technology-based interfaces to deliver legal services in some form, we will have to take UX seriously.

Don't raise the bridge, lower the water; expanding opportunities for client choice

It is not just on the lawyer to find ways to simplify their processes and develop straightforward products that fit a wide range of consumer needs even if every product is not appropriate for every consumer. The legal system, lawyers, elected officials, administrators in court systems, and consumers can all advocate for changes in the laws to make them simpler and easier to understand. Similarly, all stakeholders must work together to streamline court processes to make our courts more accessible, and possibly moving some of these processes into other fora. Those other settings must not only be accommodating and user-friendly but also must guarantee essential due-process rights. We can take the approach that one size fits many and strive to create systems that resolve simple and straightforward matters in a way that is easier and more accessible for consumers to navigate. When we offer off-the-shelf solutions to consumers, often on both sides of a dispute, it creates incentives for consumers to look for ways to utilize such solutions where both sides believe it is in their best interests to do so. More complex problems will always require more complex dispute-resolution mechanisms, but if there are more meaningful opportunities for real dispute resolution, where the parties may choose a less-expensive and more-accessible path to addressing their legal conflict, that will not just offer them outlets for effective means of resolving their disputes, it will also put less pressure on existing systems, which will have fewer matters to address. That alone will help make even more complex systems less cumbersome because judges and court personnel will have fewer matters to handle and can attend to those conflicts that require greater attention.

Alternative dispute-resolution outlets certainly exist, and they have their own significant problems: like when a company funnels its disputes with its customers to a forum that is decidedly anti-consumer and has opaque processes that actually make it more difficult for the typical lay person to navigate. They might also have to advocate with an adversary who represents the company almost exclusively before the same mediators or arbitrators. Such repeat players have a significant advantage over someone who might find themselves before an adjudicator just once. And sometimes those repeat players actually pick and compensate those adjudicators, so we can only imagine where their loyalties may lie. It is obvious that if we are going to create more effective options for consumers to resolve their disputes in fora where the processes are simpler and more accessible, those fora must serve as neutral sites that offer accessible—and impartial—means of addressing legal conflicts.

Apart from creating fora that are easier to access and navigate, there are also other ways that we could make legal problems easier to solve—or even prevent them from occurring in the first place. Legal professionals could create simple legal agreements that cover a range of consumer scenarios and provide a degree of protection for the parties to those agreements that will satisfy their basic needs. The creation of simpler contracts that can satisfy consumers' basic needs would not only reduce the need for more complex transactions, they would also be far easier to unwind and enforce than their more complex, custom-made counterparts. If we look at the Innovator's Dilemma as playing out on a microeconomic level, a lawyer might have to create a lengthy and complex document to justify their role, even if done in good faith, out of the belief that this level of complexity is needed to protect the client in every conceivable situation. It is possible, if not likely, that this type of contract is not what the client would choose if given the opportunity and if made aware of the risks associated with not having the more complex version of the agreement and the cost that is associated with adopting that version.

In the end, consumers should have a choice as to whether the simpler and more straightforward solution is one that will work for them, and they can weigh the value of having a more complex and costly agreement. We already take this approach in the market for residential mortgages. Bank regulators have blessed what is known as a "qualified mortgage." These are mortgages that have a range of basic provisions that have been vetted to ensure that they are protective of both the consumer and the lender, and the agreement has certain elements to it to protect against abusive or predatory terms towards the borrower. When the lender uses the qualified mortgage, certain benefits accrue to them, including less regulatory oversight of their activities, at least with respect to their use of these mortgages. In other words, when parties accept a vetted agreement, one that seems to balance the interests of the parties well, even in an environment in which there are great asymmetries of information, in some respects this lets the parties to that transaction greater leeway to act, freeing them from more rigorous oversight of their activities. Historically, lawyers have not shied away from complexity, in fact, complexity is often the friend of the profession. Creating that complexity is more time-consuming itself. What is more, acting in the face of such created complexity is also more complicated. Finally, should parties operating under a complex agreement violate their obligations, it will be more difficult—and costly—to resolve disputes over those actions after the fact.

In the 17th century, when economic agreements were far less complex and resolving disagreements under them was much easier, people could generally resolve their disputes without the assistance of an advocate, even if they had to do so in a court of law or some other tribunal. As life and the economy both became more complex, there was a greater need for lawyers to help create and enforce legal relationships. But after the formation of the new nation, one that was purportedly founded on the notion that all (white) men were created equal, a new aristocracy emerged: that of lawyers. Alexis de Tocqueville, in his visits to the nation in the 1830s, identified this class of aristocrats, who, he argued, served neither on the side of the wealthy nor the masses, but, stood between them.[5] The nation was also to be one of laws and not men, and, as a result, lawyers held a prominent role in society. But this aristocracy soon sought ways to strengthen its position, doing things like working to reduce the number and types of disputes decided by juries so as to ensure that lawyers had a more prominent role in dispute resolution.[6]

This sort of lawyer dominance in the resolution of legal disputes continues to this day. For example, the innocuous sounding "no-fault-divorce process" is one in which the parties to a marriage have all agreed that it should end, and seek legal recognition of its termination, just as they sought legal recognition

---

[5]   ALEXIS DE TOCQUEVILLE, DEMOCRACY IN AMERICA 332 (Henry Reeve trans. 2013).
[6]   See MORTON J. HORWITZ, THE TRANSFORMATION OF AMERICAN LAW, 1780–1860, 141–51 (1977).

of its consummation. But even in settings where the request for divorce is uncontested, in many jurisdictions it is still quite difficult to navigate the process without legal representation. In order to make other elements of a Lawyer 3.0 world function as effectively as possible, the profession should work to narrow the instances when a full-service, Lawyer 2.0 professional is necessary to address a consumer's legal problem. Remember, the consumer's job to be done is not to hire a lawyer; it is to solve an issue they face that requires a legal solution. That solution should not require the engagement of a legal professional in every instance.

New rules for a Lawyer 3.0 world

Another important pillar of a Lawyer 3.0 approach to the delivery of legal services is to restore the primacy of the consumer and strengthen client agency within the legal system. With an array of potential solutions to their legal issues available to them, and different modes of resolving legal their disputes, this will place the consumer in a better position to make decisions for themselves about how to resolve those problems. Yes, cost always factors into the equation, but consumers can decide for themselves how to proceed in different contexts if they are cognizant of the benefits and risks associated with using simpler tools to address those problems. This is in contrast to the current, bespoke approach where the lawyer offers more complex legal interventions to address the consumer's problem, and they do so at a premium. What is more, when consumers possess more information about their legal problems, even when all that does is help them understand that they have a legal problem in the first place, this will give consumers more agency in their lives. When a consumer does not understand the court system, their legal rights, and how to protect them, or cannot appreciate the ways in which their actions could have harmful consequences, they are in a weaker position to make informed choices that improve their lives. A fundamental precept of the legal profession is that the client should determine the overall goals of the particular representation. We often divide this principle up into two elements: the lawyer is in charge of the *means* of achieving what the client decides are their *ends*. But there is no bright line between means and ends. When the lawyer's bespoke plan of action for a particular client makes the lawyer's services too expensive for the client to afford, it is no less destructive of the client's ends than if the lawyer simply ignored the client's wishes in a formal lawyer–client relationship. The legal professional in a Lawyer 3.0 world will offer far more choices to consumers, and will be much more transparent about those choices, so as to place the lawyer and client on much more equal footing, and the client will have a better grasp of how to make decisions that will advance their goals for the representation.

Because of this re-orientation of the legal professional's approach to client services, the final pillar of the Lawyer 3.0 version of the profession will require a significant reform of the rules that govern the practice of law. The Lawyer 2.0 era in many ways was ushered in, at least in part, by the adoption of the Canons of Professional Ethics in 1908. Those canons established the basic parameters of lawyer regulation at the time, but many of those core parameters exist to this day. At the same time, the Canons themselves have been revised and overhauled not once but twice: once in the late 1960s and again in the 1980s. The ABA adopted the current iteration of these rules, the Model Rules of Professional Conduct, in 1983. We are now over 40 years under those rules. The ABA and individual states have certainly tweaked the Model Rules or the rules of individual states since the ABA disseminated this version of the rules, including the adoption of the duty of technology competence referred to in the last chapter. As a whole, though, those rules remain largely intact, and virtually every state has adopted some version of them, sometimes practically verbatim. The reality is, though, we are still very much operating in the world the profession created in 1983, let alone 1908.

The basic framework of the profession—that lawyers have a distinct code of ethics, that the profession is self-regulating, and that non-professionals should not delivery legal services—has calcified, and dominates any discussion related to the profession, with obvious access-to-justice implications. Lawyer 3.0 likely requires a significant overhaul of the rules of ethics that govern the profession and those outside the profession who might want to deliver services that, at present, are considered UPL. We will thus have to review not just the role of the lawyer in the delivery of legal services to ensure that other professionals can also have a hand in helping consumers solve legal problems, but we will also have to rewrite the rules where they seem to protect lawyers rather than consumers. We also need to reiterate that the purpose of the profession and the larger legal system is to ensure that all Americans can solve their legal problems in an effective, fair, just, accessible, and equitable way. That is where we should begin in any effort to reform the rules that cover the legal profession to make sure that they place the consumer at the moral, practical, and philosophical center of the legal system and the legal profession that operates within it. Re-orienting the legal profession to put consumers first will require a significant adjustment of the outlook of many lawyers; this will also require significant reform of the rules that govern the profession and those who might seek to improve access to justice in a Lawyer 3.0 world.

★★★

The American legal profession is at a critical inflection point that is no less significant than the one it faced over 100 years ago when it created the basic contours of the profession as it exists to this day. But that profession has, perhaps, exceeded its sell-by date. Far too many Americans face their legal problems without the assistance of a lawyer. This is, in part, because of the high cost of legal services, but also because legal services are difficult to access, and too many Americans do not even realize they might have a legal problem, let alone one that a lawyer can help them solve. The system the profession put in place to serve its own ends, one that offers lawyers a monopoly on the delivery of anything that comes close to the definition of the practice of law, is one that places legal assistance beyond the reach of far too many Americans. A core problem with the system that the profession ushered in over 100 years ago is that it places the lawyer at the center of the delivery of legal services, rather than the American consumer. Because of this, there is a significant gap between Americans with legal problems and the ability of lawyers to solve them. New technologies are available now that might go a long way towards narrowing that gap, if not closing it altogether, and lawyers should embrace them. But while something might be gained by using technology to close that gap, American consumers could lose a lot as well. What I have tried to offer here are the tools that can help us not only deliver services in new and more innovative ways, but can also help us understand that there are times when such tools may serve a consumer's job to be done, and others when they will not. In order to usher in the next version of the legal profession—what I have called Lawyer 3.0—we must develop the ability to discern when such tools can deliver appropriate services, at scale, to the right consumers, at the right time. I harbor no illusions that such services will displace the more traditional and full-service model of representation in every situation. A legal profession that strives to put the consumer first by adopting the job-to-be-done framework described here will also aspire to offer critical services to the community in the most effective, affordable, and accessible way possible. There will still be some situations that demand the delivery of services in a traditional, bespoke way. But there will also be many other instances where technology can deliver justice and do so at scale. It is up to lawyers, and the communities they are supposed to serve, to develop the wisdom, judgment, courage, and humility to know the difference.

Chapter 10: Key takeaways

1. Advances in technology will soon automate many routine legal tasks, leading to significant changes in how legal services are delivered. While technology has not yet fully disrupted the legal profession, it could transform legal service accessibility and affordability over the next decade.

2. UPL rules, designed to protect consumers, also hinder innovation by preventing non-lawyers from providing legal services. These regulations can stifle disruptive innovations that could offer low-cost legal assistance to consumers, particularly in cases of low complexity.

3. The legal profession must shift toward a consumer-centered model, where legal services are designed to meet the needs of consumers rather than maintaining the monopoly of lawyers. This approach emphasizes affordability, accessibility, and focuses on the consumer's job to be done.

4. Lawyer 3.0 will involve pre-packaged legal strategies that can be commoditized to serve many clients at a lower cost. This contrasts with the traditional bespoke legal services model, where each client's case is uniquely tailored by the lawyer. This shift could provide consumers with affordable, accessible options that still meet their legal needs.

5. The legal profession should work to simplify court processes and create user-friendly alternative dispute resolution fora, simplified legal agreements, streamlined contracts, and off-the-shelf solutions to make legal services more accessible, thereby reducing the complexity and cost associated with full-service representation.

6. In order to usher in the next version of the legal profession, this will require significant reform of the ethical rules that govern the profession to support the delivery of services by non-lawyers and to encourage innovation. Rewriting these rules will prioritize consumer needs and ensure that the legal system serves the public rather than protecting the lawyer's monopoly on legal services.

Index